An international guide to
Wines of the World

An international guide to
Wines of

John Bartholomew and Son Ltd
Edinburgh

*Grape treading, a scene from the Queen Mary Psalter MSS.
14th Century.*

the World

John Morrell

For my son and friend, Tim Olsen,
the man whom I would wish to be,
his Sally-Louise and Charles.

© John Morrell 1974
First published in Great Britain 1975
by John Bartholomew and Son Ltd,
12 Duncan Street, Edinburgh EH9 1TA
and at 216 High Street, Bromley BR1 1PW

ISBN 0 70281 011 8

Maps © Bartholomew Books
Filmset by Photoprint Plates Ltd, Rayleigh, Essex
Printed in Great Britain

*"O for a draught of vintage! that hath been cooled for a
long age in the deep-delved earth . . ."*

(Keats)

Contents

A vineyard scene from Piero de Crescenzi's treatise on agriculture, illuminated in Franco-Flemish style in the late 15th century.

Introduction

The consumption of wine in English-speaking countries, particularly America and the U.K., has increased enormously in the last decade and the forecast for the U.K. is that consumption will approximately double in the next decade. America also forecasts significant increases only a part of which will be satisfied with the present vineyard extension and new plantations. Wine was once a special occasion beverage, but is now regularly enjoyed by a great many people and it is, therefore, pleasing to see that a widely read wine journalist has written a book which will no doubt appeal as much to regular drinkers as to the new generation of drinkers whose enjoyment and enthusiasm about wine must surely be stimulated by reading and studying the background to the many wines from all over the world which are now available on the market.

John Morrell has been Wine Correspondent of the Sunday Telegraph for a number of years and also writes for other leading journals. His pleasing style, without the pretentious use of wine jargon has created a large following for his writings. It is therefore with great pleasure that I write this introduction and although my own ideas may not run completely parallel to those expressed by the author, I am certain that the sincerity of his writing and the recording of his very many travels to the vineyards and the descriptions of the vintners he has met, will appeal to a great many wine lovers and to those who are embarking on the journey into wine for the first time.

PETER HALLGARTEN
LONDON

1
The Glory of Wine

Wine, like love, has the power to make men and women happy, to transform their outlook and their lives, to bring contentment and tolerance, and to ease and improve their relationships. It is also a source of pleasure to the understanding because the true wine lover is so carried away by the subject that he studies all the many fascinating operations that go to produce his favourite growth.

Like other pleasures wine, when abused, will abuse the drinker, though less harmfully than one might expect. But the genuine wine lover is too fond of his wine to over-indulge. He knows that once the senses can no longer savour a splendid bouquet, appreciate the depth of colour, the supple body, the fine finish and lingering after-taste, then his interest and enjoyment have vanished.

Wine, too, is most happily drunk in civilised surroundings with good company, men and women intelligent and knowledgeable enough to discuss the wine and compare it with others they have drunk. This special aspect is not to be confused with wine snobbery, a silly and futile affectation that is gradually disappearing as more and more people elect to study wine for themselves and so confound the pompous.

Another pleasure to be found in wine is the happy effect it has on those who deal in it, from the grower in his vineyard, painstaking in his yearly ritual hoping to produce excellence from tiny shoots that successfully defy rain, hail and frost, to the shipper who makes the purchases and the shopkeeper who sells them.

The men of the wine trade in all countries are the chosen of the gods because in some strange way the miracle that turns a tiny grape into a source of worldwide appreciation and pleasure, the transformation effected by sun, soil and human care, equally gives them a good humour, generosity and friendliness that makes their acquaintance a continual reward. There are occasional exceptions, human nature being what it is, but such creatures tend to disappear from the scene as though they realised that they had chosen the wrong calling. After all, who wants to buy a source of such delight from a man who does not love his fellows? And this applies to all nations—French, German, Italian, Californian, Chilean, Australian — in every land where the vine flourishes there flourishes, too, this richness of spirit. I speak from experience.

Wine has been defined officially in all countries and always on much the same lines. In simple terms, it is the naturally fermented juice of freshly gathered grapes. But wine will differ according to the country and climate where it grows, even to the aspect of the slope on which the vines are planted, to the grape that is used, and to the way in which it is made, whether the fermentation is stopped at a certain stage or continued to its final end. It is affected, too, by the methods used, chosen by the winegrower according to his experience and that of his forefathers aided, in modern times, by the advice of great research institutions in winegrowing countries and the wine laws he must respect. Port and sherry are wines just as much as are burgundy and hock, but they are made by different processes and fortified by the addition of brandy or wine spirit during their making, so that they are stronger than the usual bottled wine that you may buy for everyday meals or for friendly social drinking.

Noah was one of the earliest named makers of wine and as the Bible relates in Genesis 'Noah began to be an husbandman, and he planted a vineyard'. Unfortunately he drank too freely of his product but after seven months in the ark floating on water he perhaps craved something a little more satisfying, and the fact that he lived to be 950 years old seems to show that his indulgence had no lasting ill effect.

The Greeks, the Persians and the Egyptians all knew wine and recorded its pleasures and it was the march of the Roman legions that took wine throughout the rest of Europe, cultivating the vines in their own way. It flourished so greatly that at one time the Emperor Domitian gave orders to reduce the number of vines by half, and so showed himself a predecessor of the wine law-makers of today whereby quality wines are limited to set numbers of gallons per acre.

Charlemagne, too, in his time encouraged the planting of vines in his great empire of the west, while in Italy the inhabitants were cultivating

An illustration to Virgil's Georgics, written and illuminated in Italy in the late 15th century.

vines and enjoying the produce 1,000 years ago. In Trier, that splendid city of history, commerce and vines on the upper Mosel, they show you Etruscan wine jugs in their museum to prove an early trade and remind the visitor that England paid her taxes here in Roman times.

The Trier museum, too, has stone carvings showing grapes and rabbits eating them, and a great sculptured ship laden with wine barrels depicting wine transport on the Mosel at the beginning of the third century. Here also is a splendid mosaic of Bacchus among the grapes, and another fine blue and red mosaic that demonstrates the follies of over-indulgence in wine. Other sculptures show grapes being cultivated in much the same way as they are today, the growers plagued by birds exactly as they suffer now, though modern vintage time in Germany is accompanied by the reports of automatic 'guns' to scare away these thieves.

Such ancient monuments help to show the grapes used and, as one might expect in this northern part of the world, the grapes depicted around Trier are white ones, not red. A greenish-white paint was used to colour them on their stone background and there is no trace of red, much as the Mosel grapes today are white wine grapes, the kind that flourish best in colder climates harassed by fluctuating weather conditions.

A Corinthian wine-jug. Discovered in Rhodes. Dating from around 600 B.C. The design showing real and imaginary animals. Height 12 in.

9

This sculptured ship laden with wine barrels depicts wine transport on the Mosel at the beginning of the 3rd century.

A stone carving showing a rabbit eating Mosel grapes in Roman times.

The growth of Christianity, flourishing mightily as the Romans withdrew, saw monasteries spread throughout Europe and then the monks, the learned men of their age, cultivated the grape and made the wine, improving on past methods and using their scholarship, wisdom and time to follow such precepts of St Paul as 'Use a little wine for thy stomach's sake and thine often infirmities'.

Cultivation was necessary to provide the sacrament, but this coincided with the need to supply a wine for meal times, a drink moreover approved repeatedly in the Bible, from the Old Testament to the New as shown by the miracle at the marriage in Cana of Galilee when the water was turned into wine.

As the monasteries and the Church grew more and more influential the devout began to leave their vineyards to ecclesiastical bodies, some no doubt out of gratitude and others as a means of ensuring an easier entrance to paradise. When Bèze was founded it received vines on land that is famous for its wine today, the vineyards being situated at Beaune and Gevrey. There is record, too, of vineyards being planted in England for the Church in Shropshire and elsewhere, and although there were to be subsequent gaps and neglect in the encouragement of viticulture, the present day has seen a revival of these skills by private growers in Hampshire, Sussex, the Isle of Wight and even in Lincolnshire, although all are at present on a modest scale.

Sir Guy Salisbury-Jones has been cultivating a vineyard at Hambledon for twenty-three years and uses chiefly the Seyve-Villard grape, a French white hybrid. Other vineyards use a cross between the German Riesling and Sylvaner grapes, among them the Merrydown company at Horam which runs a co-operative for wine-growers and presses their grapes. English wines are almost all white since red wine cannot be produced satisfactorily in northern latitudes because of the lack of sufficient sun. One of the most pleasing English white wines is Adgestone, made by K. C. Barlow in the Isle of Wight, and it flourishes, like the best of the others, on chalky soil, using Seyve-Villard and Müller-Thurgau grapes.

The achievement is in producing wine at all rather than in the actual result, although some English wines are sold in London hotels. The standard is perhaps best described as reasonable, but production is small and the price is the same, or slightly more, than better French or German wines. Interest, however, is growing and the English Vineyards Association has 330 members.

These modern wines have no active connection with the Church, and the monks are no longer such important figures in the vineyards. This is not the case in California, where the Christian Brothers have become internationally famous for their products, not only for the standards achieved, but because they export the wines to Europe. This monastic order was founded by Abbé de la Salle (after whom one of the wines is named) when he started a training college at Reims in 1685. The Order spread to California with the object of educating the poor, but the vineyards in the Napa Valley which were started in 1882 have flourished and now produce a considerable range of table wines as well as their own sparkling wine and Californian brandy. Brother Timothy, the Cellarmaster, has devoted most of his life to the vineyards, and his name is always associated with them today.

The Christian Brothers have rivals for modern wine fame in the white robed monks of La Grande Chartreuse, the Carthusian monastery in the French Alps, fifteen miles from Grenoble. Their life is one of strict devotion, but the Father Prior, the Father Procurator and three monks share the secret of two of the world's most famous liqueurs. Green Chartreuse came first, based on an elixir distilled in 1735. In 1840 the yellow variety was perfected. More than a hundred herbs go into the making and the monks carry out the manufacture at a distillery near the monastery. For part of the year they go to Tarragona in Spain to work at another distillery. On these visits they travel separately to avoid an accident that might rob the monastery of its skilled technicians.

As always, the Church is adaptable and the Monastery of the Silent Fastness is linked with a busy commercial company that has seventy civilian employees and sends the famous liqueurs all over the world.

The Chartreuse matures in huge oak barrels, each containing 100,000 litres. The herbs include saxifrage and gentian, gathered by the monks and blended, when dried, with a strong wine prepared for them in the Camargue.

Brother Timothy, Cellarmaster of the Order of Christian Brothers, holds a glass of wine to the light to assess colour and clarity.

La Grande Chartreuse, the Carthusian Monastery in the French Alps, near Grenoble.

Francois Hannibal, Maréchal d'Estrées, who gave the monks the recipe in 1605.

The manuscript containing the secret recipe for Chartreuse.

Vats of maturing liqueur line the side of the ancient cellar.

Royalties from the sales help to support the Order's twenty-six houses in Europe and the U.S.A., a worldly choice put to good use for those whose lives are lived in prayer and contemplation.

Bénédictine, too, is a liqueur that owes its origin to an elixir invented by a monk at Fécamp Abbey in 1510, using herbs and plants that are still gathered on those French cliffs by the company formed after Alexandre Le Grand rediscovered the formula. He found it in papers from the Abbey, which the monks had given to one of his ancestors for safe keeping when the French Revolution threatened them. No monks are now connected with the liqueur, but the seals in red wax that are still stamped by hand on each bottle carry the arms of the Prior and the old Abbey.

Two notable charities exist today that owe their prosperity to the vine. The first, the Hospices de Beaune, is known throughout the world because of the auction each November at which its wines are sold. Founded by Nicolas Rolin and his wife in 1443, the old buildings, with their roofs tiled in fantastic patterns of gold, red and brown, are one of the sights of the ancient wine city. It is still used as a hospital but you can visit the kitchen, with its huge copper pans, and the pharmacy. You can also view the painting of the Last Judgment by Roger van der Weiden in which the righteous ascend to heaven and the outcasts descend naked to hell; the typical Middle Ages outlook. Throughout the centuries, as elsewhere, penitent souls have left their vineyards to the hospice with the result that it owns some of the finest wine-producing acres around Beaune. Its red wines are famous for their soft, smooth, light texture and delicate bouquet.

The great courtyard of Fécamp Abbey, France.

The great courtyard of the Hospices de Beaune (Hotel-Dieu).

Nicholas Rolin and his wife Guigone de Salins from the painting by Roger van der Weiden.

Less known, but similarly interesting, is the St. Nikolaus Hospital at Bernkastel-Kues on the river Mosel in Germany, founded by Cardinal Nikolaus Cusanus who was born there in 1401. The hospital is a home for thirty-three old men, the number chosen for the years of Jesus, and has a chapel with a remarkable ceiling showing the cardinal's crest, a large red crayfish from his family name of Krebs. A single pillar with twelve ribs supports the ceiling and a fifteenth-century painting of the Crucifixion is a striking piece of work with the Cardinal and his secretary kneeling in the foreground. His library of 400 manuscripts is carefully preserved.

Like the Hospices de Beaune, the Cusanusstift, as it is known, has not lacked for vineyards and today cultivates 75,000 vines growing in some twenty acres of the best areas of Bernkastel, Wehlen, Graach and Brauneberg, all names to conjure with on the Mosel and all using Riesling grapes.

The Rector took me through his splendid cellars and told me he was extending them so that the wine could be kept in bottles rather than casks. As a theologian, librarian, guardian of the aged and priest, he has the added problems of the vineyards. Labour comes from nearby villages but is difficult to get, and the eight-hour day (so different from the dawn to dusk toil of the vineyards in the past), plus high wages, add to his difficulties. In addition he has the burden of high corporation tax, a penalty of selling so much fine wine at the quality prices it merits! Sometimes, too, the Mosel floods his cellars as in May, 1970, when the water rose three feet high there, but without damaging the wine. In 1925 the whole cellar space was flooded. Visitors are welcome, preferably with advance notice.

Wine, then, has been cultivated for thousands of years but, through the interest of the Church it has become a more exact science, with training schools and laboratories such as those at Bordeaux and Mâcon-Davayé in France, at Geisenheim and Mainz in Germany and at Conegliano in Italy.

The marriage of the future Henry II to Eleanor of Aquitaine in 1152 brought to England the rich winelands of south-western France and set the seeds for 300 years of dissension, since Eleanor, some ten years older than Henry, had previously been married to Louis VII. This marriage had been annulled by one of those processes possible then for kings but for few others, and meant that Eleanor kept her lands and added them to Henry's already considerable portion of western France.

In due course the wines of Bordeaux and the surrounding region came to England in quantity and started a relationship that has lasted ever since the thirteenth century, with slight fluctuations. The English called these red wines claret, a word that persists to this day, though it is not used as such in France. It came from *clairet*, a wine of pale red colour or even red and white wine mixed. In fact *clairet* is current in France for a very light red wine, not to be confused with *clairette*, red and white wines of southern France.

St. Nikolaus Hospital—Cusanusstift, Bernkastel Kues, on the Mosel, in Germany.

To the Englishman, indeed to the British, claret remains the name for red Bordeaux wines both great and small. It was English demand that led to expansion of these vineyards and at the same time caused a decline in the growth of the vine in England. Soon Scotland and Wales demanded their share and a regular shipping service carried to and fro the casks of what was soon to become the popular national drink.

When the stout links with Gascony were severed after the battle of Castillon in 1453 wine became less easy to ship. But the people of Bordeaux contrived to continue the trade by one means or another. Indeed the majority of them lamented the English departure. Libourne, the river port inland from Bordeaux, had particular links and boasted the proud title of Loyal Libourne which it earned as a *bastide* or fortress in the English interest. It had been founded by Roger of Leyburn in Yorkshire from which place it took its name, and the tombstone of Roger's wife is still to be seen in the district.

The British drink around ten bottles of wine per head per annum in these modern days compared with 149 bottles in France, but nobody should underestimate the island's interest in good wine as today's increasing consumption figures show.

When the supplies of Bordeaux fell off, merchants turned to the Rhine wines of Germany, and Rhenish, as it was called, became the popular drink. Similarly enjoyed was sack, or sherris sack, which was sherry from Spain and Sir John Falstaff's tipple in Shakespeare's version of the man. The name Rhenish later became hock, after the town of Hochheim on the Main, and Queen Victoria's favourite wine.

In turn came port, following the treaty with Portugal and the marriage of Charles II with Catherine of Braganza, daughter of King John IV of Portugal. Her handsome dowry brought Tangier to England as well as her country's most famous drink, interest in which rapidly developed when Scots and Englishmen settled in Portugal to develop the port wine trade.

Thus in a way Catherine of Braganza duplicated the role of Eleanor of Aquitaine and winelovers owe much to these two ladies, though neither is likely to have been aware of such marriage consequences.

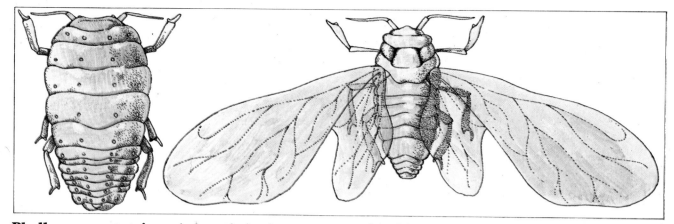

Phylloxera vastatrix —*wingless and winged stages. An insect which some years ago almost destroyed the crops in European vineyards. The wingless form attacks the roots of the vine. The winged female lays the eggs which start a complicated life cycle.*

Vineyards on the slopes beneath Burg Castle at St. Goarshausen on the Rhine.

In different parts of the world other drinks found favour. When the Portuguese discovered Madeira they fired the vast forests that covered the island and planted vines instead. From these vines and the volcanic soil came Madeira, a wine that seems to live for ever, for the effect of the warm climate is increased by its storing in *estufas* for long periods at considerable temperature. It was to become particularly popular in America in the colonial period and is still shipped to Britain although it has fallen somewhat out of favour. It is fortified with cane sugar spirit much as port is fortified with brandy, and in France it is still popular in preparing certain recipes such as *Rognons sautés au Madère*, an excellent kidney dish.

The wine story, however, has not always been an easy one and the coming of the phylloxera plague shook nearly all European vineyards. Damage by this tiny insect was particularly savage in France from 1864 onwards and a decade passed before an answer was found.

When a solution was discovered it came through an English-born American, Charles Valentine Riley, who realised that the pest, *Phylloxera vastatrix*, did not affect eastern American vines. He suggested the grafting of the stock of the great European grapes onto the hardy American roots, and this grafting has gone on ever since, in France, Germany and many other lands. I have often wondered how far General Charles de Gaulle in his anti-American diatribes, realised that France's greatest agricultural industry, and indeed the wines of much of the world, owed their continuance to an American entomologist!

2
The Golden Grape.

The average wine grape is perhaps half-an-inch long, is easily squashed and gives, when properly ripe, a sweetish juice. Yet from the bunches of this almost insignificant fruit are made the wines for which fantastic prices are sometimes bid, wines that can be stored in deep cellars for twenty years or more, so that they may reach the maturity that gives the connoisseur his greatest pleasure.

Many different vines grow all over the world yet it is one specie, *Vitis vinifera,* that provides the grapes from which the wines of Europe are made and this vine has been taken far and wide to repeat its success. It is not, of course, to be confused with dessert grape varieties, for its purpose is quite different. Yet a ripe Riesling grape, which produces the finest white wines of Germany, can be as sweet a mouthful, plucked in a Palatinate vineyard under the eye of the famous owner, Dr Albert Bürklin, as anything served with grape scissors after dinner.

But if *Vitis vinifera* is the wine-giver of the world's greatest bottlings, it comes in a number of varieties. The Riesling is king of white wines not only in Germany on the Rhine, Mosel and in the Palatinate, but also in one part of France where the Alsace vineyards hold it in similar high esteem. Its cousins flourish in Hungary, Yugoslavia and the north of Italy, in Switzerland and Austria and, further afield, in Chile and California.

While its quality is of the highest, its quantity is limited, and here the winegrower turns to a more productive grape of lesser quality called Sylvaner which also grows in Alsace, Austria, Switzerland and elsewhere.

The quality of the Riesling and the quantity of the Sylvaner have led various men to try and obtain the best of both worlds by crossing the one with the other. The result was called Riesling x Sylvaner or was known by the name of the scientist, such as the Swiss Müller-Thurgau named after its discoverer, or Scheurebe, crossed by Dr Scheur; perhaps even more successful.

The recent changes in German wine laws however now forbid the words Riesling x Sylvaner and the crossings must use officially recognised names, which sometimes are the names of the originators.

Since the Sylvaner lacks the bouquet and acidity of the Riesling and is a softer variety, it compensates only in its crossing by providing more wine, while the finesse and dignity of the Riesling is lost to some extent in the process. Which explains why Riesling wine is more expensive than Sylvaner or the various crossings.

Since, however, this is a commercial world there will always be a bigger market for a cheaper wine of quantity, and as the growers have to earn a living as best they can there will always be a temptation to plant an easier vine. All the more credit, then, to owners of great vineyards who scrupulously observe their traditions and refuse to cultivate lesser grapes. Their reward is in the names they establish and the respect and patronage of those who appreciate the best wines, balanced too by the higher prices they can rightly charge.

The German climate makes it less easy to produce red wine though the Spätburgunder, related to the great French red wine grape, the Pinot Noir, does well in various areas and particularly in Baden in the south among the Kaiserstuhl vineyards grouped round a volcanic hillside. Here the wines of the Kaiserstuhl Kellerei of the Friedrich Kiefer company are famous for their quality and now produce two million litres a year from a number of different grapes.

Among those for white wine are Weissburgunder, Sylvaner and Ruländer, which admirably suits the Kaiserstuhl conditions and is the most important grape there. Like the red Spätburgunder, it came originally from France where it is known as Pinot Gris and was first grown by a man called Ruland in the Speyer region.

Germans drink a quantity of their own red wine, although little is exported or known elsewhere except Affentaler. Affentaler is popular because of the novel bottle with its monkey decoration. The name Affentaler originates from the valley name 'Ave Maria Tal' which was later slurred to Affentaler. Affe means monkey, and this no doubt accounts for the peculiar label decoration. The red wines of the region round Bad Dürkheim, famous for its annual wine festival in September, are the best of the Palatin-

and Vine

Riesling

Sylvaner

Sémillon

Gamay

Chenin

Sauvignon

Pinot Noir   *Chardonnay*   *Cabernet-Sauvignon*

ate but again are overshadowed by the great whites grown there.

Splendid as are the German wines from the Riesling grape, the wine standards for the world are set by France. Nature has blessed France with a loving hand for the wine climate is ideal in Bordeaux and Burgundy and many other parts of the country. When a wine lover judges a wine, he tests it mentally against the French equivalent and few other wines can reach this standard, close though some of them may come to it.

The great red wine grape of Burgundy is the Pinot Noir which also plays the chief part in making champagne, a strange contrast since one is black and the other white, except for pink champagne which is really a rosé wine. If men bow in homage before an equivalent of the white Riesling when thinking of red wine, then they must kneel to the Pinot Noir for it is not blended with any other grape when making its noblest wines.

This is not to denigrate the qualities of the red wines of Bordeaux, whose elegance and finesse reach similar heights and indeed most experts give Bordeaux first place.

When all is said and done, however, Bordeaux red wines are made from more than one variety of the Cabernet vine and practically never from a single grape. Although all are grown by the same owner on his own land, the grapes are Cabernet Sauvignon, Cabernet Franc and Merlot. While the first provides by far the larger proportion, usually some eighty per cent or more, the other two grapes have their important part to play in the making of the wine, and the careful blending forms the peak of the cellarmaster's year.

Burgundy, then, is the only single-grape wine

in this context and, while no true man of Bordeaux would accept this as a reason for regarding his own product in a lesser light, it must have some influence on the purist. The great care taken in Bordeaux and the number of individual estates there, plus the fact that the area produces far more wine than Burgundy and sees carefully to publicity and promotional aspects, give the product an advantage.

Again, the great classification made of Médoc wines—the best area of Bordeaux—in 1855 has produced a grading that even the passing of a century cannot shake, despite the desire of the owners of wines of lower grades to move up one or more steps.

Under this classification there are four names of worldwide fame grouped as First Growths and a fifth name was added officially in 1973. The original names are Château Lafite, Château Margaux, Château Latour, Château Haut-Brion and the promotion from a Second Growth to join them is Château Mouton-Rothschild. The first, third and fifth all come from the Pauillac district of the Haut-Médoc, the second from Margaux, also in the Haut-Médoc, and Château Haut-Brion from Pessac in the Graves area close to Bordeaux. Their best years will currently cost £15 upwards a bottle in a wine merchant's and probably almost twice as much in a restaurant. Prices have reached these heights in the seventies due to demand in the United States, Switzerland, Belgium and Japan, countries where sufficient wealth exists for such purchases.

These wines stand supreme, not only for their own quality but because they represent the best of large estates owned by proprietors whose

Muscat   Cinsault   Grenache

names are similarly famous. Their equivalents in Burgundy might be Romanée-Conti, Richebourg, Chambertin and La Tache, but all the five Bordeaux estates are of well over 100 acres while most of the four Burgundies are well under 30 acres. What is more, the ownership is often complicated. Yet, by the lesser quantity of their production, the price remains astronomically high.

Just as the Riesling is the great white grape of Germany and Alsace, so the Chardonnay is the supreme white grape of Burgundy. It is a small grape of a brilliant green-gold colour. Sometimes wrongly called the Pinot-Chardonnay it is also not to be confused with the lesser Pinot Blanc grape. Chardonnay is its name in France and that is sufficient.

The wonder of the Chardonnay grape is that it can produce the austere, dry white wines of Chablis, the powerful dry but mellow Meursault, and the fresh, young Pouilly-Fuissé with its 'nutty' aroma, all grown over a distance of some one hundred and fifty miles in varying country. The same grape is responsible for all these and a number of others, which perhaps indicates that it is the soil itself that finally settles the character of a wine.

Such then are the four great grapes and vines of France, Cabernet and Pinot Noir for the red wines, Chardonnay and, in Alsace only, Riesling for the white. There are numerous other grapes but they are lesser examples for lesser wines and will be discussed later.

Vine cultivation is an agricultural pursuit and must be regarded as such, despite a natural inclination to look on it as being more romantic than growing turnips or maize. Technically the vine is a bush with roots that help it to breathe and feed. It grows canes on which are shoots that support the leaves, tendrils and eventually grapes.

On the shoots appear the buds and the young green leaves among which, even at this early stage, one can see miniature bunches of what will later be grapes. The flowering comes in June for a fortnight, a most crucial time for the grower when sunshine is needed and frost or rain could ruin much of his work. If the flowering fails then a state called *coulure* develops which may drastically affect the future of the grapes. The Chardonnay grape is especially prone to this.

The early grapes change in colour as, warmed by the sun, they are nourished from the roots and the leaves. The sugar is formed in the leaves and accumulates in the grape. Some seventy-five per cent of a grape consists of water, twenty per cent of sugar, less than one per cent of acids and the remainder cellulose and minerals. Warmth of the sun, good, clear light and absence of storms are necessary for the final development of the grape. August and September are vital months in the vineyard as the harvest time approaches when the grapes are taken for pressing.

Now yeast plays its important part on the skin of the grape, where its cells appear and, when the grapes are crushed and the skin broken, penetrates to the sugar inside, turning the sugar into alcohol.

The sugar content is all important. Grapes, for instance, can be left on the vines until, as in the great Sauternes, they are heavy with *pourriture noble,* shrunk into massive sweetness or, as in Germany, left to a very similar state to become *beerenauslese,* single grapes chosen specially—and

The Vine *in various stages of growth :-*

(a) In early Spring the vine sends out the first young shoots.

(b) A fortnight or so later the leaves are well-developed and tendrils appear.

(c) Towards the end of May, buds resembling miniature bunches of grapes appear. These will flower later.

(d) The all-important flowering process follows in early June, and for fine grapes to form, good weather during this flowering period is essential.

(e & f) The grafting of the vine. It is common practice to graft French vine stock onto American root stock thus producing a plant which is resistant to the ravages of Phylloxera.

(g) The ripened grapes.

expensively—for their ripeness and sugar content.

There are also areas where, in adverse weather, there is not sufficient sugar content in the grapes to make satisfactory wine.

It is, of course, possible to add sugar during the winemaking process. This is added to the must or grape juice before fermentation. Those estates that have no need for such action look down on less fortunate growers. But when maturity has not been properly reached it would be hard on the grower if he was refused a solution to his problems. The wine laws take account of this and in France the process is called *chaptalisation* after a Minister of the Interior in Napoleon's time, Jean-Antoine Chaptal, who was also at one period professor of chemistry at Montpellier.

Proper authorisation is required and *chaptalisation* done under official supervision. Water may not be added. This is not to say, however, that sugaring is not sometimes done on the side but not, one believes, by reputable firms. Wine so treated will not always compare with the best wines, but provided the process is admitted it is hard to see why the wine should not be saved in this way. Yet there is still often a vague feeling among wine lovers that it is not the correct thing to do.

Talking with a famous wine shipper in France our conversation turned to Germany. He smacked his hand on the desk. 'Do you know that in Germany they actually add sugar to some of their wines?' he asked.

'Yes, I know that,' I replied, 'but do you not also have in France the process of *chaptalisation*?'

'Oh-oh, that is something quite different,' he said and hastily changed the subject.

I must admit that a famous Mosel grower, discussing a poor vintage told me he had never known a year when they could not make wine and I merely said, 'Sugar is very useful,' at which he laughed heartily.

The period from the flowering in June to September comprises 'the hundred days' known to every child in a wine district as one of breathless anticipation while the berries develop under the threat of weather hazards, lack or deluge of rain, poor sunshine or, on occasion, perfect weather which creates a vintage of wine history.

In the past, in France certainly, it was a set tradition that the grape picking would begin one hundred days after the flowering, but nowadays local commissions make such decisions. Science is, of course, right, and the ripeness of the grape can be assessed by analysis of several kinds including, in Germany, the Oechsle measure of sugar in the must, or grape juice. Indeed I have seen Frau Jutta Bürklin bite a fine Wachenheim Riesling grape and announce its Oechsle content on the spot from her deep experience and I have no doubt at all that she was absolutely correct.

The vineyard slope is preferably to the south and here, as in all countries, the best grapes grow and the best wines are made, for this gives the best exposure to the sun. All vineyards, however, cannot be on exact southern slopes, so the south-western slopes are also favoured and lesser men making lesser wines must make do with what they can find. But even in the greatest winemaking areas you will see empty plots which you think might raise wine but have been rejected. Sometimes, too, as on the Mosel, that sharply winding river of horseshoe bends, you will see the favoured vineyards now on one bank and now on the other as the slopes are exposed in turn by the twisting river to the golden sun.

At the same time the sun must not be scorching, otherwise Spain and Italy could produce wines to rival France and Germany. It is notable that the best Spanish and Italian wines do not come from the hottest areas.

Once the harvest starts action is continuous, for air is detrimental to wine whether in vat, barrel or bottle. Especially with white, air takes away the flavour and leaves the wine flat and darker in colour. Casks of wine have to be constantly watched so that any leakage may be met, the French word being *ullage*. Thus if you have a barrel of your own you need a further supply to keep it filled up, otherwise your wine may soon turn to vinegar.

The grapes are brought as soon as possible from the vines and crushed and destemmed. The juice and the pulp are delivered into the fermentation vat. This juice and pulp is called the must. As fermentation proceeds it is important to keep the temperature steady at about 75°. The liquid is carefully stirred occasionally to break up the chapeau of grapeskins that accumulate at the top of the vat taking care that too much air is not stirred into the mixture, as inferior wine may result from this. The red wine colour comes from the skins of the dark grapes and after sufficient colour has been extracted the liquid is drawn off and run into barrels with loose fitting bungs in which the fermentation process continues. The remaining material in the fermentation vat is termed the pomace and this material is then transferred to a press and further juice is extracted. This liquid gained in this manner is stored in other barrels and kept apart from the first juice because this second extraction, the result of pressing, produces far inferior wine. The wine juice that runs away freely from the pomace is termed 'free-run juice'. The extra yield is called 'press wine.'

White wine is produced by a similar process. The grapes which may be either light or dark are delivered to the crushing and stalking machine and the grapes, stalks and branches are then delivered to the horizontal press, there being no

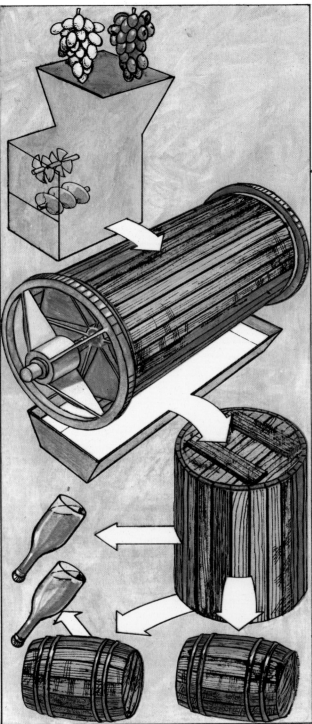

The Fermentation Process

Red Wine.

The fully ripe grapes have their stalks removed, and are slightly crushed in the process. The crushed grapes are then delivered to the fermenting vat and fermentation proceeds with temperatures around 20°–30° Centigrade. The free run juice is then racked off the lees and fermentation continues in cask. The lees are then transferred to the vertical press and the juice from this pressing is also racked off into casks. The must from this second pressing produces inferior wine, due to the presence of more tannin containing materials in it. It is sometimes used to make cheap brandy or occasionally blended with the 'free run' wine.

White Wine.

The grapes, which can be white or dark, are de-stalked crushed and pressed. The must is allowed to settle and the bright clean must is then racked into clean casks and care is taken to remove any dark grape skins which could colour the wine at an early stage. After fermentation, which may last several days, the juice is racked into other storage casks to start maturation. Special procedures are necessary when making German wines to preserve their sweetness.

separation of the fruit and tannin containing materials. The must is run into sulphured hogsheads and allowed to settle, the unwanted solids from the grapes accumulating at the bottom of the casks. The bright, clean must is then racked into clean casks, pure yeast is added and fermentation allowed to proceed. The casks are sealed with special bungs which allow the carbon dioxide to escape freely but which do not allow air to be drawn into the casks. The process of racking is repeated several times during the time the wine is kept in the cask.

Fermentation is a noisy, violent process with the wine juice rumbling and bubbling in its great cask. Hefty volumes have been written by French and German scientists on the way to handle the process but only the essential details are easily followed by the layman. There are many tricks of the trade that may or may not be involved. Why not natural wine with no additions, you may well ask? I have drunk wine made naturally, without chemicals on the vine, the land or in the vats. Alas, it did not please me as much as the wine made by recognised techniques. This may be due to the fact that we are all accustomed to the result of modern production methods and dislike anything very different.

During the resting period the wine may now be subjected to further processes such as fining, in which particles in suspension are removed by adding white of egg or modern aids, and filtering. It is still too young for drinking and must rest in cask, white wines for comparatively short periods but reds of the highest quality for years.

The modern trend, particularly in the big co-operatives of France and Germany, is to use stainless steel tanks, but although these are also increasingly common in Burgundy and Champagne, older growers still have faith in the qualities of the oak cask. They feel the wines gain from contact with the wood and 'breath' through it, particularly the reds, and so find qualities missing in glass-lined or plastic tanks.

During the period when the wine matures much care is needed and it is now that great houses justify their reputation. Each year the vintage brings its own problems and calls for different skills.

Just as the vine in the vineyard requires constant attention, and must be sprayed, fertilised and protected against pest and insect, wind and frost, so the wine in the cellar must be given similar care. Wine is often called a living thing and this is because it changes constantly and can be saved or killed according to the ability of the men who look after it.

The modern winegrower works under many pressures. He is urged to make his wine by quicker methods and to sell it sooner because the merchants who buy also want to sell quickly and so avoid tying up their capital. Indeed the vigneron himself has much outlay before he receives his reward. The longer he leaves his wine to mature in his cool, quiet cellars, hearing it stir each year at the coming of spring and sleeping again with winter, so much longer is his own capital idle.

Casks in the cellar of Louis Jadot, Beaune.

Yet there are many such men who will refuse to sell their wine before it is ready. I remember talking to old Louis Clair, master winemaker of Santenay, as we sipped in his cellar.

'A good wine must wait at least two years before anything is done with it, often much, much longer,' he recalled. 'I had this splendid wine of 1966 and they kept coming to me and urging me to sell it to them. I refused once, twice, even more often. But then in a weak moment I allowed them to persuade me. So I agreed to bottle it, but even as the *camion* drove out of the yard I felt a great pain in my heart.

'I swore then I would never give way again for I knew I had done myself an injury that the silver they had left me would never repay. That wine, I knew, would be sold within a few days and those men would make their money as they had left me my money. They were merchants and they would go off to buy more wine somewhere else, but I was left with my conscience. I had bottled and sold a wine that would never reach its very best, its full potential, because it had been torn from me too young and that was a wicked thing I did.'

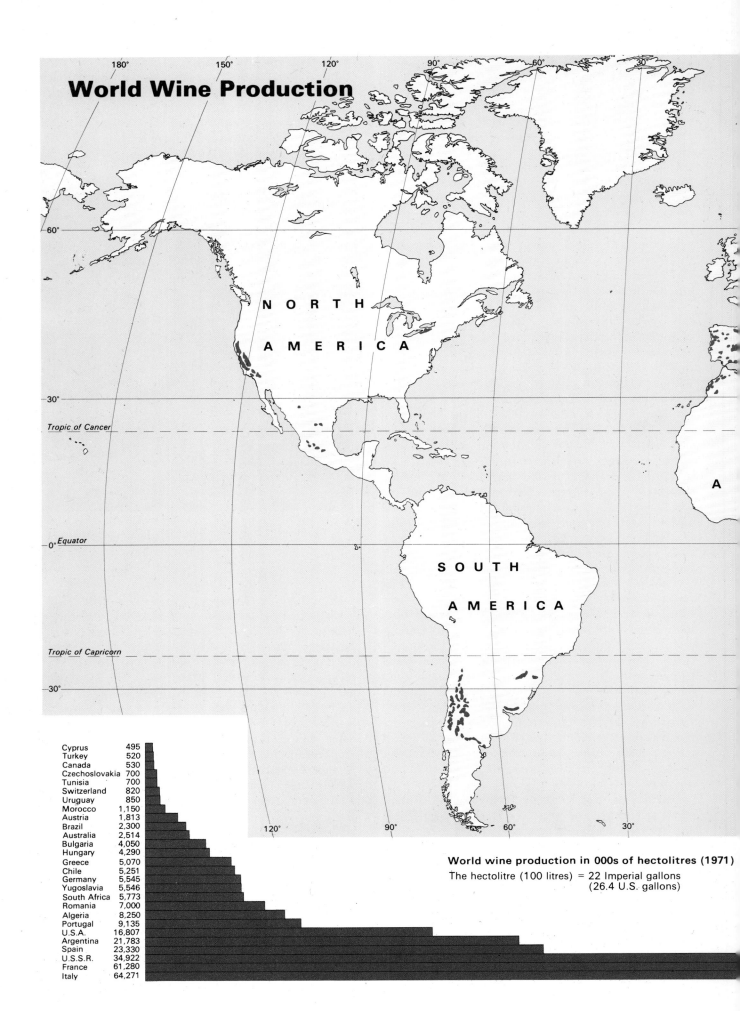

World Wine Production

Cyprus	495
Turkey	520
Canada	530
Czechoslovakia	700
Tunisia	700
Switzerland	820
Uruguay	850
Morocco	1,150
Austria	1,813
Brazil	2,300
Australia	2,514
Bulgaria	4,050
Hungary	4,290
Greece	5,070
Chile	5,251
Germany	5,545
Yugoslavia	5,546
South Africa	5,773
Romania	7,000
Algeria	8,250
Portugal	9,135
U.S.A.	16,807
Argentina	21,783
Spain	23,330
U.S.S.R.	34,922
France	61,280
Italy	64,271

World wine production in 000s of hectolitres (1971)

The hectolitre (100 litres) = 22 Imperial gallons
(26.4 U.S. gallons)

Major wine-growing areas

Bartholomew's "The Times" Projection

His wonderful brown, sun-tanned face broke into a smile. 'It all sounds foolish I know,' he went on, 'but if you love your vineyard and your wine you feel like this. I have to live with it.'

Although the broad principles of cultivating grapes and making red and white wines are mostly the same, procedures differ in different areas. The grapes along the Mosel, for instance, are trained higher and more upright than those of Bordeaux. Along the Weinstrasse in the German Palatinate the method is again different and at the end of every row you see a support wire fastened round a big oblong sandstone let into the ground to take the strain.

In Burgundy the distance between the rows is narrow and much less than in the Jura, where on some estates you can drive a motor car between the lines of vines. And that is how the vines are cared for, with tall, spiderlike narrow tractors that can move up and down the rows, the driver perched so high that he can see far over them. Yet the land on which the vines grow varies tremendously. The great reds of Burgundy grow in a rich, ruddy-brown earthy soil of clay and silica that always reminds me of the red soil of Devon.

Philippe Cairol is one of the most famous *courtiers* or winebrokers for the great Vosne-Romanée wines and he lives in the village itself. A youngish man, he dresses very dapperly in corduroy and drives his big car fearlessly round the vineyards. Pressing his foot on the accelerator he roared me from his front gate up the steep track, bumpy with big stones, to the exclusive Romanée Conti plot high above us. It only takes up four-and-a-half acres and every inch is carefully cultivated to produce an average harvest of 1,250 gallons from the Pinot Noir grape.

I got out of the car and walked a little way by myself until I was quite alone, leaning on a low wall and looking down on this priceless holding.

Its produce is world famous, treasured and respected by winedrinkers and winemakers from London to Alaska and from New York to Peru. To its left lay the twenty acres of the great Richebourg and to its right the fifteen acres of La Tache. Within sight were the twenty-two acres of Grands-Echezeaux, another superb burgundy to which I was first introduced by the late Guy Prince, a prince indeed of London wine merchants and head of Lebègue & Co. Beyond again lay the vineyards of the lesser but noble Nuits-St Georges.

What a prospect for anyone who knows something about wine to enjoy! The even rows, the carefully cultivated ground, the village itself, the peace of the countryside broken only by the faint humming of a passing car, here was an earthly paradise that represented bottled contentment for the world or at any rate those who could afford its products. And who, knowing the wines, could not afford them?

Yet, for all they represented in money and pleasure, there were no guards or sentries, no police or machine guns to protect them. They lay under the warm afternoon sun secure in their personal prestige.

Some time later I was in Chablis visiting another winegrower, Michel Remon, whose office is in the grounds of a Victorian house, *'une belle propriete'* as an old woman told me when I asked her the way.

Here again all was peace, with the town of Chablis and its ancient walls, arches and battlements undisturbed in the background. We went down to his cellars in the garden and he opened bottle after bottle to sample for our joint delight.

First of all a 1970 Chablis Grand Cru Blanchots, a wine of superb quality, full in the mouth and with a wonderful finish, an exceptional, lingering aftertaste. Chablis is a dry wine, noted particularly for its fine accompaniment to oysters and shellfish, but this wine was not dry in the normal sense of the word. It was at the same time mellow, lemon gold in colour, full of mingling flavours, a great experience.

Michel turned to a bottle of 1970 Chablis Grand Cru Bougros, another great offering but one which did not strike quite such a chord with me as its predecessor. My host, with his lifelong knowledge, assured me that it was the equal of the first but took longer to develop.

As a final sacrifice, he offered me a 1969 Chablis Grand Cru Les Preuses that surpassed even the Blanchots. It was such a wine as words finally fail to describe, with all the qualities of the first two plus an extra smoothness and elegance that only a truly great year can provide, an experience that only comes very occasionally to one.

A visitor who had called on the cellar and been given a glass begged for the opportunity to buy half a dozen cases but Michel could only smile sadly and shake his head. We were drinking one of the very last half dozen bottles that he had retained. The rest had gone down the throats of an appreciative world and left only their memory to stir the growers to renewed efforts that might, the weather and the gods being willing, result in five or ten years time in another such growth.

But the point is this—these superb Grand Crus were three out of the seven that total some 18,000 gallons a year. And they all come from soil that, using the white Chardonnay grape, produces this splendour from marl and limestone.

I have climbed the back-breakingly steep slopes of the Mosel and have leaned at a precarious angle among the slabs of slate that cover most of the ground. They are highly valued for the way they reflect the heat of the sun on to the grapes. It is an infertile soil but good vines flourish on

A Jura vineyard, where vines are planted some distance apart to enable a tractor to drive between the rows.

A Burgundy vineyard showing the distance between the rows of vines.

A typical Bordeaux vineyard.

A typical vineyard in the lush Palatinate area.

difficult land partly because they have to thrust their roots down vigorously if they are to live. It is much the same on the slopes of the Rhine, but very different in the lush Palatinate.

Down the Rhône I have trodden the big, bulky stones that litter the vineyards producing the full wines of Chateauneuf-du-Pape and Gigondas. They are round and white and heavy and grow hot enough under the sun's rays to burn your fingers. Except for their powers of reflection they are different again from the slate of the Mosel. Yet to the Syrah and Grenache grapes they are as valuable as the Mosel slate is to the Riesling.

So one must conclude from all this that the soil must suit the grape, and the grape must fit the soil. The Pinot Noir does not flourish in the granitic earth that produces the splendid quaffing wine of Beaujolais, which comes only from the Gamay grape, and the Gamay grape proves a poor thing when planted in the land that best supports the Pinot Noir.

Nature has given a choice of grapes with a lavish hand, but they must be planted where nature has provided the best setting and they must be cultivated by methods that suit the district. That, after all, is the basis of the wine laws of all countries that grow wine. The legislation is only restrictive in the sense of securing the best produce from the land it governs, and the conditions it imposes are basically those of good and successful husbandry.

For every vigneron or winegrower, however, there are five other men engaged in buying, storing and selling for the wine trade of his area and so on across the world. Yet it is an intimate industry. Take any wine town such as Bernkastel or Beaune, Jerez or Verona and in that region the quality and value of every man's wine will be common knowledge. His methods, idiosyncracies, failings and successes are familiar to all.

The buyers and sellers have known one another for many years. With the larger firms it is not uncommon for an agency or a connection to last for fifty years or more, often with nothing in writing. So the stranger coming to make a purchase will do well to arrive with introductions. And that is why the unknown purchaser who hopes to buy a barrel to send home will never get the best wine available. He will not pay any less than the other buyers either, and he may even have to pay more, but the best of the cellar goes to the houses who have bought there for as long as anyone can remember.

Every big French shipper has his agents or *courtiers* in the regions where his interests lie. There are also *commissionnaires,* rather superior and older gentlemen who only deal in large quantities. Both maintain contacts between their clients and the winegrowers, tasting and reporting

Parade of wine guilds and banners in a wine-tasting hall at Bordeaux.

and making this their life work. They have their own association with an annual conference and their success depends upon their palates.

The system in Germany is similar, but here the gentlemen are called *kommissionäre* and are to be found at the advance tastings which precede the great wine auctions, such as those of the 'Trierer Verein von Weingutsbesitzern der Mosel-Saar-Ruwer', held in the hall of the Treviris restaurant in October. And what a sight that is!

The printed catalogue of wines, a substantial handbook, glistens with the great names of the area: Willi Haag, S. A. Prüm, J. J. Prüm, Dr H. Thanisch, Otto Van Volxem and many more. These are obviously kept afterwards as records, for each page lists the grower, the number of bottles offered, the details of the growth such as year, vineyard, and distinctions like *Kabinett* or *Auslese,* the price estimated and the buyer's name, plus a large space for notes.

The advance tasting is picturesque too, for the bottles are ranged in orderly rows, with baskets of sliced dry bread to cleanse the palate between each tasting.

In France members of the trade, like the cellarmen, carry their own *tastevins,* silver convoluted shallow cups shaped like small saucers and held by a tiny ringlike handle.

In German tastings a glass stands before each

A German wine auction held in the casino at Wiesbaden.

A tastevin as used at wine tastings in France.

bottle, perhaps half filled, and each taster sips from it in turn, spitting out the wine into a convenient bucket or a sawdust channel. If you question the hygiene of sharing a single glass for each wine among so large a company you are told that wine is naturally antiseptic and there is no risk attached. Who are you to quibble?

With Rudolf Bernhard, a former wine dealer now converted to the pleasure of publicising Trier and its wines and history to the visiting public, I moved down the long tables. These were wines of that great vintage, 1971. Some say it is the wine of the century, but the century is far from over! Wonderful wines they certainly are, however. A sip of a great Wehlener Sonnenuhr Auslese from S. A. Prüm, followed by a full, smooth Urziger Würzgarten Auslese with a fine bouquet from Hugo Berres. Then an Erdener Prälat Auslese from the cellars of Elisabeth Christoffel-Berres of Ürzig, a smooth rich Riesling; a splendid Graacher Himmelreich Auslese from J. J. Prüm; and a big, bold and fruity Bernkasteler Doktor und Graben Spätlese with a special nose from Dr H. Thanisch.

It was a tasting that could, it seemed, have gone on for ever, ending with some magnificent *eiswein* examples made from grapes frozen when picked.

While I tasted for pleasure, the *kommissionäre*, young and old, sipped industriously. They would report back to their clients, Herr Bernhard told me, and make recommendations of what to bid for at auction. The client might instruct on their word alone or come and sip for himself.

'But,' I asked carefully, 'what happens if a *kommissionär* has several clients? How does he decide between them if he finds one special wine?'

Herr Bernhard looked serious. 'Such a situation would not arise,' he said finally.

'But it could,' I persisted, 'it could.'

Herr Bernhard shook his head. 'No,' he said, 'it could not. A good *kommissionär* would never let it arise.'

That seemed to me to be true German logic.

3

How to Care for .

Storage:

Wine bottles should always be stored on proper racks, of which there are many on the market at moderate prices. If you do not have a wine cellar, then under the stairs or at the back of a deep pantry are convenient places for storage. Large bins of the kind illustrated are available if there is sufficient space to accommodate them. Care must be taken to ensure an even temperature, around 55 degrees Fahrenheit, and darkness is always an advantage. Bottles are stored on their sides so that the corks are kept moist. If the corks become dry, air may enter through them and adversely affect the wine. Heat and air are enemies of good wine. Should a bottle be seen to be seeping wine, it should be opened and drunk. All wines, even the cheaper ones, benefit by resting in this way and usually a week at least is advisable before drinking them. Spirits should be kept upright.

If you buy vintage wine to lay down, a cellar is really essential to get the best results, since the bottles should remain undisturbed. The alternative is to buy matured wine from a good merchant, but this of course, is more expensive, or you can also pay for storage by your merchant until it is ready. Merchants, however, are often pressed for space. Wines do better in darkness and an even temperature and should be segregated from anything that might taint them by its smell. Discipline yourself to keep a cellar book, giving date of purchase and price.

Decanting is certainly necessary with old vintage port. Avoid shaking the bottle, draw the cork carefully, and pour into the decanter against a light, preferably a candle, so that you can see when the sediment approaches the neck. Then stop pouring and do not start again!

Matured claret and burgundy are usually decanted, almost always by wine shippers when showing them at luncheons. You may think it wise to follow their example, though I confess to a fondness for seeing the bottle on the table with its label clearly visible to tell you so much about the wine. Decanting should take place not less than one hour before drinking.

Don't be impressed by a restaurant that has

Open fronted bin.

Terraced bin to fit under a staircase.

racks of wine near the customers. The heat in a restaurant and the lighting itself will affect wine kept for any length of time in this way. Your wine waiter should supply you from the cellar and show you the label for checking before he draws the cork. Since, however, red wine should be opened in advance to breathe at room temperature for an hour or more, you can seldom ensure this in a restaurant unless you order beforehand and can trust the owners' reputation.

and Serve Wine

Glasses:

The wine may taste the same but having the right glass makes a considerable difference to your enjoyment.

Top row left: Red wines are served in plain glasses with stems the same length as the bowls, suitable for both Burgundy and Bordeaux. Hocks and Alsatian wines are traditionally served in green or amber stemmed glasses.
A long stemmed 'tulip' glass.

Bottom row left: A 'tulip-shaped' glass for Bordeaux. A port glass. A liqueur glass. A copita-type sherry glass. Your glass should never be overfilled, about three-quarters full is right. This allows the wine to be swirled around and its bouquet enjoyed to the full.

Bottles:

Wine bottles are nearly as interesting as the wine they contain and vary in shape and colour according to their region of origin.
Top row left: A slim long-necked German Rhine Bottle. A typical sherry bottle. A brown glass Italian bottle for Piedmont wines. A 'clavelin' bottle for Jura wine.
Middle row left: A club shaped Beaujolais Pichet. A slim necked green Alsace bottle. A flagon of Portuguese Mateus Rosé—a flask shape which has been adapted from the traditional 'bocksbeutel' used for Franconia, German wines.

Bottom row left: A magnum of champagne. A high shouldered green bottle for red wine of Bordeaux. A Rhone wine bottle. A Chianti bottle in a straw flask. A high shouldered port bottle.

32

Choice:

All wines are not suited to all dishes. Some blend rather better with certain foods than others. Nobody in France would drink wine of any kind with hors d'oeuvre, or dishes with French dressing, but many Italians like to sip the sparkling wines of Asti Spumante with dishes that contain mayonnaise, egg sauces and salads, so this advice cannot be taken as firm rules.

Aperitifs:

This should not spoil your palate with its sweetness. A *brut* (dry) champagne is ideal, if expensive. A *fino* (dry) sherry, or a medium-dry if you must have something less austere is also acceptable. A dry vermouth from Cinzano, Carpano, Noilly or one of the other houses may just be permissible.

Soups:

With soups, whether thick or clear, a dry sherry or a dry Madeira is acceptable. With *Vichysoisse* one might drink a dryish white wine, a German Riesling or an Alsatian Muscat. Paté goes well with these white wines.

Fish dishes:

Red wines generally do not go with fish, although some insist that a *rosé* wine may be drunk with salmon and red wine with kippers. A Muscadet from the Loire makes a happy accompaniment to most fish. Oysters are traditionally associated with Chablis. For simple fish dishes choose from Alsatian and German Riesling, Pouilly Fumé from the Loire and Pouilly Fuissé from the region south of Mâcon, an Italian Soave, a Yugoslav Riesling, a South African or Australian Riesling—all white, dryish wines. Fish of a stronger flavour, like salmon or turbot, or those served with a rich sauce require a bolder wine, and Puligny-Montrachet, Bâtard-Montrachet, Chassagne-Montrachet or Meursault are all excellent. A fine Mosel makes a contrast, or, one might be tempted by the flowery, if spicy, bouquet of an Alsatian Gewürztraminer.

White meat:

For pork and veal the first choice would be among white wines though the lighter reds are also appropriate. The white wines should be medium dry; a Sylvaner from Germany or Alsace, or a Californian white wine such as the Chenin Blanc of the Christian Brothers or a Paul Masson Emerald Dry, both excellent wines that can well rival European products. If you choose a red wine, it could be a Zinfandel from California, a Valpolicella from Italy, a Cabernet from Australia or Chile, or a Beaujolais or Bordeaux from France.

Red meat:

Foreign dishes are best matched to a wine from that country, *boeuf bourguignonne*—beef stew made with red wine—would call for a Burgundy. A better Beaujolais such as a Moulin-à-Vent or a Brouilly a Côte de Beaune or a Pommard would thus go well. An Italian dish like *Osso Bucco*—knuckle of veal in a stew seasoned with herbs—comes from Lombardy and should have a red Valtellina wine, or a Piedmont Barbaresco or Barbera. With a Normandy dish in cider, drink Normandy cider. For roast beef if red burgundies such as Chambertin or the lesser Gevrey-Chambertin are too dear, turn to a Rhône wine such as Châteauneuf-du-Pape, Gigondas or a Côtes du Rhône. With roast lamb, choose a good Bordeaux, or choose from among the Bourgeois wines of which the best, like Château Gloria, are almost as good. Italian wines like the great Barolo or Chianti Classico are also suitable with roasts as are the Hungarian reds.

Poultry and Game:

With roast chicken a claret is a good accompaniment and a Médoc wine is simple but effective. Cold breast of chicken is pleasant with a dry white Riesling. Roast goose or roast duck—rather greasy dishes—call for a wine that will retain its flavour. A Bourgueil from the Loire is appropriate or perhaps an Italian Barbera.
Roast pheasant or roast partridge require a claret. Roast grouse, with its strong flavour, is better suited to a good burgundy like Echézeaux.

Cheeses:

Wine, although forbidden with cream cheese, goes well with many others. Stilton always calls for port, Roquefort for Burgundy, though with Brie I would prefer Claret. With Gorgonzola I would hope to have some Barola left in my glass and with English cheeses like Cheddar and Cheshire, red wine—preferably Burgundy.

Sweets:

Here again, choose by the ingredients and nationality—for Zabaglione there should be Marsala. A semi-sweet sparkling wine, a spätlese hock, or a Sauternes goes well with fruit. If your stomach is still in good condition, you will probably be ready to end with a good port, cognac or armagnac.

4

The Laws of Wine

There are three types of wine throughout the world in the sense of the colour that grapes produce. They are red and white and *rosé,* the latter most properly made by leaving the grapeskins in contact with the wine for only a short time, though sometimes achieved by mixing white and red wine. It is the fact that the black grapeskins are left with the juice or 'must' during the fermentation, and for a number of days after, that produces red wine. On the other hand the grapeskins are not left with the juice when making white wine but are removed beforehand.

Again, the dryness or sweetness of a wine depends not only on the grapes and their sugar content which the fermentation converts into alcohol, but on the actual process used in making wine. Fermentation, for instance, can cease naturally or be arrested by various methods and, since the grapes used for sweet white wines often have a considerable amount of sugar, ending of fermentation when sufficient alcohol has been reached may leave sugar in the must that provides further sweetness in white wines. Temperature is crucially important in winemaking and must be kept to the level at which the yeast cells can work best in transforming the grape juice into wine.

There are only too many other hazards such as fermentation stopping too soon, invasion by bacteria from the air which, in extreme cases, could turn wine into vinegar, faults in the wooden vats, even mysterious ailments which afflict the wine once it is in cask and have to be watched for by regular sampling, filtering and racking.

The guardian of the wine against all these ills is the cellarmaster, a veteran of many years' experience and a highly respected figure in his local community and the wine trade in general.

Even the proprietor must recognise that he comes second to his cellarmaster, however famous his own name. He may, in some few cases, know as much about his wines as his employee, but it is the cellarmaster who devotes his entire life to the service of his master's wines and uses his skills, inherited and acquired, to further their good name.

The more famous the vineyard, whether it be *château* or *domaine,* the more deserving is the cellarmaster of credit. Raise your hat to him at least metaphorically and acknowledge that without him your favourite label would be so much the less appealing.

It is seldom that you will meet a young cellarmaster or even a well-dressed one. They usually come shuffling out of some dark, unlit passage in the cellars, inevitably drawing a stained and battered *tastevin* from the pocket of the leather apron they wear as a badge of their trade. You are honoured to share the same rim as these old lips that have sipped so many immortal vintages and, of course, you may luckily be in a cellar that produces wine glasses when there are ladies in the party.

Which reminds me that never have I found a woman cellarmaster. Here is one opening that has escaped Women's Liberation and it is perhaps too lonely a life to attract their attention in any event. The cellarmaster is as devoted to his vats as the hunchback of Notre Dame was to his cathedral and rummages about them in much the same way.

What the cellarmaster has to understand are the wine laws of his country and, since they greatly affect wine drinkers, it is as well to know how they operate. While all countries producing wine of any quality have laid down laws to control the growth of the vines and their processing, the laws of France, Germany and Italy are the most important on the general wine scene. The European Economic Community has also made its own wine laws, and the individual laws of the member countries have to conform to them though, in fact, they are usually even more detailed.

In France the wine laws followed the First World War when, in the turbulent aftermath, less scrupulous growers exploited well-known names with offerings that were far from genuine, made from hybrid grapes that produced quantity rather than quality.

An area that suffered particularly in those days was that of Côtes-du-Rhône, running down the Rhône valley, but it produced a man to match the hour in the late Baron Le Roy de Boiseaumarié, a noted proprietor who loved his region.

PRODUCE OF FRANCE

1970
CHATEAU LAGRAVE-GENESTRA
SAINT-LAURENT
APPELLATION HAUT-MEDOC CONTROLEE
SOLE SUPPLIER
Mᶦⁿ MARCEAU
A BORDEAUX (GIRONDE) FRANCE
Shipped & Bottled by Rawlings Voigt Ltd.
London S. E. I. 7 BE

PROPRIÉTÉ EXCLUSIVE
LOUIS ROEDERER
CRISTAL CHAMPAGNE
1966
CRISTAL-CHAMPAGNE
BRUT REIMS
FRANCE
HO R.30 0108 PRODUCE OF FRANCE — REGISTERED TRADE MARK N. M. 3.642.242

1970

GRAND VIN
1970
Cruse
LES COUBERSANS
marque déposée
MÉDOC
RED BORDEAUX WINE
APPELLATION MÉDOC CONTROLÉE
CE MÉDOC RACÉ PROVENANT DES MEILLEURES
ORIGINES A ÉTÉ SÉLECTIONNÉ A VOTRE INTENTION PAR
SHIPPED BY
Cruse & Fils Frères
NÉGOCIANTS A BORDEAUX (GIRONDE)
RUTHERFORD OSBORNE & PERKIN
GREAT WEST ROAD, BRENTFORD TW8 - 9DY

PRODUCE OF FRANCE
Châteauneuf-du-Pape
APPELLATION CHATEAUNEUF-DU-PAPE CONTROLÉE
DOMAINE DE MONT-REDON
HENRI PLANTIN, PROPRIÉTAIRE-RÉCOLTANT A CHATEAUNEUF-DU-PAPE (Vse)
Shipped and Bottled by J B. REYNIER LTD., London, S.W.1
Shippers REYNIER Shippers

ROSÉ JEBERRE
Appellation Cabernet d'Anjou Contrôlée
PRODUCE OF FRANCE
Shipped by
Reynier
LONDON S. W. I.
REGISTERED TRADE MARK

C.M. 7.916
COTES DE PROVENCE
VIN DÉLIMITÉ DE QUALITÉ SUPÉRIEURE
Damelière
MARQUE DÉPOSÉE
V.D.Q.S. LABEL
DG-702
CANNES
ST RAPHAËL
ST TROPEZ
TOULON HYÈRES
PASQUIER-DESVIGNES
AU MARQUISAT DEPUIS 1420 - NÉGOCIANTS A SAINT-LAGER (RH) FRANCE

36

CABERNET
ROSÉ JEBERRE
D'ANJOU

SERVE COOL   SERVE COOL

Produce of France
Bottled in France

SAINT - VÉRAN
APPELLATION SAINT - VÉRAN CONTROLÉE

PASQUIER-DESVIGNES
AU MARQUISAT DEPUIS 1420

PASQUIER-DESVIGNES · NÉGOCIANTS A ST-LAGER (RH.) FRANCE

Grands Vins   de Bourgogne

FLEURIE
APPELLATION FLEURIE CONTROLÉE

Mis en bouteilles dans nos caves en Beaujolais

Au Marquisat depuis 1420,
Pasquier Desvignes
Négociants à St-Lager (Rh.) France

Cuvée des Saints Pères
Grand Vin Rouge de France
CRUSE
SHIPPED BY   RED WINE
Cruse & Fils Frères   11°
NÉGOCIANTS A BORDEAUX (GIRONDE)
Imported by
RUTHERFORD OSBORNE & PERKIN LTD - GREAT WEST ROAD
BRENTFORD TW8 9 D.Y.
PRODUCE OF FRANCE

LEBÈGUE
FRENCH COUNTRY WINE
Carcassonne
A SOFT, FULL-BODIED RED WINE PRODUCED IN THE DÉPARTEMENT OF
AUDE IN SOUTHERN FRANCE
VIN DE PAYS

PRODUCE OF FRANCE
SELECTED SHIPPED AND BOTTLED BY J. L. P. LEBÈGUE & CO LTD LONDON S.E.1

REGISTERED TRADE MARK
Tavel Rosé
APPELLATION   CONTRÔLÉE
Shipped by REYNIER London S.W.1.
PRODUCE OF FRANCE

SEC   DRY
MUSCADET VALOIS
Appellation Muscadet Contrôlée
PRODUCE OF FRANCE
Shipped by
Reynier
LONDON S.W.1.
REGISTERED TRADE MARK

It was through him that Châteauneuf-du-Pape, that fine wine of body and bouquet from the robust Syrah, Grenache and other grapes that flourish here, became the first to have regulations regarding production, an example followed later in the laws of 'Appellation d'Origine' that now apply throughout France. This first effort has done much for Châteauneuf-du-Pape, a fine red wine that comes close to the better burgundies and must be made to a minimum alcoholic strength of twelve-and-a-half per cent.

The vignerons applied as far back as 1923 for these regulations, led by the Baron, and a historic decision was eventually given by the courts sitting in Orange. This laid down that the grapes must be pruned in a certain way, the soil must be of a defined nature, the wine must be red or white and never *rosé*, and the minimum strength as above. In addition, it was stipulated that a certain proportion of the grapes must actually be rejected when gathered, though they might be used to make a wine not entitled to the great name.

This decision came at the same time as wine laws were generally accepted in other parts of France. Soon after the court at Orange gave judgement, the Civil Tribunal of Dijon defined the wine areas of Burgundy in April, 1930. And although there had been laws in France as far back as 1905 against deceit in the quality, origin and names of wines, these had been too general in their application. It was in the 1930s that the sources of origin were controlled and the 'Institut National des Appellations d'Origine' came into power, created by the law of 30 July, 1935. It links the officials concerned with the repression of frauds with the winegrowers and the shippers or *negociants*. The Institute lays down the regulations from choice of grape to the method of vinification and much more. It looks after the interests of both consumer and producer and can enforce its decisions with surprising severity. A less known aspect of its work is the protection of the great wine names of France. In this respect it has successfully protected the use of the name Champagne but has not yet succeeded with others like Burgundy, Chablis and Sauternes which are commonly, and wrongfully, appropriated by many other wine-producing lands, though happily there is some sign of voluntary reform in this abuse.

When wine leaves a French vineyard it must take with it an official receipt, known as an *acquit,* printed on distinctive green paper, and essential in any sale to a wholesaler or for export. If the wine is sold at home to restaurants or individuals the permit is called a *congé.* These papers go with the wine, however often it is sold, and are the proof of its genuine origin. The middlemen selling wine have to keep a book in which they enter details of their purchase and its resale.

There is also an official check twice yearly on wine stocks and the 'Service de la Repression des Fraudes' has similar access to the records. So it is worth knowing the terms used and printed on wine labels.

The top grade of French wine is shown by the words 'Appellation Contrôlée'. Between these two words is often printed the name of the region or, for better wines, the actual district of production. 'Appellation Bordeaux Contrôlée' would signify a wine from the huge Bordeaux region that had been made according to the legal requirements, but 'Appellation Haut-Médoc Contrôlée' would be even better as showing a particular region of recognised prominence. Better still would be 'Appellation Pauillac Contrôlée', one of the top districts of the Haut-Médoc where such very great wines as Châteaux Latour, Lafite and Mouton-Rothschild are made, though the labels would also carry their names in the case of these fine offerings.

In Burgundy there would be similar phrases. 'Appellation Bourgogne Contrôlée' would indicate the more general, and therefore lesser, wine with 'Appellation Beaune Contrôlée' as the indication of a better region and 'Appellation Romanée-Conti Contrôlée' as the great and famous wine of a very small district. In Burgundy, in fact, it is common practice merely to use the words 'Appellation Contrôlée' and also print the name of the wine, such as Richebourg or Clos-de-Vougeot, in larger type.

On the Loire and in the Jura much the same procedures are adopted. In Beaujolais the label may carry four different descriptions according to the quality of the wine. Lowest is Beaujolais, then Beaujolais Supérieur, then Beaujolais Villages, made in only thirty-six named villages, and, top of them all, the nine Crus (or Growths) of Beaujolais which are Brouilly, Chénas, Chiroubles, Côte de Brouilly, Fleurie, Juliénas, Morgon, Moulin-à-Vent and Saint-Amour. The names of the Crus also appear on the labels of their bottles. Sometimes the grade is simply referred to as A.C. or A.O.C. and it is not used for Champagne because that word alone is sufficient indication of standards enforced, and is, in effect, an appellation of origin.

One of the most interesting things about A.C. wines is that the production is limited to so many litres per hectare, or two-and-a-half acres. If this is exceeded, the surplus is declassified, which means that a man making too much Beaujolais Villages would have to sell the surplus by a lesser name such as Beaujolais Supérieur or Bourgogne Grand Ordinaire and, of course, at a lesser price. The object of the limitation is to discourage over-production and so only get the best from the vines, but better methods or better weather can foil legal intentions. Currently revision of the declassification laws is being discussed to make them less severe and Commissions are proposed to taste the surplus and, if approved, give it classification again.

The A.C. laws also act against the temptation of blending. If wines of different appellations are blended, such as Beaune and Pommard, the result must be called Bourgogne, again fetching a lesser price than if it was called by one or other of the two names involved. The next lower step would be simply calling the wine *vin rouge*.

In the next category come wines bearing the initials V.D.Q.S. on their labels, standing for 'Vins Délimités de Qualité Supérieure', of which there are some sixty. An interesting thing about V.D.Q.S. is that the wines have to submit themselves to an official tasting, which is not the case with A.C., though such a step is under consideration. But V.D.Q.S. wines, though a number are of high standard, come below A.C. wines, despite the efforts of their devotees who sometimes claim that they are equally good. In some cases they may well be, but they come in general from recognisably lesser areas, the majority in the deep south of France where very hot sun and poorer soil do not encourage the vines like Bordeaux and Burgundy. Improvement is coming, however, especially in Languedoc and Roussillon.

There are some centres of note, such as Corbières, Costières du Gard, Minervois, Côtes du Ventoux, Côteaux du Tricastin (these two recently promoted to A.C.) and Côtes de Provence. Two come from Lorraine, in the north-east, which is recognised as being lesser than Alsace, its neighbour. The Lorraine two are Côtes de Toul and Vins de Moselle, the latter near Metz. There are also the Vins du Bugey from near Belley, birthplace in the Ain of the great gastronome Brillat Saverin, and Savoie, near Chambery. Others are the Côte Roannaise near Roanne and the Vins du Lyonnais. However the great restaurateurs of Roanne, such as the Troisgros Frères, and of Lyon, such as Paul Bocuse and Georges Blanc of Vonaas, turn to the Crus of Beaujolais, for example Fleurie, for their regional specialities rather than the lesser wines on their own doorsteps. More and more V.D.Q.S. wines of the better grades are on sale in Britain.

With the increasing prices of 'Appellation Contrôlée' wines there has been increased marketing of V.D.Q.S. wines outside their areas. Nicolas, the great French wine firm with its huge chain of retail outlets, now markets twenty-seven Vins de Terroir, most of which are V.D.Q.S., and a number of these are sold in Britain. Incidentally, Nicolas is not only a seller of blended or branded wines. Some forty per cent of its monetary turnover is in fine wines and I have seen aged vintages from many great *châteaux* in the Nicolas cellars, including an 1870 Château Mouton-Rothschild.

Most leading British shippers now import their own selections of V.D.Q.S. wines. By and large, V.D.Q.S. wines are those not considered good enough to merit the full A.C. status by the authorities, though they may be promoted to it, but their quality is above that of branded *vins ordinaires* and they are often quite strong alcoholwise. They are made from regional grapes but these include in some cases the Syrah and Grenache, used in the A.C. Châteauneuf-du-Pape, and efforts are being made to persuade the growers to plant more of these two and give up some of the minor varieties which, while producing quantity, do not provide the same quality. In the south of France, however, tradition is deeprooted and change slow.

Still lower is the term 'Vins de Pays', used for wines of local origin, grown and drunk in their region in most cases and often quite good value for their moderate price. Some of them do not travel well, so seldom leave their area, but others are quite suited for shipping. In recent times Lebègue of London, well-known shippers of fine French wines, have selected a group they call 'French Country Wines' ranging from Montrichard, a medium sweet *rosé* from the Loir-et-Cher, to Carcassonne, a full-bodied red from the department of Aude in southern France.

The words *vin ordinaire* have no legal force and refer to the sort of wine you will be served in a carafe or unsealed bottle if you ask for '*Un pot de rouge*' or '*Un pot de blanc*'. One firm, however, has taken up the phrase and given its authority to the name. This is Nicolas already mentioned. 'It is a wine one drinks daily, which complements all dishes, which does not hold any particular pleasure in its origin or vintage, but has the same taste always,' is their definition. 'We do not expect it to have particular individuality, but it should always be of perfect standard quality though it is impossible to tie together individuality and continuity.'

Thus where area of origin and vintage are specified, the wines are described as 'fine wines' and may be so even if the area of origin is not accompanied by vintage. Without area of origin and without vintage the wine becomes a blended wine. In all blendings the responsibility rests on the shoulders of the blending experts, men of great experience with a firm appreciation of the need to preserve the standards of their firm's good name.

All great French wine producing areas maintain the idea of origin and vintage, though the weather in every wine year will greatly influence the quality of the wine made. This is a law of nature that must be accepted and explains why one year, such as 1961, will be accepted as a great year while another, for example 1968, is a year of indifferent quality though some wines will prove an exception.

QUALITÄTSWEIN
MIT
PRÄDIKAT
RHEINGAU
A. P. Nr. 26026 015 72
1 9 7 1 er
Schloss Johannisberger.
Rosalack
AUSLESE

Erzeuger-Abfüllung
Fürst von Metternich
Domäne Schloß Johannisberg

RHEINGAU
1969er
Aßmannshäuser
Höllenberg
Spätburgunder
Faß Nr. 22
Silberne Preismünze Hess. Landesweinpr. 1972
CABINET
Verwaltung der Staatsweingüter Eltville
Eigener Kellerabzug und Korkbrand

MOSEL · SAAR · RUWER
QUALITÄTSWEIN
A. P. Nr. 19070032173
BEREICH
BERNKASTEL
Green Label
BOTTLED IN GERMANY BY
Deinhard
KOBLENZ AN RHEIN UND MOSEL

MOSEL · SAAR · RUWER
19 **71er**
BERNKASTELER DOKTOR
SPÄTLESE
QUALITÄTSWEIN MIT PRÄDIKAT · A. P. Nr. 1576281373
Erzeugerabfüllung der Gutsverwaltungen
Deinhard
Oestrich / Rheingau — Bernkastel - Kues / Mosel

SCHLOSS ELTZ
Gräflich Eltz'sche Güterverwaltung Eltville a/Rh.
Original- Abfüllung
1969er Schloss Eltz
Cabinet
Eltviller Sonnenberg Riesling
WOLF, ELTVILLE
RHEINGAU

WEINBAU
IN DER
Weingut Winzermeist
Qualitä
Amtliche Prüfun
Nierstei

Produced and bottled in Germany

ARTHUR HALLGARTEN G.mb.H.
GEISENHEIM (RHEINGAU)

GEISENHEIM

NIERSTEINER GUTES DOMTAL

QUALITÄTSWEIN - RHEINHESSEN

Amtliche Prüfungsnummer 4 907039 31 74

"DOMGARTEN-BRAND"

registered trade mark

PRODUCE OF GERMANY

BEREICH BERNKASTEL

MOSEL · SAAR · RUWER

Moselgold ®
QUALITÄTSWEIN
ARTHUR HALLGARTEN
WEINGROSSHANDLUNG
GEISENHEIM / RHEINGAU

A. P. Nr. 502 - 23 - 72

B A D E N

B A D E N

Durbacher Schloß Staufenberg

Riesling x Silvaner (Müller-Thurgau)
Qualitätswein mit Prädikat - Auslese
Eiswein
MAX MARKGRAF von BADEN
Markgräflich Badisches Weingut Schloß Staufenberg, Durbach

"Keller Katz"   "Cellar Cat"
Qualitätswein b. A.

Amtliche Prüfungsnummer 2 907039 129 73

Zeller Schwarze Katz
"BLACK CELLAR CAT"
ARTHUR HALLGARTEN G.M.B.H.
Geisenheim / Rheingau
Produce of Germany

FAMILIE
SEIT 1696

...ich Selp, Nierstein / Rh.

...Prädikat
...82 263 / 18 72

...ofenberg

...SSEN

Scholl & Hillebrand
RÜDESHEIM AM RHEIN

KONZERT
LIEBFRAUMILCH
QUALITÄTSWEIN

Produced and bottled
by:
Scholl & Hillebrand

2,0 L.
PRODUCE OF GERMANY

COCK RUSSELL AND SPEDDING LTD.
SOLE IMPORTERS, LONDON S.W.1

GEWA BINGEN

K 4030

In poor years the winegrower can meet adverse conditions by changing his methods of vinification and the date of the grape-picking will be adjusted to allow for maturity of the grape. This is another reason for choosing the wines of a grower of repute when purchasing dearer wines.

If area of origin only is the stipulation, then the grower with two or more seasons' harvest in his cellars can blend the wine so as to make certain of continuity in the flavour and quality of his wine. This has led to a growth of brand names or names of *marque* or trademark, under which a merchant of repute may offer wines that declare their area of origin without specifying a particular vintage or year.

This is the practice with champagnes that are non-vintage. The name of the champagne house is sufficient guarantee in itself of the quality of production of these non-vintage blends, while the house reserves part of the best vintage to sell as vintage champagne with the year specified and the price, of course, dearer.

Germany is another country with strict wine laws dating back for centuries, since Charlemagne in his day banned the blending of some vintages and down the years there have been similar prohibitions.

In the eighteenth century Baden had laws regulating wine making and forbidding various additions. The first detailed German wine law was passed in 1892 and was followed by others in 1901, 1909 and 1931 with additions up to 1958.

A comprehensive new German wine law came into effect with the 1971 vintage, and although older German wines are still to be met labelled under the previous laws, these will of course gradually disappear as they are consumed.

The 1971 German wine law separates German wines into three grades. These are, the lowest first, 'Tafelwein', then 'Qualitätswein', and finally the best of all, 'Qualitätswein mit Prädikat'. The word *Prädikat* may be translated as 'title' or distinction, and this is shown by the addition of certain words on the label. These begin with Kabinett, now as in the past an indication of distinction; Spätlese, which means late gathered fully ripe grapes; and Auslese, the special selection of late vintage fully ripe grapes, and their separate pressing. Even higher are 'Beerenauslese', a selection of over-ripe grapes; 'Trockenbeerenauslese', a selection of late grapes left long on the vines until they are shrunken and highly concentrated with richness; and 'Eiswein', grapes that are gathered when frozen and ice-covered very late indeed, usually in December. These last three take much time and labour to make and are accordingly expensive.

The second grade, 'Qualitätswein', is also sometimes given with two other words *'bestimmter Anbaugebiete'* or as QbA, these words meaning 'defined regions'. They must have the typical taste of the region among other factors. To ensure this they have to be submitted to a tasting commission which grants them an official number after passing the necessary tests both before and after bottling. This number is called the Prüfungsnummer.

The wine in the second grade is made from approved grape varieties. It must be of average quality with a minimum alcoholic strength and representative of its grape flavour. The wine may be named after a village or vineyard in the defined regions. Like the top grade, the Prüfungsnummer is a guarantee of conformity with the wine law and the standards demanded.

'Tafelwein', or table wine, does not carry the vineyard names which are permitted only on the labels of the two quality wines. It is a pleasant, light wine for ordinary drinking and has not got the quality appeal of the other two. It comes, however, from delineated areas, larger than the others, and has to be made from approved grapes. Names shown on the label as already explained will be those of such regions as the Main, Neckar or Rhein and Mosel.

Some of the former descriptions used on labels are now banned, among them *feine* and *feinste*, rather vague phrases meaning 'fine', and *natur* and *naturrein* which meant that sugar had not been added. In the latter case 'Qualitätswein mit Prädikat' must by law be made without the addition of any sugar and use only the sweetness of the grapes concerned. Even the mention of prizes and medals is subject to restrictions. If called Deutscher Tafelwein it must be a hundred per cent German wine.

The German sparkling wine called Sekt also has to meet new requirements under the 1971 wine law. Strangely enough the Germans claim that this name originates from the English word 'Sack' which in England is regarded as being linked with sherry.

When France, following the First World War, was able to ensure that champagne could only be used to describe French sparkling wines of that well-known region, the Germans chose to use either Schaumwein or Sekt to describe their own sparkling wine, and it is as Sekt that this is known all over the globe. With Teutonic thoroughness the experts defining the new law investigated the use of the name Sekt and satisfied themselves that consumers expected to receive a German sparkling wine when they ordered Sekt.

As a result the new law has imposed more stringent regulations for the making of Sekt. It must now have an alcoholic content of at least ten per cent; it must not have more than 250 mg/litre of sulphur dioxide (used to hold the sweetness and for other purposes); it must be made through the process of a second fermentation; it must be stored for at least nine months with a carbon dioxide pressure of at least 3·5 atmospheres; it must be satisfactory as to bouquet, colour and taste; and it must have a prüfungsnummer. It can also be described as Qualitätsschaumwein, for the title of Schaumwein alone can be used for a sparkling wine made to less severe requirements. Another term that may be used is Prädikatssekt provided that the Sekt is made from at least sixty per cent of German wine (Common Market wine laws are less stringent on certain aspects of blending). The closed tank process is used and the Deinhard plant at Koblenz is a very impressive example.

The new German wine law also applies to spirits produced from wine and under this the word Weinbrand is restricted to German brandy. Here again the name Cognac was restricted to French brandy after the First World War and Weinbrand was used for the German variety, a very pleasant spirit of fairly moderate price in its native land, just as in Spain the Fundador brandy is familiar everywhere.

The name Weinbrand gets official recognition in the new law but must now meet equally firm requirements. For instance the product must be made from approved grape types as defined by the Common Market (EEC) and it must be stored in oak casks for at least six months in the distillery. If the age is given in descriptions it must be at least one year. The colour must be within a certain range of gold and brown. Weinbrand has to be approved as to bouquet, colour and taste and it must carry an official number certifying that it conforms with these requirements.

Incidentally, the new law lays down that both Sekt and Weinbrand must be used as names for the respective products when they are sent for export, so that those drinking them know they are officially guaranteed.

The wines of Italy took an important step forward in June 1963, when a presidential decree approved a law controlling the names of origin of Italian wines under the title of 'Donominazione di Origine Controllata' (DOC), simply translated as Controlled Donomination of Origin.

Again, there are three grades of control. The top grade is Controlled and Guaranteed Denomination of Origin which is particularly stringent, though this year should produce several wines with the necessary qualities. The lowest grade is Simple Denomination, provided for lesser wines.

The DOC title is the one to look for on your label. It is reserved for wines of 'particular reputation and worth' and it is not awarded lightly. In 1972, for example, it was stated that some 105 typical Italian wines had the right to proclaim themselves DOC while twenty-one wines had been refused permission. Today, there are many more Italian wines permitted to call themselves DOC.

In fact DOC has much in common with the French 'Appellation Contrôlée', at any rate in its aims. It seeks to protect wine names that have gained recognition for their quality arising from a particular combination of climate, soil, grapes and wine-making methods, and to prevent use of these names by lesser wines. A wide range of wines of differing quality and character is covered.

Wines carrying the Italian DOC label must be from the named region, made by traditional methods and produced from the stipulated proportions of different grapes. A maximum grape production is specified for the vineyards concerned and the yield of wine per ton of grapes has to be within stated limits. DOC also shows that the wine has been inspected while maturing and under storage by official inspectors, and that the sales have been recorded in ledgers open to similar inspection. The wine must be entirely from the vintage year given and the labels must not mislead. Finally, the wine has to meet the requirements of the 'National Committee for the Protection of the Denomination of Origin of Wines' as regards bouquet, colour and taste, as well as chemical composition and alcohol and acid content.

The National Committee is made up of growers, wine producers, dealers, state experts and consumers' representatives. Although it works under the authority of the Ministry of Agriculture, which has its own inspectors, there are only five civil servants concerned with the Committee.

Italy is the largest wine producing country in Europe, France coming second, with Spain third, and this is also the world order although Argentina is closing on the leaders. Italy is a country where wine is grown in every conceivable part, and some of the wines such as Chianti, Barolo, Barbaresco, Valpolicella and Soave are of top standard. But there is also a tremendous amount of lesser and local wine. The names used are often of places or grapes and, far more so than other countries, the same name may confusingly apply to both red and white wines.

The 1971 Italian wine production was sixty-four million hectolitres or 1,408 million gallons, of which 187 million gallons were exported, half of it to Germany, followed by Switzerland and USA. But exports to France and Britain are rapidly increasing also and one of the objectives of the DOC law is to improve standards and labelling for sale abroad. The Common Market has enormously increased the potential for Italian wines and this, coupled by rapidly increasing prices for French wines and, to a lesser degree, for German wines, presents the Italians with a tremendous opportunity that they are cleverly exploiting by publicity of all kinds.

The climate, sunshine and soil make wine production comparatively easy in Italy, as in most warm climates, but the need is for care in production, maintained standards of quality, and provision of those wines that the importing countries require. Italy is undoubtedly set for a great expansion in its overseas sales. Britain, for instance, imported nearly four million gallons of Italian wines in 1973, more than four times the amount of 1971. The total Italian wine production in 1973 was a very high one of seventy-four million hectolitres.

In the past Italy has been accused of carelessness in its wine production and a familiar and unfair gibe has referred to rows of cabbages being planted between rows of vines. A country producing so much wine from so many small growers was bound to have to contend with varying standards, but the 1963 decree was by no means the first effort to control quality. The regulations for Chianti Classico (Classico is from the best area, Riserva is quality wine at least three years in cask) go back to 1932 with the registration of a Consortia of growers, an example followed in many other districts as time went on.

As far back as the 1860s, Baron Bettino Ricasoli, who was also Prime Minister of the time, conceived the blend of Sangiovese, Canaiolo and Malvasia grapes which provides Chianti with its special appeal.

More estates are coming to the fore, and even individual vineyards, while winegrowers' co-operatives are working to market the wines of their areas on similar lines to those of France and Germany. The Consortia regard themselves as banded together for the defence of typical local wines and often have their own label with the words to that effect, 'Consorzio per la Difesa dei Vini Tipici'.

Spain, too, has its wine laws, and the name 'Denominacion de Origen' translates itself. Although we are inclined to think more of sherry than anything else in Spain, wine is being increasingly exported in bulk to sell under branded names abroad. There are also quality wines, such as those of Rioja, sold with certificates of origin, but there is room for much more organisation in this respect. Given such increased supervision there is no reason why Spanish wines, as distinct from sherry, should not find a much larger place in European, if not world, markets and, with the country's huge production, perhaps in time vie with Italy in this respect.

The wine laws of the principal producing countries are given at this length because they provide important indications of quality and authenticity. They are not as confusing as they might seem at first reading. A little study will implant them in the mind and, for those who really care about wine, must be well worth while.

5

France

The wines of France set the standard for the rest of the world. Their superb creation, the work of centuries, is aided by rich soils of different kinds, a climate that is neither too kind nor too severe, and slopes and valleys that provide ideal settings for the grapes that have come to their highest perfection under French hands, grapes that are transplanted across the world, but never with such results as they achieve at home.

Nobody can judge satisfactorily the wines of other countries unless he has a sound grounding in the better French wines, both red and white. This does not mean that he must automatically recognise the vineyards, or even the areas, of the French wines he tastes, but he must have undergone the pleasant educational experience that only French wines can provide so that he can tell when a wine is big or little, fat or thin, worthy or unworthy.

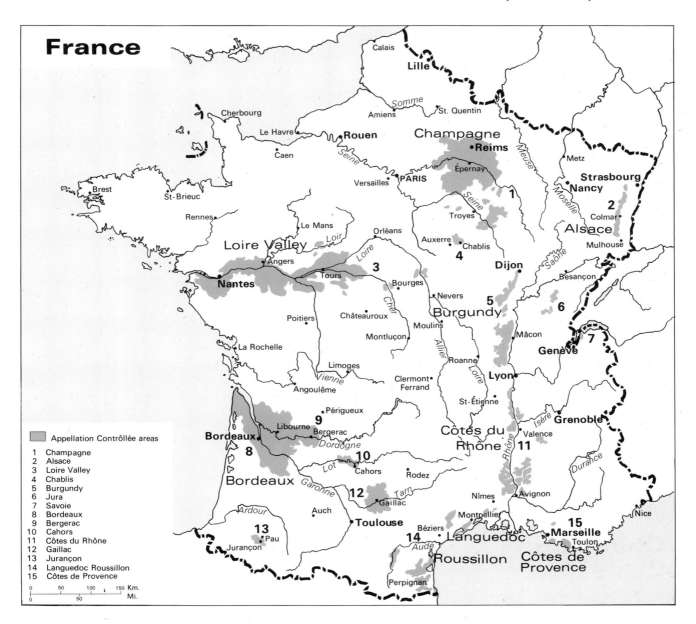

France

Appellation Contrôllée areas

1 Champagne
2 Alsace
3 Loire Valley
4 Chablis
5 Burgundy
6 Jura
7 Savoie
8 Bordeaux
9 Bergerac
10 Cahors
11 Côtes du Rhône
12 Gaillac
13 Jurançon
14 Languedoc Roussillon
15 Côtes de Provence

Champagne

French wines begin with the most northerly wine region. Champagne produces the supreme festive wine which bears that region's name. The vineyards lie on chalky hills to the south of the lovely old city of Reims with its great, grey cathedral, and production is centred both on Reims and the crowded, bustling little town of Épernay, even further south. At Épernay vineyards are grouped both to the north and in the area beyond the southern outskirts.

The wine itself is made from a blend of Pinot Noir and Chardonnay grapes, the former a blue-black grape used in Burgundy to produce superb red wine, and the latter a green-yellow grape that is used for all the great white wines of Burgundy. In each case, of course, the juice is colourless. Only when the black skins are left with the juice in the vinification process do they produce red or *rosé* wine.

The proportions vary according to the different champagne houses and the ideas of the expert blenders, but are approximately three-quarters of Pinot Noir to one-quarter of Chardonnay. The

A cross-section of the earth structure, which is typical of this region, showing the bed of chalk beneath rich alluvial top soil.

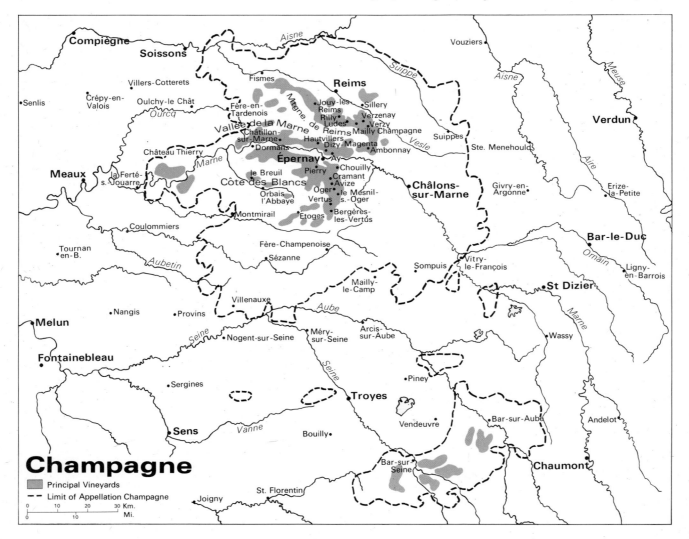

Champagne

Principal Vineyards
- - - Limit of Appellation Champagne

This immense cask, the largest in the world, has a capacity of 200,000 bottles of Champagne, and even when empty weighs 20 tons.

higher the proportion of the first grape, the more body, colour, alcoholic content and bouquet can be expected, summed up in the French word *corsé*. With more of the Chardonnay grape the resulting wine is lighter both in body and appearance, till one arrives at the Blanc de Blancs champagne, made entirely from white grapes. This is a speciality of the area south of Épernay known as La Côte des Blancs, with such famous winegrowing communes as Cramant, Avize and Le Mesnil-sur-Oger. The Pinot Meunier is another black grape, also used.

Nobody can visit the great champagne cellars running for miles under the chalk hills, some so vast as to require miniature railways to transport both wine and visitors, without hearing of La Montagne de Reims where such immortal communes as Sillery, Mailly, Beaumont-sur-Vesle and Verzenay lie on the upper section. There is also a lower section with other vineyards. Your guide at Reims will simply refer to La Montagne and take it for granted that you understand the importance of this name, for here grow essential vines.

Pink champagne is also made, the colour being obtained by leaving the blue-black skins with the wine for a short period as part of the process, but amusing as this may be in the context of what may

Abbey of Hautvillers, the birthplace of Champagne.

be called *liaisons dangereuses*, as Joseph Berkmann, restaurateur and winelover applies the phrase in one of his writings, this is not champagne at its best.

These great celebration wines are made by a long and carefully supervised process, which explains their cost. It is called *methode champenoise*, and while it is also used in other sparkling wines, usually over a shorter period than the six or more years required for the best champagne, nothing can really compare with the genuine article. The name champagne applies only to wines made in Champagne and is legally protected, both in France and abroad.

The wine was originally a still one, made sparkling through a discovery traditionally associated with Dom Perignon, a cellarmaster of the Abbey of Hautvillers between 1670 and 1715. His wonderful phrase voiced when he first tasted his invention, 'I am drinking stars,' has no doubt given him more fame than other equally worthy winemakers of his day. His discovery was that the addition of a calculated amount of sugar to the still wine brought about a second fermentation in the bottle, resulting in a sparkling wine due to the extra carbon dioxide and alcohol thus produced. A sediment is also left and to rid the wine of this the bottles are placed neck down in *pupitres*—chesthigh racks attended to regularly by the highly skilled *remueur* whose daily process of shaking the bottle in its rack and slightly turning the bottle by its base, called *remuage*, sets the deposit sliding down on to the cork. This deposit will eventually be carefully ejected in the action of *dégorgement*, when the cork is released, and pops out with the sediment attached, aided by a preliminary freezing of the bottle neck. The wine is then topped-up with wine of equal quality from another bottle and the *dosage* given, a sugary syrup with some wine and brandy, varying according to the practice of the house. For *brut* (very dry) champagne this is a small percentage, but for *doux* (rich) can be as high as eight per cent.

With the *dosage* and the dry or sweet quality of the champagne decided, the final cork which must bear the word 'champagne' on its side is inserted.

The bottles now go back to the cellar and are

The remueur manipulates the bottles in such a way that the sediment gradually slides down to rest on the cork.

A period of rest follows during which the bottles are stored en masse, neck downwards.

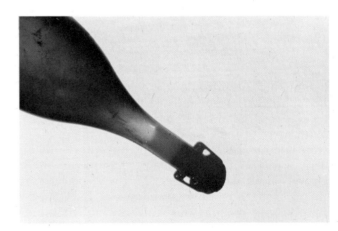

The removal of the sediment is made easier by freezing the neck of the bottle; the pellet of ice that forms enables the sediment to be separated from the wine.

A vintage scene in Pommery and Greno's vineyard at Reims.

Chablis

Travelling directly south, one crosses the Seine and after some hundred miles arrives in the Chablis area. There is no finer white wine for shell-fish, from oyster to lobster, than the produce of this most northerly wine district of Burgundy. Yet, although it cultivates that same Chardonnay grape for its wines as provides a share of champagne to the north, and the full content of the great white burgundies of the Côte de Beaune, in Chablis the wine has a nobility of its own. This is especially so in the superb Grand Cru of which Europeans must, alas, lament that eighty per cent now goes to the United States. Although the Premier Cru is a very fine wine it does not come much above the shoulder of the Grands Crus, exemplified in the produce of one remarkable slope which bears seven small vineyards—Vaudésir, Grenouilles, Blanchots, Bougros, Preuses, Les Clos and Valmur—whose names should be in letters of gold on any wine list.

Small as they are, ownership is large for it is shared among a number of people. One of them is Peter Reynier, who inherited his portion from his French father. It produced a number of very valuable barrels each year, distributed from his London headquarters. It is strange that Peter, an English agent for some of the best French wines, should have received the Military Cross for fighting against the Vichy French when he took part in the capture of Madagascar. The defending French commander was so impressed by Peter's spirit, despite wounds, that he sent a letter to his conquerors recommending Peter for a decoration.

The Premier Cru or First Growth vineyards come next and include Fourchaume, Monts-de-Milieu, Les Forêts, Vaillon, Beugnons, Les Lys, and fifteen more, while in the lower categories of Chablis and Petit Chablis the wines must come from twenty other communes to earn the right to carry the appropriate *appellation*.

It is not difficult to say why the Grand Cru wines are superior once you have tasted them. All Chablis are dry and all have a green-gold tinge, but the dryness of a truly great Chablis is not bone dry. There is a fascinating depth, almost a mellowness, a flavour of such elegance that it is as different from ordinary dry white wines, where mere acidity is often taken for dryness, as a gold chalice is from a tin mug. The Premier Cru have some of this nobility. A Fourchaume 1970 that I tasted with Ralph Gilbey, that connoisseur of this region, had a wonderful nose yet its flavour was a medium dryness, and the Vaudesir 1969 and Grenouilles 1970 with which we compared it had a mystique and breeding in their richness that left it behind. The finest wines inspire the finest reactions, they stimulate the taste buds and the imagination in a way that is beyond lesser offerings.

One of the best-known growers and merchants

---

watched to ensure that the *dosage* is successful, remaining for varying further periods in the cool depths of the cellars, perhaps beneath the very vineyards that gave birth to the wine.

Today the great French champagne houses continue to maintain their traditions of quality, integrity and superb hospitality. Their noble *châteaux* close to the cellars and vineyards are the centre of a unique blend of business and entertainment, lavishly staffed and generously run. Such great Anglophiles as Prince Guy de Polignac of Pommery et Greno, Marquis Hérard de Nazelle of Veuve Clicquot, charming Madame Odette Pol Roger of Pol Roger, are at once kindly hosts and widely-travelled negotiators. Champagne is famous for its 'widows' and besides the historic Madame Veuve-Clicquot-Ponsardin, whose firm claims that she invented *remuage*, there are Madame Pol Roger herself, Madame Lily Bollinger, recently retired from active command, and Madame Camille Olry-Roederer.

While Pol Roger declare that their champagne was the favourite of Sir Winston Churchill, Pommery also supplied his cellars regularly, and all the houses are accustomed to visiting royalty and presidents from the USSR to the United States. Yet for all the wealth and tradition there is a pleasant informality. When I had luncheon with Prince Guy de Polignac white-gloved footmen handed round the dishes and no less than four different champagnes, whilst his 88-year-old mother discoursed on the problems of modern living and asked my wife if she had much trouble in getting cooks and servants, an increasing problem in Reims. To know champagne is to love it and to know the proprietors, one and all, is to feel a deep affection for them, as well as an appreciation of their way of life.

A view with Chablis in the distance.

The town of Colmar, centre of the Alsace wine industry.

in this fascinating old town of narrow, winding streets, historic walls and arches, is Michel Remon, still a young man, of whom I have written earlier. His humour is as quick as his palate and he has ready stories about his customers. One client had arrived out of the blue in his Rolls Royce and bought five cases of Blanchots because he had enjoyed it the night before at a neighbouring hotel and pestered the proprietor until he revealed his source.

Although so much of the best Chablis goes abroad, there is good news from the area. In the past vineyards have been allowed to go out of cultivation, partly because the weather is so varied and hard that cultivating the vine is a real struggle, and partly because of the drift of workers to the cities. Now, with prices much increased, it is worth the effort to bring the abandoned areas once more under cultivation and to take advantage of their *appellation.*

The growers of Chablis are farsighted and have formed a commission with the shippers to fix the price of each grade, Grand Cru excepted, after every harvest. They take into account the quantity, quality and market conditions, and genuinely try to set a price that is fair both to themselves and the consumer. The need for such consultation is shown by the varying amounts of past harvests. In 1969 the yield was 22,000 hectolitres, followed by the bounteous year of 1970 which reached 78,000 and then fell again in the good but sparse vintage of 1971 to 25,000 hectolitres. In this way the men of Chablis can maintain a balance between good and short year prices. One hopes other areas may follow their example.

Alsace

About one hundred and fifty miles east of Chablis lies another very individual French wine area, that of Alsace. Like many other French wine names, Alsace has its dramatic connotations. The black-draped statue in Paris after the region was lost in 1870, the moving story of *La Derniere Classe* in which Daudet told of the village school's final French lesson before the German masters imposed

their language, and the agony of villages and vine-yards in 1944 when the tremendous tank battles of the Colmar pocket devastated so much land, must move every lover of France. Some, like lovely Riquewihr, 'the pearl of Alsace,' survived virtually unscathed whilst others, such as Mittelwihr, have risen, rebuilt, from the holocaust. Vineyards have been replanned and replanted and now produce better wine than perhaps Alsace ever knew before.

I would not group Alsatian wines in a German chapter, as others have done, because I believe both the wines and their proprietors have an individuality that is essentially French rather than German. After 1870, too, German rule called for vines producing quantity rather than quality, to use in German blends, and Alsace suffered accordingly. But after 1918, the Alsatian growers made a determined effort to restore their vineyards to former individuality, and dug out the poorer vines to replace them with quality stock. This was a wise and farsighted decision, whose true fruits are to be seen today.

Unfortunately, despite the French lamentations for lost Alsace, the return of the province after the First World War did not provide the concrete advantages hoped for by the Alsace growers. In 1920 France already had too much mediocre wine, and growers in other parts of the country decried the Alsace wine both from jealousy and from fear of competition.

These things are still remembered in Alsace, as is the courage of the grandparents of the present generation in planting the quality stock now flourishing today. So the Alsatians are rather inde-pendent in their outlook and that is what their chequered history has made them. Our generation has come to think of Alsace as something torn from France in 1870, as indeed it was. But although originally inhabited by the Gauls it became Germanicised after the Roman conquest and later joined the Holy Roman Empire until part of it was surrendered to France at the peace of Westphalia in 1648. The rest was seized by Louis XIV in the seventeenth century, so there is more to the tug-of-

The picturesque village of Hunawihr in Alsace.

war over this beautiful region than appears at first sight. Even the determination to regain Alsace and Lorraine shown in 1918 was in part due to the realisation that Lorraine alone held a tremendous store of iron ore which had greatly assisted German strength.

It is not surprising, therefore, that the Alsatians are very individual and even their way of training the vines is different from other areas of France. Certainly, as you drive through the villages with their black-timbered houses with steep, tiled roofs, glimpsing occasionally a proud stork on its nest, and enjoying the full, lush food, one is inclined to feel more in Germany than in France, irritating as such a thought must necessarily be to the French.

But the vines that are so famous today are largely

names that spring readily to the mind for their German origins. The greatest is the Riesling, that superb white wine grape of the Rhine valley. It does splendidly in Alsace, fragrant yet dry, quite as notable in its own way as any German example, although the soil and weather are different and experts can readily differentiate between them.

Sylvaner, again found in Germany, is a light and fruity white wine, not so classically dry as Riesling. But the wine that is growing more and more popular as a product of Alsace is that from the Gewürztraminer grape, again a white wine but this time with a most haunting, heady bouquet, spicy and, for some people, even perfumed. It is so remarkably different from other white wines, and so well made in Alsace, that it could prove to be the ultimate restorer of Alsatian fortunes. It goes well with seasoned, powerful dishes.

Until recently there were both Traminer and Gewürztraminer wines, both from the same grape, but the Gewürztraminer being selected from spicy, flavoured examples as, indeed, Gewürz indicates. From 1973, however, only Gewürztraminer has been permitted as a name, a sensible decision since the demand has been increasingly for this type and the use of Traminer as a title only led to confusion.

Gewürztraminer is a wine for occasions, but worth the slightly higher cost compared with other Alsatian wines. No white wine is quite like it, and although it is a splendid refreshment on its own, it comes through superbly with lusher dishes such as *Lobster Cardinal*, where it can stand up to the stronger flavours with its own aromatic taste.

Muscat is another excellent product of Alsace, but not related to the sweet dessert wines made from the Muscatel grape in other countries, or to be confused with Muscadet, the light, dry white wine of the Loire that goes so pleasantly with fish. Muscat has its own dry spicy flavour, less pronounced than Gewürztraminer, and is an excellent wine for a mid-morning drink. I remember a 1970 Les Amandiers Muscat, drunk in Riquewihr with Guy Dopff of the notable firm of Dopff & Irion; it was lightly chilled, gently encouraging our conversation. And that is how a wine should remain in the memory, recalled as a token of a pleasant occasion.

There are other Alsace wines too, though not so noteworthy, such as Chasselas, Pinot Blanc (or Clevner) and Pinot Gris (also known as Tokay d'Alsace but having no connection with the Hungarian Tokay). This latter is a suitable accompaniment to *foie gras*, where its mellow fullness matches the great Alsatian dish. Alsatian wines take their names from the grapes used and these appear on the label, a safeguard in itself, with the words *'Appellation Alsace Contrôlée.'* Edelzwicker denotes a blend of the 'noble' or better wines, while Zwicker is a blend of lesser quality grapes. Vineyard names are little used and one depends on the famous

Rodern, a town in Alsace with Château du Haut-Koenigsbourg on the hill in the distance.

Foie gras.

shippers. Such houses as Dopff, Dopff & Irion, Hugel, Schmidt, Beyer and Faller are reliable but in recent years the growth of the co-operatives has produced fine wines from such cellars as the Cave Vinicole de Turckheim, where the special Gewürztraminer, which I have enjoyed on the spot, is called 'Baron de Turckheim'.

The Jura

South-west from Alsace one finds more hills, but whereas the Vosges mountains protect the Alsatian vineyards on the eastern slopes from the winds and rain of the west, the Jura vineyards in the foothills of their region are more exposed. Their variety is interesting and while Alsatian wines are almost all white, those of the Jura are equally divided between white and red, with a famous *rosé* from Arbois.

Indeed the wines of the Jura have not had the recognition they deserve but, with other French areas becoming more expensive, they may yet be given a more prominent place. The great wine name here is that of Henri Maire, a veritable giant of a man both in stature and in business. His family have made wines at Arbois since 1632 but it took Henri to make them nationally famous. He chose his Vin Fou, a white sparkling wine of medium-dry flavour, put it in a bottle with a gay, dazzling label, and placarded France with brightly coloured posters showing masses of bubbles and four words: 'Vin Fou, Henri Maire'. These put their official rivals enjoining 'Sobriété, Securité' and 'Alcool Tue', to shame but added to the gaiety of the nation.

When I met Henri in his huge, glass-walled offices, a highly-modern building equipped with computers and electronic devices to carry on his business, he took me into his own more traditional study and opened a bottle of Vin Fou with his own big hands. The firm claims to grow and sell every year seventy per cent of those wines carrying the 'Appellation Contrôlée' in the Côtes du Jura, Arbois and Château-Chalon vineyards. The great specialities of the Jura are Vin de Paille and Vin Jaune, both demanding wines to make, and correspondingly dearer. The first takes its name, 'wine of straw', from the way it was traditionally made. Over-ripe grapes were left to become even riper on straw mats in the sun for up to three months.

Vin de Paille is an after-dinner wine to be drunk with dessert or on its own and, since fermentation is technically difficult and comparatively little is made, you will be lucky to find and drink this particular nectar.

On the other hand Vin Jaune is produced in a number of vineyards, led by Château-Chalon, Arbois and L'Etoile. Its name comes from the unusual yellow colour and its dry, 'burnt' and nutty flavour. The grape used is the Savagnin and this is late-picked with a consequently higher sugar content giving increased alcohol. After pressing, the wine juice goes into old casks for six years. The *flor* from the yeasts spreads across the surface of the wine like a film, glinting eventually with the yeast colours. This film provides the special taste, not unlike amontillado sherry and indeed the process has similarities with that used for the fino of Jerez. Again the wine is costly due to the long process, but it is not uncommon.

Other grapes of the Jura are Trousseau and Poulsard, both for red wines. As with most of Henri Maire's wines they carry distinctive names. His big, robust red is called Frédéric Barberousse, while his Cendre de Novembre, which translates to 'November ashes', is a *rosé* of strength and full flavour.

Like Alsace, the Jura region is an attractive holiday centre, and those who visit Arbois should call at Henri's tasting rooms in the main street. They are known as Les Deux Tonneaux, because the front is shaped like two barrels, and here films can be seen and wines tasted, and ordered from the sometimes rather importunate salesmen! Almost next door to the tasting rooms is the Hôtel de Paris of my friend André Jeunet, worthy holder of a Michelin star for cuisine which includes *Coq au vin jaune et morilles*, made in the famous yellow wine. Jeunet, as big as Maire, has a jovial approach to life and is an excellent host.

Burgundy

Now, however, one turns slightly north-west and drives inland to arrive at Burgundy which, with Bordeaux, forms the two most important wine areas of France. When one thinks of French wine, it is of one or other of these regions, and particularly of the red wine. Their rivalry is centuries old and one of nationality, too, for the Burgundians were allies of the English when the latter fought Joan of Arc and occupied a vast area round Bordeaux and the south-west of France.

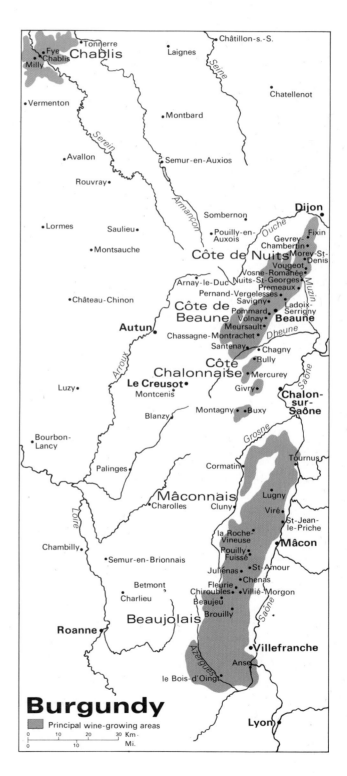

Burgundy

Principal wine-growing areas

0   10   20   30 Km.
0   10   Mi.

53

Sometimes I feel the English are unduly maligned over Joan of Arc, for she was undoubtedly captured by the Burgundians near Compiègne and just as undoubtedly handed over by them for her imprisonment and trial. When one visits Burgundy it is not surprising to find a warmth and heartiness that is akin to our own, since the Burgundian is closer to the soil and village life than are the great estates of Bordeaux where *Châteaux*, large and small, abound, and the proprietor is still very much the *seigneur* in his locality.

As one great vineyard owner of Bordeaux explained to me, he had no problems with local Communists. 'I merely told the villagers I would buy a new tractor for communal use,' he said. 'The local Communists dare not cause too much trouble because the other villagers naturally wanted the tractor, and as such things require renewing from time to time and I am ready to foot the bill, we all get along surprisingly well. From my point of view it is a modest payment that saves many difficulties.'

In Burgundy such a situation would scarcely be possible, for nearly every man there is his own proprietor and has his few acres. But Bordeaux has some 110,000 acres (44,534 hectares) of vineyards, producing over sixty million gallons of wine a year, whereas Burgundy, where vineyard acreage has drastically declined in the past century, produces much less than half that amount. With rising demand, Burgundy may revive some of the lost vineyards but it will take much time.

That the rivalries exist, however, it would be silly to deny. In Bordeaux, the pretty girl of twenty who drove me from the airport to the Maison des Vins asked me how well I knew France, and when I mentioned Burgundy she slowed down her sporty Italian car and said to me very solemnly, 'Monsieur, please do not mention Burgundy when you are in Bordeaux'.

Again, when I last dined in the excellent Marché restaurant at Beaune, that lovely old town where a score of top wine shippers can be found, I was interested to see that every one of these great houses was represented by several of its best Burgundies in the wine-list, a necessary and tactful step as it is here that the merchants bring buyers to do business. But when I turned the page to find the section covering the wines of Bordeaux, only three were listed—a humble Bordeaux Rouge, a St-Émilion of a blended trademark name, and a Château Beychevelle of 1963, a poor year!

What, then, is the difference between Burgundy and Bordeaux? As has been mentioned earlier, the great red Burgundies are all made from one grape, the Pinot Noir, whereas the great Bordeaux reds are made from a blend of three, even though all are grown on the same estate. The purist, however, might be wrong to think that the single grape offering was necessarily better. The truth is that each wine has qualities of its own.

For me, the appeal of Burgundy is that the best products are really 'big' wines. They have a great bouquet that rises from the glass before your nose is well in it. They have a deep, warm, dark colour. Their flavour fills your mouth immediately, clothes the palate entirely, and lingers there most royally once you have swallowed your first tasting.

A great Bordeaux is a wine of more finesse, perhaps of more individual flavour, depending on its vineyard, certainly of more refinement and breeding, in the French sense of *racé*, or thoroughbred. It will appear, weighed against the Burgundy, as a lighter, even thinner, wine, less bold and voluptuous, but balancing this by other qualities of taste or flavour, of more individual bouquet and variable colour. These terms are descriptive, not critical. The best of both take longer to mature than other wines.

In short, each of the two regions has splendid and noble qualities of its own, the Burgundy big, hearty and inviting, the Bordeaux selective, refined and very individual. It will depend on your nature which you prefer, but if you are wise you will enjoy each in its own part of the world with the dishes of its background. And, as I have shown, you will probably find it impossible to obtain a top specimen of either when you are in the rival's territory! At home you will choose for yourself.

Chablis, already described, is technically in Burgundy but its white wines are so much in a style of their own that most winelovers regard Burgundy as beginning with the wines of the Côte d'Or, that splendid range of gentle, golden slopes which lie between Fixin, near Dijon in the north, and Santenay, near Chagny in the south.

The Côte d'Or is divided into two parts. The first or upper part is called the Côte de Nuits and the second, or lower, which begins just above Beaune and runs south to Santenay, is known as the Côte de Beaune. Both produce superb wines in their individual ways, the Côte de Nuits producing the great red wines such as those from Chambertin, Vosne-Romanée and Nuits-St-Georges, and the second the lighter and smoother red wines of Corton, Beaune and Volnay, and the outstanding white wines of Montrachet and Meursault.

In the Côte de Nuits the vineyards are called *climats*, a word that indeed means climates and reflects the difference in soil and position which, in conjunction with the weather and the age of the planted vines, makes the wine great or modest. The skill of the cultivator and the winemaker are equally important, but standards here are, in general, as high as the rewards. In the cellars I have seen an old *vigneron* compare the flavour of one cask with another, distinguishing with his palate the wine of young vines from that of old. Easy enough for him, perhaps, for he had lived with them all his life, impossible for most others.

The best vineyards are found looking south-east

A vineyard at Vosne-Romanée.

from the twelve-mile-or-so range of hills, for here the sun strikes them early in the day and gives its fullest intensity at noon. The soil of Clos de Vougeot is nearly half silica and more than a third clay, with limestone and ironstone added. This produces a great red wine from Pinot Noir grapes. Yet for Montrachet, some thirty miles away in the Côte de Beaune, the finest of white wines made from the Chardonnay grape, the soil composition is one-third silica, just under one-third limestone, and twenty-eight per cent clay. On this basis even a geologist might hesitate to draw conclusions before forecasting a harvest.

Fixin is the first village of the Côte de Nuits and its wines are rated by some with those of Gevrey-Chambertin, a couple of miles away. Not so by me, for they seem to lack the depth of the best of the latter, although they have good colour and

alcoholic content. The two *premiers crus* are Clos de la Perrière and Clos du Chapitre, both from twelve-acre vineyards, and worth while drinking, though because of the relatively small quantity not seen as far afield as they might deserve.

Gevrey-Chambertin originally made itself famous in the mid-nineteenth century when the perceptive village fathers tacked the name of the great red Burgundy on to the word Gevrey by which the village was known. It is a rather narrow place made notable by the Rotisserie du Chambertin, which has a Michelin star and attractive decor in ancient wine cellars.

The addition of the magic name enabled most vineyards round Gevrey to call their wine Chambertin, which proved too much for the rest of the world to accept. As a result the locals eventually agreed to the use of Chambertin only for the classic vineyard of that name and for its neighbour, Clos de Bèze. The latter's labels in fact usually appear as Chambertin Clos de Bèze. These are the two great Chambertins, made from thirty-two acres and thirty-seven acres respectively, wines without peer and correspondingly expensive. There are a number of owners, all devoted to their product.

Unless you are wealthy, or happily privileged, you will not be able to drink them often. Recently I drank a Chambertin 1955 and a Chambertin 1952 with Peter Reynier, whose firm had bottled them. They were both excellent, the first at its full and splendid peak, the second still maturing. And here is one of the problems of drinking great wines, for only by opening one of your few and expensive bottles can you find out if the wine is finally ready for drinking!

Gevrey-Chambertin is the permitted name, under regulations, for wines of the commune and I have seldom been disappointed in them. The winemaking standards and traditions are high, the body good and big, the *robe* or colour splendidly black-red, the bouquet full and enticing. Prices, alas, have started to go up and are double what you might have paid only a few years ago. Certain grades can add a vineyard name and other vineyards entitled to be called *Grands Crus* can couple their name with Chambertin such as Charmes-Chambertin, one of the leaders.

The next commune is that of Morey-Saint-Denis, a very interesting township, seemingly half-asleep, a collection of little old stone houses that nobody disturbs. This is quite untrue and yet only one aspect gives it away. The town that a few years ago had ancient Renaults, battered and broken-down outside its doors, now boasts spanking new Citroën IDs, Mercedes and similar emblems of luxury. Within the modest houses new furniture abounds, television sets of enormous size fill the small living-rooms, and wallets are bulging. The canny vineyard owners who live here, however, still wear their old leather jackets and drab blue jeans that were jeans long before modern youth had adopted them.

Morey-Saint-Denis was never really poor, but its wines were certainly overshadowed by Chambertin to the north and Clos de Vougeot to the south. Now the world has woken up to wine values and realised the enchantment of two, at least, of its Grands Crus. These are Clos de Tart and Bonnes-Mares, though most of the latter lie next door in Chambolle-Musigny. Clos de Tart is owned by Jean Mommesin. All are slow-to-mature, big, noble red wines, the two above undoubtedly names of the future and worth laying down, Bonnes-Mares in particular.

It was a Bonnes-Mares 1953 that Hubert Piat, of the famous Macon shippers, selected when we visited The Sanctuary in his cellars where the best wines are kept. There was no attempt to warm it,

A vineyard scene at Vougeot.

or let it stand open for an hour or two, or put it in a fancy cradle. Hubert whipped out his corkscrew and the deed was done, the bottle stood on an upturned barrel in its dusty glory while we sipped the gorgeous achievement of the Piat cellarmen, so full of power, sumptuous but individual, long and lingering. In those cool *caves*, in the dim light, with Hubert's smiling face and our readily recharged glasses the setting was quite as appropriate as any Guildhall function.

So it is in Chambolle-Musigny that one finds much the greater acreage of Bonnes-Mares. Here Les Musigny is the other cru held in high regard, and it shares this same soft, well-rounded appeal, a more feminine attraction than that of the bigger Chambertin, though the minimum alcoholic strength demanded by its *appellation* is the same 11.5 degrees. These degrees represent percentage alcohol by volume on the Gay-Lussac system of this French chemist. 'A wine of silk and lace' is how the red Musigny has been described.

After great Bonnes-Mares the leading Premiers Crus are Les Amoureuses and Les Charmes, whose names alone would seem to win them popularity. Both must be preceded by the name Chambolle-Musigny on the label, and whereas Bonnes-Mares

Clos de Vougeot.

single word Vougeot or as Bourgogne, and one would expect the growers to choose the first for the name has magic. But it is important to note that this name is not to be confused with Clos de Vougeot, as wine-list prices will soon show you. Clos de Vougeot is red and must be made to 11.5 degrees, whereas Vougeot only requires 10.5 degrees, and has also a white wine called Le Clos Blanc de Vougeot.

As you drive south, the great Château of Clos de Vougeot stands on the right-hand side of the road, presiding over the 125 acres of rich vineyards around it which are owned by sixty or so different proprietors. Its splendid four-square appearance, with corner towers and arched entrance, is unmistakable and the drive to the great doorway, through the carefully tended vines on their rich brown soil, is memorable indeed.

The *château* dates from Renaissance and is open to visitors. You walk through the great courtyard and see the historic thirteenth-century wine-press, one of several, once operated by the monks of Cîteaux who owned the vineyards. It is a massive affair of great timbers and wooden screw, and was in some danger during the Second World War when German prisoners housed there tried to chop up the wood for fires in the cold winter. The property of the Chevaliers du Tastevin, the famous Burgundy wine guild, it is the scene of their meetings and particularly of dinners held in the great cellars, when new members are admitted with lavish ceremony and much singing of Burgundian songs and drinking of Burgundian wine.

Among the stories associated with the *château* is the tale of a Colonel Bisson making the men of his regiment present arms as they passed the vineyard, and most wine books repeat the fable that French soldiers maintain the tradition to this day. Alas, it is not so. Those who live on the spot told me that the glamorous legend originated with a local militia's commander, who called his men to the salute as they passed on the way to a nearby field for drill. The French army today roars past the *château* in canvas-topped *camions*, as I have seen on several occasions, with never a salute in evidence.

One of the great dinners is held when the Chevaliers celebrate on the third Saturday in November, the eve of the sale of the Hospices de Beaune wines, held in aid of the Hospices charity on the next day. A visit to Clos de Vougeot gives you some insight into the long history of Burgundy and its wine-making. The *château* itself is unique in this part of the world, and perhaps in all France, for while you can find wonderful buildings in Bordeaux and Champagne that are linked with wine, there is nothing really comparable in age and history.

Another revered name lies within a short distance to the south. Mention Vosne-Romanée wherever good wine is appreciated and you will

may only make 264 gallons to the acre under the wine laws, the other two can make up to 308 gallons. Since restrictions are intended to ensure quality one draws the obvious conclusion, excellent as they are in the glass.

With the next commune of Vougeot one is back to 264 gallons to the acre under the stipulations for the 'Appellation Clos de Vougeot', a historic name. Any surplus here may be sold either as the

A vineyard at Romanée.

still the conversation, for this commune, in poker parlance, holds a straight flush with Romanée-Conti, Richebourg, Romanée, La Tâche, and Romanée-Saint-Vivant. They are precious not only because they are so superb, but because their areas are so small.

Romanée-Conti is only four-and-a-half acres and was replanted after the Second World War, when new grafted vines were planted, and wine-making resumed in 1952. It is now, twenty years later, that the vines have aged sufficiently to bring out their best. Personally Richebourg is my favourite among these wines. It comes from twenty acres and is a true emperor, velvety smooth in texture, of tremendous, full bouquet and a glorious deep colour. The aftertaste is so long and lingering, the warmth of the mouth-filling flavour so overwhelming, that one can only sit back and thank God for this splendid gift to compensate men for the woes of the world.

Others sing the praises of La Tâche, another great wine, which comes from fifteen acres, while Romanée has only two acres and so is unlikely to come your way. Romanée-Saint-Vivant, with twenty-three acres, is similarly notable but not to the same extent as the others perhaps. And there are still Grands-Echézeaux with twenty-two acres,

and Echézeaux with seventy-five acres, fine, full wines in each case. I learned to love the former, as I have said, with the late Guy Prince, whose care and attention brought the London house of J. L. P. Lebègue to the forefront of shippers of French wines in the post-war period. Grands-Echézeaux is a truly magnificent wine with a full flavour and brilliant ruby colour, very suave and with elegant finesse. If Richebourg had not captured me early in life I could well be a slave to Grands-Echézeaux.

The next name of note on the Côte de Nuits is linked very clearly. It is Nuits-Saint-Georges, which also legally includes certain vineyards from the neighbouring village of Prémeaux, and this is a wine which was long favoured in Britain and still would be had not the price risen so much in recent times. Some think the Saint-Georges part of the title has given it a special appeal to England, but this is probably due as much to the quality as the reasonable prices for which it has in the past been famous. In addition, it covers a large area, nearly a thousand acres, which makes it very marketable.

The leader of the Premier Cru vineyards is Les Saint-Georges, and what a fine roll the words have, Nuits-Saint-Georges Les Saint-Georges. Close to

A vineyard at Aloxe-Corton.

this comes Les Vaucrains, Les Cailles and Clos de la Maréchale, all of which I have enjoyed at one time or another. There are some thirty-five others of these First Growths and certainly this is a wine to look for when your pocket will not stretch to a Richebourg or a Chambertin. It is not quite so big as those wines, but has more body than simple Chambolle-Musigny and nobody could complain of the colour, deep and dark. Les Porets and Les Argillats are others to buy. Faiveley is one of several outstanding growers here. But it is particularly important to look for the words *appellation contrôlée* on Nuits-Saint-Georges labels for the wines have been exploited by the unscrupulous in the past.

The Côte de Beaune would be famous even if the ancient city of Beaune, splendidly embraced by high stone walls and battlements, its streets still narrow and cobbled, did not exist. For while the wines called by its name are excellent drinking there are other fine wines nearby, such as the Premiers Crus of Volnay, Pommard and Aloxe-Corton— pronounced incidentally Alosse-Corton. Apart from these red wines, the Côte de Beaune grows some of France's noblest white wines from the Chardonnay grape, among them the leader, that superb wine known simply as Le Montrachet (without pronouncing the first 't'). Its cousins are Chevalier-Montrachet, Bâtard-Montrachet, Puligny-Montrachet and Chassagne-Montrachet, lesser but worthy and certainly more likely to meet your pocket.

One starts, however, at the junction with the

Côte de Nuits, and in the commune of Aloxe-Corton one meets the great powerful red wines of Corton and the white wines of Corton-Charlemagne. The wines sold as Aloxe-Corton are pleasant but, unless accompanied by a vineyard name, are simply commune wines.

Le Corton is the great name here, with the red much in the majority. Regulations for Corton and its Corton-Charlemagne white neighbour call for 264 gallons to the acre and a minimum strength of 11.5 for red and twelve degrees for white. For Aloxe-Corton wines the degrees are one less and the yield is 308 gallons to the acre. Some of the Cortons come from the neighbouring commune of Pernand-Vergelesses, a rather fascinating hill town overlooking the vineyards. The best wine under this title is the Premier Cru, Ile-des-Vergelesses, and I well remember a discussion with Charles Piat in his great cellars at Mâcon after drinking a splendid bottle. Was there or was there not an island at Vergelesses? Due consultation of wine books such as Poupon and Forgeot's *The Wines of Burgundy*, searches of road maps and a local atlas brought the conclusion that there is no island as such.

One now comes to Beaune and nobody should leave without visiting the famous Hospices with its red, brown and gold tiled roof and interesting painting of the Last Judgment by Roger van der Weiden, with the righteous ascending to heaven and the winebibbers going to hell. The wine museum in the fine house of the Dukes of Burgundy is another essential sight.

The shops are nearly as interesting and, in my experience, blessed with particularly courteous and helpful assistants. Here you can buy souvenir *tastevins*, figures in the robes of the Chevaliers du Tastevin, coloured plates, ashtrays with amusing advice and postcards depicting the wine life from optimistic angles. There are excellent bookshops, all specialising in wine and food volumes which, although in French, are not difficult to follow.

Among hotels there is the Poste, where I have stayed comfortably but found the prices rather high for my pocket. The hall includes a list of proprietors from 1660, and the service, food and wine are good. The Marché, looking over the cobbled central square, is more moderately priced and I have eaten excellently there. Both have Michelin stars.

But what a history of the French wine trade one can read into the names on the often modest doorways! Here you will find Louis Latour, Louis Jadot, Joseph Drouhin, Marcilly Brothers, Calvet and Cruse, with any one of whom you might do business and be well satisfied. The Syndicat d'Initiative is a large, well-run office near the Marché restaurant, and can advise you on what to see and where to go. What is more, Beaune remains a natural, normal French town despite its fame and attractions so you can sit happily at one of the cafés and enjoy the passing scene in comfort.

The great courtyard of the Hospices de Beaune (Hôtel-Dieu).

When I had difficulty in finding my way to the Poste hotel because of temporary diversions, I went into a café to inquire the way and a young man there finished his drink and offered to accompany me. After we had driven there he courteously refused a drink or a lift back! Such memories warm one's heart to a nation.

Since there are so many variations of the name Beaune on a wine label, it is worth memorising some of them. The name Beaune alone may be followed by the words Premier Cru (First Growth), or the name of the *climat* or vineyard growing the wine. There are thirty-four classified First Growths, among them such *climat* names of fame as Les Clos des Mouches, Clos du Roi, Les Grèves, Les Bressandes, Les Marconnets, Les Teurons, Les Epenottes etc. Practically all are red wines with a minimum alcoholic strength of 10.5 degrees and made at a maximum yield of 308 gallons to the acre. Each has its own charm, and standards are high for these First Growths. Then come two *appellations* which are entirely different and yet similar enough in title to lead to confusion. Both rank below the Premier Cru above. The first is Côte de Beaune and this name on a label without any vineyard or village name indicates a good wine grown in the area of recognised Beaune production with another twenty-two acres added. It is not as good as the wines with Beaune alone in the name. At the same time it is better than wines with the *appellation* Côte de Beaune Villages. This latter is quite different, being given to red wines blended from villages in the area outside the Beaune wine district. Drinkable enough, they are not comparable in breeding with the other two.

The three wines described above, almost alike in name but so differing in quality, are an example of the complications of wine buying and drinking, and the need for a little study of the subject. The chance to taste many of the best in their cool cellars at Beaune I owe to André Gagey of Jadot, Jean-Pierre Robin of Calvet and André Marcilly.

One leaves Beaune reluctantly, for it is an enchanting city, but there are notable names to the

Vineyards at Beaune, in the Côte d'Or.

A vineyard at Pommard.

south. First is Pommard, another area where a popular name has made it necessary to choose with care. The red wine is of good deep colour but rather lighter in strength than its neighbours. There are twenty-six Premiers Crus, of which the leaders are Les Epenots, Les Rugiens-Bas and Les Rugiens-Hauts. Once again the minimum strength is 10.5 degrees and the maximum yield 308 gallons to the acre. The Rugiens crus have the best body, but in general one does well to look for the name of a good shipper.

The next name is that of Volnay and though these wines again have a lighter touch they are well-bred with fine bouquet. Perhaps Pommard is better known outside France because it travels well and ages well. Most people who know both would prefer the elegance of the Volnay, and the 'nose' alone as one sniffs slowly in the glass is rewarding. The leaders of the Premiers Crus are En Caillerets, Caillerets-Dessus, En Champains, and En Chevret, the only area I know where the word 'en' precedes the vineyards. The bouquet is sometimes likened to violets, and Volnay is linked to Les Musigny as representing the best of their respective Côtes, though I would not agree!

One now comes to the region of the greatest white wines of the Côte d'Or and, indeed, of

A vineyard at Volnay.

France, with Chablis as a possible exception. Meursault is the first of these communes, and, though some red wine is made, all reverence here goes to the noble whites from the Chardonnay grape. This change of colour is even seen in a certain lightness of the soil and of the vine itself. I have always liked the town of Meursault and the stone spire of the church, for it is one of those placid places which wear their fame easily. The name is said to come from the Latin for 'rat's leap',

not a very happy link, but balanced by the smooth, mellow product.

The colour is of pale straw with hints of green and the wine is big as befits its place among the great dry whites of France. The Premiers Crus must have 11.5 degrees of alcoholic strength, and since many exceed this the wine is powerful. Such wines cannot be cheap, but if ever there was a case for investing in true satisfaction it is here. Hoarded money provides no memories.

I have drunk some of the finest wines of this region at the table of Peter Reynier, generous prince of London wine shippers. Well do I remember a 1966 Meursault Premier Cru from the Perrières *climat,* or vineyard, which we drank with a wonderful soufflé prepared by his treasured chef, Mrs Eileen McCarthy, in his dining room at Tachbrook Street over the well-filled cellars. He warmed the glass with his hands to bring up the bouquet and what a treasure it was! Words, alas, only convey a fragment of such pleasures.

The leading growths, then, are Les Perrières, Les Charmes and Les Genevrières but there are also Les Caillerets and La Goutte-d'Or which I like, though I confess the name of the latter alone— the drop of gold—would attract me. Minimum alcoholic strength is 11.5 degrees and maximum production 308 gallons to the acre. These figures change with the next commune, that of Puligny-Montrachet and home of Le Montrachet, acknowledged as the greatest dry white wine and sometimes weighed against Château Yquem, the acknowledged leader of sweet white wines from Sauternes near Bordeaux. Personally I think they are so utterly dissimilar, both in colour as well as in flavour, as to make any linking undesirable.

It was Le Montrachet which inspired the greatest tribute ever paid to a wine, Alexandre Dumas's immortal words: 'It should be drunk kneeling, with the head bared'. And Le Montrachet is one of the few examples of a wine or person justifying its tribute.

It is made at a maximum of 264 gallons per acre and a minimum alcoholic strength of twelve degrees. The savour is rich, surprisingly so for so dry a name, and the bouquet subtle. Visiting Harvey Prince, at that time head of J. L. P. Lebègue and worthy son of Guy Prince, I drank the Montrachet of the Marquis de Laguiche, for there are several proprietors. To own part of the Montrachet area is like owning a part of Clos de Vougeot—a privilege as well as a perquisite—and my friend René Fleurot of Santenay also has a superb example which I have enjoyed in his cellars.

Since less than a thousand cases are made available each year and these are in great demand, you will not often meet Le Montrachet, but there are other neighbours of fine quality, to be bought as domaine-bottled single-vineyard offerings. Bâtard-Montrachet makes a much larger quantity, some seven thousand gallons, and Chevalier-Montrachet 2,600 gallons, to the same high *appellation* standards as Le Montrachet, to which both come close.

The requirements for Puligny-Montrachet and Chassagne-Montrachet are a little less stringent. The first has two splendid Premiers Crus in Le Cailleret and Les Combettes, and many a bottle of the latter have I drunk. They are great dry wines, these whites, fruity and full of breeding, but a little less than the others mentioned. The last bottle of

A cellar at Meursault.

the second I drank was Chassagne-Montrachet Morgeot 1969 from the Marquis de Laguiche, once more at Peter Reynier's table, and truly excellent it was.

With all these white wines, however great, there is a time factor and the ultimate is six years, though I would drink them in five for safety's sake. They will, of course, last longer but they will not stand up to life like red wines and tend to maderize as they grow older. The green-gold turns to dark gold and then to brown and they lose their life. You can experience the same thing with champagne which, in addition, loses its sparkle and becomes flat.

One has to be aware that good red wines are also produced under some of these names, such as Chassagne-Montrachet. So be sure you look under the right section of the wine-list when you give your order!

At the end of the Côte de Beaune one comes to Santenay, making some hundred and thirty thousand gallons of very satisfying red wine per year, lighter in body than the reds of the Côte de Nuits but of velvety texture. It is strange how the reds decline in 'size' all the way down the Côte d'Or, but they have other features to make up for this and Santenay has a fine bouquet and can be quite fruity. The best Santenay approximates to Volnay, and the leading Premiers Crus are Les Gravières, Clos-de-Tavannes and La Comme. In the past Santenay has been neglected, but now that the top burgundies have risen in price Santenay is in considerable demand as an honest wine.

One of the leading growers is Louis Clair, with whom I have several times sat on wine juries at the French National Wine Fair at Mâcon, tasting entries for medals and diplomas. Conscientious, full of integrity and yet with a rich sense of humour, I have written of him earlier and his red, weather-beaten face with its slow smile. His old brown jerkin and cap come to my mind as I think of him. Talking of the use of chemical sprays by some growers on their vines he shook his head and said, 'Soon it won't be Beaune '75 but BP '75'.

Having left the two sections of the Côte d'Or one reaches Mercurey, an intriguing wine that always

A statue at Mâcon depicts the Burgundy wine harvest.

has, for me, a slight pepperiness in the bouquet. It is grown in the Chalonnais district, again using the Pinot Noir grape, with a minimum alcoholic strength of 10.5 degrees (eleven degrees for Premiers Crus) and a maximum yield of 308 gallons per acre. A pleasant wine, it is again less than its rivals further north. Similar red wines are Rully and Givry, though here I find the bouquet normal.

More white Rully is made than red and much goes to making the sparkling wine famous in the area for over a hundred and fifty years. It was around 1820 that the first attempts at the *methode champenoise* were made in Rully and in Nuits-Saint-Georges. So was Bourgogne Mousseux born, and it soon spread to other towns. Today more than six million bottles are produced yearly and the Syndicat des Producteurs de Vins Mousseux de Bourgogne, centred on Beaune, claim this represents a fifth of French production of this wine type. There is also a sparkling red burgundy which sells abroad.

Adjoining Givry is Montagny, which makes a very pleasant dry white wine with a tang that refreshes the mouth. Some fifty thousand gallons are harvested and it is worth knowing. Its *appellation* stipulations are more severe than those applying to the white wines of Mâcon further south.

These Macon wines are famous in both their red and white forms, thanks to the very energetic and skilfully directed publicity of the Comité Interprofessionnel de Mâcon et Bourgogné and its allies. Their ambassadors of Mâcon wine have spanned the world from Italy to California, and the green plaques urging the public to drink the good Mâcon product can be seen in many lands.

Much as I love the Mâcon life and wine, I have to admit that Montagny and Pouilly-Fuissé are both better whites and Beaujolais is a better red. However, there is a vast amount of Mâcon wine made, some seven hundred and fifty thousand gallons a year; the growers and the cellarers are skilful, and they bring out the best qualities. In some cases, such as the white Mâcon-Villages, with the addition of the commune name, they are quite superior, and the white Mâcon wines of Viré, Lugny and one or two others are notable. Viré is seeking the right to use its name as an *appellation contrôlée* without the name of Mâcon attached. It is made mostly by a co-operative from the Chardonnay grape and the big bar at the co-operative is worth a visit.

The best white wine of the area comes from the region some six miles south of Mâcon called Pouilly-Fuissé. It is again made from the Chardonnay grape which grows here in chalky soil, the best of it from Pouilly and Fuissé and high quality also from the communes of Solutré, Vergisson and Chaintré. At Solutré a great white rock, shaped like the prow

La Roche de Solutré, in the Mâconnais country.

of a ship, rises above the valley and the masses of crushed bones at the foot are said to have come from horses driven over the top by hunters seeking food many thousands of years ago. The bones may or may not have fertilised the ground, but some of the best vineyards are here.

Called 'Polly-Fossy' by the cellarmen of one London merchant, the name has intrigued Americans also and led to great demand and higher prices. Much cheaper than the best Chablis it has made some inroads on that market also. The flavour is somewhat of hazelnuts, though others describe it as flinty. There is a vigour and freshness that makes it superior to Mâcon Blanc, and the colour is a light gold with hints of green, as in Chablis, though less pronounced. It goes admirably with chicken, veal and sea-food dishes, and comes from one of the loveliest countrysides in all France. The minimum alcoholic strength is eleven degrees, with twelve degrees for First Growths, and the maximum yield is 396 gallons per acre. Made to the same standards are Pouilly-Vinzelles and Pouilly-Loché from adjoining villages, but somehow not quite of the same quality, and lighter.

Between Pouilly and the Beaujolais country to the south there was created in 1971 a new white wine *appellation*. This was Saint-Véran, also from the Chardonnay grape and on similar soil in the villages of Chânes, Chasselas, Davayé, Leynes, Prissé, Saint-Amour and Saint-Vérand plus some vineyards in the Solutré district. They form a belt round the Pouilly-Fuissé area and their wines will rank between those of this region and Mâcon Blanc.

In the past the wine could be called either Mâcon Blanc or Beaujolais Blanc, but the growers petitioned for the new name of Saint-Véran because they believed they merited their own title, in the same way as the growers of Mâcon Viré hope to achieve an *appellation*. I have visited the vineyards since they got their wish and was impressed by the determination to use the greatest care and highest standards in cultivation. Saint-Véran must undergo an official tasting and approval before it can be labelled and sold.

Some of the villages in the Saint-Véran area are already famous for other vineyards growing the Gamay grape which produces Beaujolais, for long the most famous, moderately priced, red wine in the world. Alas, it is now going up in price. It is the wine of 'Clochemerle', Gabriel Chevallier's immortal book of village life in the beautiful Beaujolais country with its rolling, wooded hills, carpeted by rich, brown, granitic soil and green slopes dotted lower down with vineyards, all growing the plump, black grape.

Today the men of Beaujolais are plumper and more sophisticated than they were in the 1920s when 'Clochemerle' appeared with its story of the village winegrowers' rivalries over the building of a *pissoir* next to the church. They will tell you that the book is no longer a true picture of their life, if it ever was, but don't be too sure. I have walked through Vaux, which proclaims itself the original setting, and seen a thin, elderly man dancing around the rain puddles with an inside-out umbrella held above his head! Certainly Vaux has the public lavatory from which the local youths wave, with their free hand, at passing coachloads of goggle-eyed tourists. And it was at Chiroubles, within a short distance, that a villager told me he discovered his wife with her lover and beat her up, not for what she was doing—that, he explained, was natural, *bien sûr*—but because she had opened two bottles of his best wine for the scoundrel.

There is no doubt that Chiroubles *is* a very good wine! It is one of the nine Crus of Beaujolais, the others being Brouilly, Côte de Brouilly, Chénas, Fleurie, Julienas, Morgon, Moulin-à-Vent and Saint-Amour. The growers must not make more than 356 gallons per acre, with ten degrees minimum of alcohol and eleven degrees if they add the name of the *climat* or vineyard. Côte de Brouilly minimum is 10.5 degrees.

The big area of ruddy, granitic soil favours the Gamay grape—*gamay noir à jus blanc* to give the full name—which is as unsuitable to the great Côte d'Or as the pinot noir grape would prove in Beaujolais. So does nature shuffle around her marvels. The wine that results is wonderfully fresh and youthful though, for a red, its keeping qualities are limited to some four years and it is best drunk at a year or two old. Some gimmicky publicity has been given to Beaujolais Primeur, wine made within four weeks of the official release of the vintage in November. If the harvest is good this may be done successfully but with a late harvest of poor quality, as in 1972, the Primeur, or Nouveau as it can also be called, needs more time and can be too acid. The 1971, however, was very good indeed. It is only because Beaujolais does not require so long to mature that this Primeur is possible, and yet the Primeur, hastily made and immature, costs more than one of the good Crus a year old simply because it is fashionable for a brief period.

Just below the high standard of the nine Crus comes the wine called Beaujolais Villages, made in thirty-six communes, many of whose names are inscribed on a plaque above the entrance to the tasting cellars at Beaujeu, once the capital of Beaujolais. This is made at a maximum of 396 gallons per acre and a minimum of ten degrees alcohol. The third grade is Beaujolais Supérieur and the fourth Beaujolais, each with less stringent regulations for their making. Among leading growers and shippers are Pasquier-Desvignes, Jean Mommessin, Georges Duboeuf and Charles Piat, with all of whom I have enjoyed their wines.

While the nine Crus will keep for up to four years, the other grades should be drunk young, and are sometimes truly called 'quaffing' wines for their very freshness, fruity flavour and pleasing bouquet makes one tilt the glass very readily. The greater wines of the Côte d'Or, however, have such body and deep 'nose' that one approaches them with some reverence and prefers to sip and savour with, perhaps, an appropriate dish. It is worth paying the slightly higher price for the Crus and the Villages grades, and one should choose those of a reputable shipper. In the past Beaujolais has been 'nourished' with lesser wines to improve the quantity at the expense of quality, despite all the wine regulations.

A view of the countryside around Beaujolais.

Côtes du Rhône

Beaujolais is technically in Burgundy though, like Chablis, its wine is so different as to make it a self-contained community. We now leave Burgundy and enter the increasingly important area south of Lyon known as Côtes du Rhône, which runs for some hundred and fifty miles to Avignon. It has always been famous for its big, impressive red wine called Châteauneuf-du-Pape, lacking, however, the sophistication of the great burgundies, and Hermitage, another red wine of quality. Both have the advantage of the best positions in their respective areas to catch the sun, and here in the very south of France the sun is powerful indeed. Moreover the vineyards are tough to work because they are covered with great pebbles, the size of a man's fist or bigger, which, like the slate in the Rhine vineyards, reflects the sun's heat and rays on to the vines themselves. When one first sees the stony vineyards one can hardly credit that vines grow there at all.

The Rhône has its own grapes, too, with names like Grenache, Syrah, Cinsault and ten others used for Châteauneuf-du-Pape, producing its body and bouquet by their skilful blending. Hermitage uses chiefly the Syrah grape to achieve its velvet softness and rich bouquet as it slowly matures.

Pont de St. Bénoget at Avignon.

A vineyard at Hermitage.

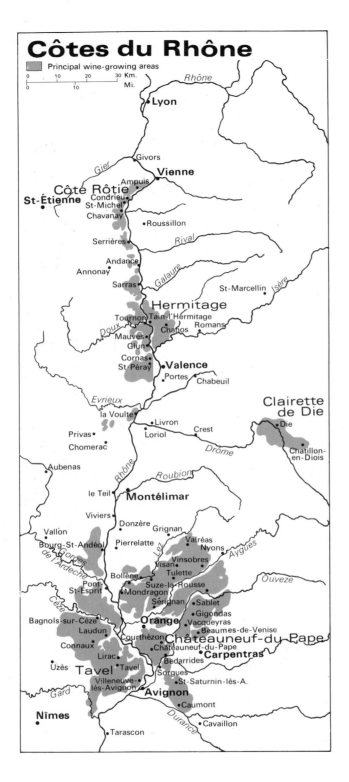

Côtes du Rhône

Principal wine-growing areas

0 10 20 30 Km.
0   10   Mi.

Rhône
Lyon
Gier
Givors
Vienne
Ampuis
Côte Rôtie
St-Étienne
Condrieu
St-Michel
Chavanay
Roussillon
Rival
Serrières
Andance
Annonay
Galaure
Sarras
St-Marcellin
Isère
Hermitage
Tournon
Tain-l'Hermitage
Doux
Chanos
Romans
Mauves
Glun
Cornas
St-Péray
Valence
Portes
Chabeuil
Evrieux
la Voulte
Clairette de Die
Livron
Crest
Die
Privas
Loriol
Chomerac
Drôme
Chatillon-en-Diois
Aubenas
Rhône
Roubion
le Teil
Montélimar
Viviers
Donzère
Grignan
Vallon
Bourg-St-Andéol
Pierrelatte
Valréas
Nyons
Aygues
Gorges de l'Ardèche
Visan
Vinsobres
Bollène
Tulette
Ouveze
Pont St-Esprit
Suze-la-Rousse
Mondragon
Sérignan
Sablet
Bagnols-sur-Cèze
Gigondas
Cèze
Orange
Vacqueyras
Beaumes-de-Venise
Châteauneuf-du-Pape
Laudun
Courthézon
Connaux
Châteauneuf-du-Pape
Carpentras
Lirac
Bédarrides
Uzès
Tavel
Tavel
Sorgues
St-Saturnin-lès-A.
Villeneuve-lès-Avignon
Gard
Avignon
Caumont
Nîmes
Durance
Cavaillon
Tarascon

Vineyards between the towns of Gigondas and Sablet.

The village of Châteauneuf-du-Pape.

A typical vineyard at Châteauneuf-du-Pape, showing the large stones which cover the red-brown soil.

Both make dry, distinctive white wines as well as the perhaps more famous reds, now coming to even greater prominence as substitutes for the dearer burgundies and Bordeaux wines. Gigondas is a third red wine that has come to the front. It is grown near Orange where, in summer, men dare not walk outside the shade, and it again uses a variety of local grapes. Like the local sunshine these wines are strong, invariably 12.5 degrees or more, and should be drunk with caution after the first bottle.

The name 'Roasted Slope' indicates temperature again and the Côte Rôtie wine near Vienne centres on Ampuis, where Pontius Pilate was once the governor. The wine he undoubtedly once drank is big and long, lingering in the mouth with Syrah bouquet reminiscent of raspberries. Near Ampuis is Condrieu, and nearby the famous Château Grillet vineyards, making a white wine in small quantity from a grape called Golden Viognier. It is a late harvester, therefore not as dry as one expects, and is much sought out by connoisseurs for

A vineyard at Tavel, note the specially designed tractor which straddles the vines, leaving them undamaged.

its unusual flavour.

Other white and red wines are Saint-Joseph, now being exported more and more, and Lirac, which also has a pleasant *rosé*. It is made near Tavel, not far from Avignon, and for a long time was over-shadowed by Tavel, which is perhaps the finest *rosé* of them all with its orange-pink colour and full dry body, often twelve degrees of alcohol or more, and surprisingly strong for a wine whose colour leads the public to think otherwise.

The whites are sometimes found too dry, but there is a superb dessert wine made in the region that must certainly be mentioned. This is Beaumes-de-Venise, made from hundred-year-old vines of the Muscat grape, the examples I know best being those of J. Vidal Fleury, which I have enjoyed with Ralph Gilbey of J. R. Parkington, the London shippers, and Yapp Brothers of Mere, Wiltshire, who sell them.

The vines grow in some twenty acres and are aged in cask and offer a fine example of fortified wines of natural sweetness. The colour is as golden as Chateau Yquem and I would be hard put to choose between them, but certainly Beaumes-de-Venise has a splendid aroma and a wonderful taste that is not sickly in any way, while the price is currently a third of either Yquem or the great sweet German hocks. A marvellous dessert wine to love, cherish and obey.

Côtes de Provence

One cannot leave the south of France without looking at the wines of Provence, again an area gaining prominence as public interest grows. The white wine of Cassis is full and dry and powerful, and goes well with such dishes as *bouillabaisse*, or the local fish which you can watch the fishermen land as you lie on the pebbly beach. It is made from such vines as Ugni Blanc, Pascal Blanc and Doucillon. There are also red and *rosé*, but since each kind is at least eleven degrees they are powerful. From vineyards near Cannes comes Pradel Rosé which goes well with cold meat dishes and has a V.D.Q.S. *appellation*. The vineyards of the Côtes de Provence wines run from near Marseilles to outside Nice and have the V.D.Q.S. designation. No doubt they will improve as growers respond to the market, but they are usually not up to the Cassis or Bandol wines. Many of them come in attractively shaped flasks, however, and the prices are reasonable. The *rosés* are the best choice.

A view of the Bay of Cassis.

Bordeaux

Since this is a geographical survey of French wines, Bordeaux comes in the middle, but most connoisseurs would put it first. Only Burgundy can rival its quality. Each, as I have said, has its own powerful attractions, but there is a certain snob element in claiming Bordeaux to be first for it has a much larger area and has many great and gracious *châteaux* with well-bred, courteous and wealthy owners. Burgundy is inclined to be a land of bourgeoisie, risen from the peasant background of toiling and tilling their own little vineyards, something few Bordeaux owners have done regularly.

The classification of the best Bordeaux wines into five growths has already been explained and, although this took place in 1855 and has been disputed ever since, nobody has yet produced a better order. By and large, it is still justified, a tribute to the wine knowledge of the men who made it. The growths are listed at the end of this chapter.

Bordeaux itself is a fascinating city unequalled in Burgundy, for Lyon is not a wine city in the way that Bordeaux has grown to be, and Beaune is much smaller. First of all Bordeaux is a great port, with all the magic of quays and cranes and ships, a large part of them employed in the task of housing and moving wine. But it is also a city of broad, handsome boulevards and noble buildings, a setting of fine

The city of Bordeaux.

aspects peopled by friendly, bustling men and women who reflect the prosperity around them. Like Lyon, it has famous restaurants and a cuisine of its own, the most famous dish being lampreys cooked in red Bordeaux wine. You pause to admire the beautiful eighteenth-century Grand Theatre, now restored to its first golden white stone, pass through the splendid Esplanade des Quinconces looking out on the broad river Garonne, and turn along the Quai des Chartrons, home of the cellars of so many famous names. All the way your nostrils and taste buds are stirred by the heady odour of good wine and the aroma of perfectly cooked food from the *caves* and eating-houses that you pass.

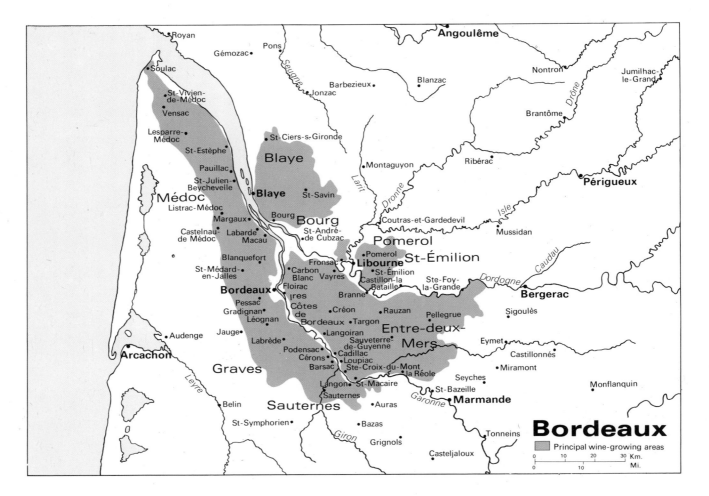

Yes, Bordeaux is a city offering all the true pleasures in life, and if it is necessary to have a few francs in your pocket to enjoy them, then so much more is the justification for work at all.

But apart from the five classified growths there is much other good wine in Bordeaux and its district. The lowest grade is Bordeaux with, slightly better, Bordeaux Supérieur, and these come as red, white and *rosé*. Then come regional names such as Médoc, where the best wine is grown, Graves, and Entre-deux-Mers, while in separate nearby areas are St-Émilion and Pomerol, homes of fine wines.

On the north side of the river Dordogne, where it joins the Garonne to unite as the Gironde, lie the three red wine districts of Fronsac, Bourg and Blaye, making good wine of moderate price that is steadily improving under increased care as more famous Bordeaux names grow costlier and leave wider openings on the market.

But the greatest area of Bordeaux is the Haut-Médoc, the lower half of the Médoc area, which peters out in comparison at the upper northern end. In the Haut-Médoc one finds nearly all the great names, wines made with finesse and character and with wonderful flavours. The fact that three grape varieties are used puts more individuality into the resultant blends and gives the cellarmaster even greater opportunities for his skills than elsewhere. As with so many other wine areas, the soil here would be despised by any normal farmer. It is sandy and covered with pebbles and flints, yet admirably suited to the local vines, much as the Mosel and the Rhône respond to their own different vineyards.

The Médoc wines need time to develop and when one drinks them young they are austere, even tart, quite different from the later result of fifteen or so years' care and maturing. So wine buyers need particularly skilled palates when they go purchasing in the months following the harvest here. As they age, the great Médocs acquire a harmony, a body from their tannin, which is a product of the skin, pips and stalks and makes for long life, and a splendid *robe* or colour. The Cabernet grape is noted for its tannin, but tannin itself requires care from the winemaker. If it is in too great quantity it leads to a heavy deposit which can be met by *collage*, or fining of the wine in which gelatine or egg white sinks down through the wine to remove particles, by filtering and other technical treatments. So one slowly descends the length of the Haut-Médoc, raising one's hat to all the famous names met on the way.

The word given to a parish in Bordeaux is commune, and these names are renowned wherever wine is drunk, firstly in a general district sense and secondly because in each commune there are vineyards and *châteaux* with the noblest qualities. St-Estèphe is one of the first, with wines of splendid body, slow to reach greatness but, once that is acquired, worthy of drinking at an emperor's wedding. From here comes my favourite growth, Château Cos d'Estournel, run close by Château Montrose and Château Calon-Ségur. One could write a book on each name. The first two are Second Growths in the great 1855 classification and Calon-Ségur is a Third Growth.

Cos d'Estournel became the property of Fernand Ginestet in 1919 and later passed to his son Pierre Ginestet, famous for his skill and the fact that he is also the owner of Château Margaux, one of the five First Growths. To hold two such aces, should make a man happy for life, and certainly wealthy. Among his attainments Pierre can name the Grand Chancellorship of the Academy of Wine of Bordeaux; I regard it as a compliment to his talents that I would sometimes as soon drink his Second Growth wine as his First. But whereas poor Cos d'Estournel has no actual *château* at all, Margaux has a most sumptuous building with a classic, pillared façade and splendid staircase.

Château Montrose does have a building and so beats Cos d'Estournel, but it is a poor thing compared with Margaux's, and not as impressive as that of Château Calon-Ségur, which rises nobly with squat towers above a sea of vines. Calon-Ségur boasts itself 'Premier Cru de Saint-Estèphe' but Saint-Estèphe is not the Médoc, where it ranks as a Third Growth, as I have said. These three wines are all noted for the regularity of their quality. Even in poor years they have a certain dignity, and in great years they are superb. Cos d'Estournel land is said to be so exactly drained, by reason of the sub-soil, that there is never too much water on it in winter, while the mixture of pebbles and sand serves to retain humidity in the hottest days of summer. Its wine for me has sufficient body, velvet texture, generous flavour, bouquet and all round balance, to make it a superb example of Bordeaux genius at its best. Montrose seems to me more overpowering, a harder wine, than Cos, strong, even pugnacious. Calon-Ségur has not always, for me, the distinction of the other two, though it is rounded and can on occasion be vigorous. It is certainly well made, though somewhat lacking in real lustre. But having made these remarks, let it be recorded that all three are well worth buying and drinking, particularly in the best years. None of them will let you down in themselves, whatever the wine waiter may do to them.

Now comes Pauillac, a resounding name, probably the greatest of the Haut-Médoc districts, for here reside Château Lafite and Château Latour, those two great First Growths and their newly promoted rival, Château Mouton-Rothschild, formerly the leading Second Growth in the classified lists whose owner, in season and out of season, trumpeted his claim to be a First Growth. I do not normally like trumpeters, but Baron

Philippe de Rothschild sounded his blasts with some cause and has now obtained his wish. His wine is excellent and he lovingly tends it, even if he also produces lesser wines which to my mind ought to be given more clearly different names, for Mouton-Cadet, good value at its price, is a wine blended in his cellars but far from a Château Mouton-Rothschild. The Baron is a public benefactor, however, not least in the excellent wine museum he has established. Famous artists, including Cocteau, Braque, Dali and Henry Moore, have been engaged to design labels for his greatest wines, a worthy form of art patronage indeed. A little, voluble man, the Baron looks rather like Picasso himself.

The Baron also owns a Fifth Growth called Château Mouton-Baron-Philippe. Its previous name was Château Mouton-d'Armailhacq and it usually so appears in the classified list. It is a tribute to Baron Philippe's thrusting vigour and energy that I should have written so much about his wines before dealing with Château Lafite-Rothschild, usually called simply Château Lafite, and Château Latour, which are the original two First Growths from Pauillac.

Monsieur Raoul Bloudin, Cellar Master at Château Mouton-Rothschild, tasting the wine.

Château Mouton-Rothschild.

Château Lafite.

Lafite, like Cos d'Estournel and a number of other vineyards, was once in British ownership in the early nineteenth century. In recent years it has owed much to Baron Elie Rothschild, a cousin of Philippe, but since he performs his genuine wonders in a quieter way one does not hear so much of them. After all Lafite is a name to conjure with on its own, to silence reverently a dinner table as T. E. Lawrence's Arab allies were silenced when the name 'Damascus' dropped from the air in their conference tent.

Lafite has some hundred and sixty acres of vines compared with Latour's 115 and produces the most wine of any First Growth. That, alas, does not make it any cheaper. All First Growths are currently very expensive, since speculators have followed up heavy American and Japanese purchasing and much of the greatest Bordeaux wine seems destined to linger in cellars for many years. It must eventually be sold at maturity and will then no doubt be drunk by a more or less worthy owner. A poor year, such as 1965 or 1968, might just possibly be within your reach, but I would scarcely recommend it. To my way of thinking the great names in poor years are a waste of money except for curiosity. Much better to buy a Second or Third Growth of a good year and enjoy its quality.

Château Latour has a most splendid label—a squat, battlemented tower surmounted by a lion—yet a simple one. 'Mis en Bouteille au Château', it says at the top, meaning the wine was bottled where it was grown and made. 'Grand Vin de Château Latour' run the largest letters, rather thin and spidery. Then underneath, in small capitals, 'Premier Grand Cru Classé', the slightly snob way of telling the world you are the greatest of your kind, the magic letters of a great year, 1966, and finally *'Appellation Pauillac Contrôlée'*, these latter being words which much lesser wines may also carry.

The Chaise at Mouton-Rothschild showing the new wine in cask.

73

The vineyards of Latour with the Château and tower in the background.

Château Pichon-Parempuyre in the Haut-Médoc.

I love Château Latour because it is as solid and honourable as its tower and seems to me to make more effort to control its prices. Because, also, a friend once provided two of its noblest bottles to celebrate an occasion which, in the end, was not an occasion, though the memory of the wine lingers on. Château Lafite is more a lady, with a wonderful perfume; Château Latour, the simple man of quiet dignity. Both are truly great, but while the first will turn your head and dazzle your vision, and sometimes prove fickle, the second will be your reliable friend and counsellor. Come to think of it, these Latour qualities are very British, and no wonder since twenty-five per cent of the property is owned by Harveys who, earth of earthiness, are part of Allied Breweries.

Both *châteaux*, incidentally, produce second wines, that of Lafite being called Carruades de Château Lafite-Rothschild, and that of Latour named Forts de Latour. These are not inexpensive and have not caught my fancy in the same way as their superiors, due no doubt to their being made from the younger vines of the estates. Vines, it must be noted, have to grow old and mature like the wine itself, and men who work among the vineyards can tell the age differences very well from sipping samples in their *tastevins*. Incidentally, the Rothschilds are good at picking *châteaux*, and Lafite has a handsome example with a delightful tower that appears on the label. Latour has little to show, hence perhaps the reason for the simple label.

Pauillac has two noted rivals among Second Growths. These are Château Pichon-Longueville-Comtesse de Lalande and Château Pichon-Longueville-Baron. They face one another, even glare across the road since each has a handsome *château*, but the Baron's version has more towers.

Once, indeed, they were part of a splendid whole but now go their separate ways, the Comtesse making the more delicate wine and the Baron the manlier—not indeed unlike their two greater rivals, Lafite and Latour, with a label difference of course—the two Pichons may only call themselves Grand Cru Classé, the front rank word Premier not being theirs to use.

Another Pauillac dear to my heart is Château Pontet-Canet, not only for its splendid, deep purple wine with heart-throbbing bouquet, but for the kindly hospitality of the Cruse family and particularly Edouard Cruse. I remember meeting several Cruse relatives at the great Bordeaux Wine Festival in 1971. They provided refuge and refreshment in a suite at the handsome new Hotel Aquitania where the champagne flowed, as champagne should.

Pontet-Canet at the head of the Fifth Growths is ample proof that, after the First and Second Growths, the classifications have come to mean less in some cases than they should. To me Pontet-Canet is a candidate for promotion, and certainly the splendid cellars and the way they are run are recommendations in themselves.

Pauillac has so many fine wines. Châteaux Batailley, Grand-Puy-Lacoste and Lynch-Bages are other fine estates. One expects much from Pauillac, of course, but one is seldom disappointed.

Below Pauillac lies St-Julien, a commune whose name rings bells for me because it was one of the first Bordeaux wines I drank. The name was simple and stood, as it does now, for wines of good body with a touch of delicacy. Looking back it seems one chose wines then for their popular names, like Beaune and St-Émilion, a thing I would have said was impossible in these more knowledgeable days, but of course in pre-war years relatively few wine books were available to impart knowledge. Some that I find excellent and interesting reading now would have seemed, if read in those days, pretentious and precious.

Château Léoville-Lascases has some claim to be the greatest of the St-Juliens. It comes first among them in the Second Growths, followed by Léoville-Poyferré and Léoville-Barton. I drank a splendid bottle of 1964 Léoville Lascases with Philippe Müller, an executive of Nicolas of Paris. We were in the excellent Le Galant Verre restaurant of Monsieur Girard in the rue de Verneuil, a restaurant not to be confused, incidentally, with that other Michelin starred Paris eating-house, l'Auberge du Vert-Galant on the quai Orfèvres. Monsieur Girard's house is a mixture of light brown beams decorated with wine barrel spigots, red table cloths, brassware, panelled walls, pretty girls and young Frenchmen. From the alacrity with which Monsieur Müller rose to greet a boyish gastronomic critic he spotted at another table, I could see that writing on *la grande cuisine* gives one an eminence in France that is somewhat missing in England. During the meal, when we had praised the wine, discussed its qualities, and admired its *robe*, Monsieur Müller casually asked me for my preference among clarets. I suggested Cos d'Estournel and, on our return to Nicolas, there stood a bottle of 1955 Cos d'Estournel to be tasted against a 1952 Haut Brion, the great First Growth from Graves. What hospitality!

But, also, what a compliment to a guest. I hope, and think, it was not out of courtesy that Philippe Müller, expressing his opinion before mine, was prepared to say that the Cos d'Estournel came out of the competition first. It was a close run thing but the Second Growth was so full and yet soft that it provided once again a wonderful memory. The two years are rated similarly for quality, at number two where number one is top in vintage charts; very good against excellent in first place. And while some affect to despise vintage charts, they do have their uses as a broad guide, particularly for those who have not the time, desire or, indeed, memory to master the literature of annual wine reports.

Still journeying south the next commune is Margaux, a magic name because here is the home of Château Margaux, the First Growth already mentioned. I shall never forget seeing a simple sign on a wooden column, very naturally carved, saying 'Château Margaux' when I alighted from the car ferry that crosses the Gironde from Blaye on the right-hand bank. The ferry was captained by a dark, handsome hero in his early forties, the living image of Laurence Olivier, watched wistfully throughout the voyage by most of the women passengers. Margaux is a land of *châteaux*, fine, delicate wine, and hot rivalries, for few communes have known so much argument and legal battle

Bottles of wine maturing at Margaux.

over the right to use the *appellation*. Margaux wines are particularly noted for their exceptional, quite distinctive, bouquet and their suavity. Château Margaux, incidentally, also produces a relatively small quantity of white wine called Pavillon Blanc de Château Margaux. It is fresh and dry with some individuality.

The Margaux area, however, has also a particularly British interest because here is to be found Château Lascombes in which Bass Charrington Vintners have the majority holding.

Château Lascombes is a wine to be proud of, being well up among the best Second Growths, delicate, perfumed, and of a splendid deep claret colour. The fact that it claims to be the largest-selling château-bottled claret in the United States is a tribute to the activities of Alexis Lichine, that remarkable talented Frenchman who is not only grower and seller of fine wines, but also a distinguished author of deeply researched volumes on the subject.

In 1971, the Bass Charrington group, with admirable taste, acquired over seventy per cent of the shares of Château Lascombes S.A. It had been owned by Lichine and some American friends, several of whom retained their shareholding. Alexis Lichine et Cie was bought by the Bass Charrington interests in 1964, which gave them the exclusive franchise for Lascombes wine in the USA. In fact Lascombes was owned quite recently by the Ginestet family, owners of Château Margaux, and acquired by Alexis Lichine and his friends in 1952. Its ownership entitles the *château* to fly the Union Jack but in fact Bass Charrington preserve the European spirit and fly the flags of many nations to welcome visitors.

Château Lascombes is in the best area of

Margaux and produces some fourteen-thousand cases of wine a year. It shares the famous Margaux reputation for bouquet, the aroma often being likened to violets, not so fanciful a comparison as it sounds. The cellars also make a Rosé de Lascombes, a dry wine slightly paler than most *rosés*. The name is said to come from La Côte, a reference to the knoll of Margaux, the highest part of the commune, an advantageous position. The vineyards run close to those of Château Margaux, and the estate has its own *château* of some character, which figures on the bottle labels.

The commune of Margaux has just as many notable names as the others. Among the Second Growths are Château Brane-Cantenac and two similar names but differing wines, Château Rausan-Ségla and Château Rauzan-Gassies. Brane-Cantenac takes its name from a Baron Brane who rejoiced in the local nickname 'Napoléon des Vignes' in the early nineteenth century. Perhaps he wasn't as clever as his friends thought, for he sold his other vineyard, Brane-Mouton, in order to concentrate on the first and in due course Brane-Mouton became the great Mouton-Rothschild, already described. However Brane-Cantenac does not lack distinction and is a biggish wine, fruity without the delicacy of Château Margaux. Lucien Lurton, the owner, also has the Second Growth Château Durfort-Vivens, a suave wine of fine *robe* and flavour, and, has inherited his father's and grandfather's skills and devotion. There is also a Third Growth called Cantenac-Brown and another named Boyd-Cantenac, both good wines, the first now undergoing a revival after a change in ownership in 1968 and the second also under skilled management, less widely sold but worth buying in good years when available since it is the best of two linked vineyards.

Château Rausan-Ségla is considerably more distinguished than Rauzan-Gassies, though the two vineyards were once one. It has had ups and downs but is at present in an upswing and much work has been done on the vines and also on their promotion. Rauzan-Gassies certainly tries hard and deserves to get better results. An advertisement I saw recently boasted three gold medals in Paris but the dates, alas, were 1878, 1889 and 1900!

By and large I would be more inclined to recommend Margaux Third Growths like Château Palmer, where Sichel has a British interest, named after an English general of Wellington's wars who once owned it; Château d'Issan, run by the Cruse family who also own Pontet Canet, Haut-Bages-Libéral, Laujac and other sound, well-made vineyards; or Château Giscours now in a thriving period.

I have often ordered Château Giscours because I have such happy memories of this lovely hundred-year-old *château* with its pillars and ascending broad front staircase that reminds me a little of Margaux

Château Palmer.

itself. Over a hundred and fifty years ago the vineyards had Americans in ownership and in more recent times belonged to the famous Cruse family to whom I have already referred. Some years ago it was purchased by Nicolas Tari, who moved there from Algeria, and it is now in the hands of his enthusiastic son who has increased its area and standing. Pierre Tari is also secretary of the 'Syndicat des Crus Classés du Médoc', the association of owners of wine classified in 1855. As such he was subject to frequent forceful visits from Baron Philippe de Rothschild as part of his long-standing campaign to get Mouton-Rothschild made a First Growth. Pierre was well able to look after himself in such encounters, but it was certainly rather ironic that he, managing a vineyard that some of my French friends think has its own claim to a higher classification, should be in such a position.

My invitation to Château Giscours came from Pierre's sister, the charming and good-looking Mrs Thomas J. Heeter whose American husband lives with her in the *château*. Pierre and his family are there also, another example of gracious living with the source of wealth all about them and a splendid atmosphere of old guns, hunting horns, boars' heads, hunting prints, carved wood and, by the door, a stand of old walking sticks, well used on the countryside. Pierre also administers two other *châteaux*, one belonging to his mother and the other in his wife's family, Branaire and La Roque. After a family meal of simple dishes with which we drank some splendid examples of Giscours, wonderfully perfumed and elegant, a wine that improves very soundly, we walked in the extensive grounds, picking *cêpes*, those broad, flat mushrooms, for the evening meal. Yet within two hours I was landing at Heathrow airport outside London!

Since there are sixty-two Classified Growths and at least two thousand properties round Bordeaux, one cannot consider them all and I have written of those that I know and like best among the Médoc.

Château la Mission Haut-Brion.

But some others must find place. Château Talbot, for instance, a Fourth Growth Saint-Julien, takes its name from the Earl of Shrewsbury who fell at the battle of Castillon in 1453 when the English were virtually driven from France. You will find this wine fairly easily in Britain, perhaps because of the name, and it is a sound, full wine, not of course the greatest but priced accordingly. The same owners have Château Gruaud-Larose, a Second Growth St-Julien.

There is Château Beychevelle, another Fourth Growth St-Julien, making some of the best wines in the area, and said to get its name from the shouts in the estuary of 'Lower the sails' or *baisse-voile*. The owners claim that the sails were lowered as a tribute to the great wine of these vineyards, but rival growers say that the sails were adjusted while the ships manoeuvred in the tricky river conditions. Château Beychevelle is a long, low, *château* with large, smooth lawns decked with flower beds in front of it.

A Fifth Growth I have enjoyed is Château Camensac, in a rather flat area. It has in recent years received considerable attention from the owners, who have rebuilt the cellars and the vat room. Camensac only produces a small amount of wine but some of this comes to England and I have got it from André Simon Wines in London. It is not a boastful wine, but its flavour and colour are attractive and it has price advantages.

Strangely enough, one of the wines growing in popularity since other prices have risen is only entitled to be known a a *bourgeois* growth. This is Château Gloria, full, deep and rewarding, with a splendid dark colour and tantalising bouquet. I have frequently found it more pleasing than several Classified Growths at tastings.

The secret undoubtedly lies with the distinguished gentleman who makes it, Monsieur Henri Martin, who is not only the proprietor of Gloria but the manager of Château Latour itself, President of the Bordeaux Wine Council, Grand Master of the 'Commanderie du Bontemps de Médoc et des Graves', the famous Bordeaux wine guild, and, last but not least, Mayor of St-Julien-de-Beychevelle. It was a great pleasure to be the guest of Monsieur Martin and his colleagues on the Wine Council in 1971 at the first wine festival to be held in Bordeaux since 1909, and to hear his splendid declaration to the crowd of many thousands, including a score or more berobed wine guilds: 'Bordeaux wine is *joie de vivre!*'

He made his declaration from the handsome three-storey Maison du Vin in the centre of Bordeaux as the climax to three days of feasting, wine-tasting, music and dancing, all of which did indeed show that Bordeaux wine is *joie de vivre*. It was an occasion never to be forgotten in the great halls of the tasting hung with many coloured wine banners, where splendid food and bottles were set before the guests, some four thousand in all.

Another unclassified growth which, however, puts on the label '*Grand Cru Exceptionnel*' by way of compensation, is Château Siran owned by the Miailhe family, who are also proprietors of the Second Growth Pichon-Longueville-Comtesse-de-Lalande already described and the Fifth Growth Château Dauzac. Since Dauzac is next door to Siran one would expect similarities and the proprietors have recently put much time and money into improving the wines. Both are well worth attention, though until recently it appeared easier to get Siran. They have the characteristics of the Margaux area, being light and fragrant. There is every reason to think that their quality will improve even further and current Dauzacs show this.

Nor may one forget Château Loudenne in the upper half of the Médoc, which has been part of W. & A. Gilbey since 1875 and is now one of the Gilbey Vintners—I.D.V. properties, a Cru Grand Bourgeois of sound quality. The estate covers 500 acres and is among the largest in the Médoc. It also makes a white wine from the Sauvignon grape.

One now travels south of Bordeaux to Graves, which is the home of the fourth First Growth, Château Haut-Brion, in the commune of Pessac. It is rather strange that the men of 1855 chose to link this wine so far away from the other three in the honour of First Growth, an indication of its reputation at the time, which has been fully justified since.

The name is often suggested by English writers as being linked with O'Brien, but French sources give its origin as d'Aubrion, then changing to Hault-Brion and finishing as Haut-Brion. As far back as 1529 Jeanne de Bellon, daughter of the Mayor of Libourne, that former English citadel, brought the domaine of Hault-Brion as her dowry, and nearly 300 years later it was in the possession of Talleyrand, the famous French Foreign Minister. Today it is the property of a company formed by Clarence Dillon, the US banker who acquired it in 1935. The Bordeaux suburbs threaten to encroach on it.

One of the reasons for the quality of Haut-Brion is found in the deep pebbly gravel that reflects the heat and equally allows rainwater to disappear quickly, much as happens at Cos d'Estournel. Perhaps these similar conditions give the wines something in common for, being a devotee of Cos d'Estournel, I find something similar in the great Haut-Brion. It is a big wine with a flowery bouquet, in which some people find hints of raspberry, and has other fine qualities of concentration and vigour that assure its reputation.

Again one has to differentiate between Haut Brion and a vineyard called Château La Mission Haut-Brion on the opposite side of the road. This comes within yet another classification, that of the Official Classification of the Red Wines of Graves made in 1953. It is good wine but lacks something of the gravelly flavour of Haut-Brion, though why this should be nobody can really explain. Haut-Brion, too, makes an excellent dry white wine called Haut-Brion Blanc, though it is rather expensive considering the range of white wines available to purchasers. La Mission does not make any white.

Another excellent red Graves is Château Carbonnieux which has been making wine in the same spot for some five hundred and fifty years. Great care is taken in choosing the vines for planting, and the reds develop splendidly as they age, fine and generous, with something of the breadth of Burgundy wines. However, Carbonnieux is perhaps even more famous as a dry wine of great elegance, with long finish for a white. It then uses the Sauvignon grape. Personally, the red is good enough for me and a wine that I would always consider carefully when selecting from a wine list though it is not always there. There is a good story about the white, however. The monks who made it wanted to sell some to the Turks who, as Moslems, were forbidden to drink wine. They labelled their bottles 'Mineral Water from Carbonnieux' and the Sultan who tasted it nodded approvingly and remarked to his courtiers, 'If the French can make such excellent mineral water, I wonder why they bother to go to the trouble of making wine!'

Among other notable red Graves are Château Smith-Haut-Lafite, (not to be confused with the First Growth Château Lafite), Château Olivier, Château Pape Clément, with a typical regional nose, and Domaine de Chevalier which, though classified with the Graves red, does not proclaim itself Château.

South to east of Graves, going up-stream along the river Garonne, one comes to Sauternes where all the greatest sweet white wines are made, principally from the Sémillon and Sauvignon grapes, the first giving smoothness and suavity and the latter body and bouquet, though some wine-

Château Yquem.

makers add small proportions of other grapes.

The leading communes are Barsac and Bommes, but Sauternes, Preignac and Fargues are also permitted to use the Sauternes *appellation*. Barsac, however, is quite sufficient on its own and denotes a wine of superior standing, sweet but not sickly sweet. Sauternes as a general name is usually of slightly less quality and sweetness, unless it is from one of the several outstanding châteaux, crowned by the wine of Château d'Yquem, far and away the greatest sweet white wine of France. The present owner is the Comte Alexandre de Lur-Saluces, who recently succeeded the Marquis Bertrand de Lur-Saluces, a most dapper but friendly figure, for many years at all great wine occasions. The fame of Château d'Yquem is more than three hundred years old and until it has been tasted nobody can feel qualified to speak or write on sweet wine. It is a superb though expensive experience, but while there are other excellent sweet wines in Sauternes such as Châteaux Guiraud, de Suduiraut, Climens, Coutet, Rieussec, Filhot and Haut-Bommes, none can capture the magic of Yquem, excellent as they are in their own way.

This great domain was brought by Joséphine de Sauvage d'Yquem when she married Count Louis Amédée de Lur-Saluces in 1786, it having been in her family since the sixteenth century.

So recognised is the superiority of Château d'Yquem that it is put in a class of its own and nominated Grand Premier Cru de Sauternes, while the other châteaux wines reach no higher than Premier Grand Cru de Sauternes. Rather strangely, the gold and white label is very simple and carries only the words 'Sauternes Appellation Controlée', the *château* name and the year. Modesty *in excelsis!*

The secret of Sauternes is not only that the wines are naturally sweet, but that the grapes are only picked when they are over-ripe and in the state of 'noble rot', in French *pourriture noble*, resulting from the action of the valuable mould *Botrytis cinerea* under which they shrivel and only produce a little

The Sauternes vineyards of Château Yquem.

Sauternes vines and a specially-built tractor for harrowing between the rows.

Vineyards at Entre-Deux-Mers.

precious juice. The wizened grapes at this time might not seem to indicate the wonderful wine they will provide, but that is their secret. The German word is *Edelfäule* and refers to the similar state of the Auslese and even richer grapes left on the vine. These sweet Sauternes, whether great or minor, are suitable only for drinking with dessert, or by themselves, perhaps on a summer morning if a lady whose beauty matches the standard of the wine is there to give you her company.

Across the river and under the trees, where Hemingway never went, is Ste-Croix-du-Mont which uses the same Sémillon and Sauvignon grapes to produce from late-picked grapes rather lesser sweet white wine. This district on the right bank of the Garonne never reaches the high standard of the Premiers Crus of Sauternes, but it is very moderately priced. Thus, among the middle range wines of Sauternes and Ste-Crois-du-Mont, you are likely to find better comparative value when you go shopping by selecting from the latter place.

One further white wine area remains to mention, and that is the rather attractively named Entre-Deux-Mers, a wide stretch of land and vineyards behind Ste-Croix-du-Mont, and between the Garonne and the Dordogne. It produces a great deal of cheap but, alas, rather ordinary white wine. When I first knew it the wine was sweetish, which in those early days pleased my taste and slender means. Today it is made in drier style to suit the

changing fashion. It is still cheap, but there are other dry white wines which are more pleasing.

Crossing this wide region and the river Dordogne on its northern side, one reaches an area of red wines that, if it was not for the superb growths of the Haut-Médoc, would be as good as anything from Bordeaux. It is divided into two neighbouring regions around Libourne, that old wine-shipping bastion, called Pomerol and St-Émilion. When you visit the latter and buy coloured postcards showing the famous Jurade de Saint-Émilion in their scarlet robes and flat caps, you also wander up and down the narrow, picturesque streets where the ninth-century chapel is carved from a huge rock. Standing outside the hillside cellars you can look down on the sea of green-blue vineyards all around you and recognise a perfect setting for living, if only men would make life so.

If you are so fortunate as to be admitted a member of the Jurade you will swear to defend faithfully the renown of St-Émilion and its vineyards by your words and your example, and to produce only wine of very high quality that will magnify the virtues and safeguard the traditions of your fathers.

There are also the Hospitaliers de Pomerol, but they only date from 1968 and are not so famous. When the Jurade 'revived' early traditions in 1948 they were quick to say that they were descended from the times of the Kings of England as well as France, and that Richard Coeur de Lion no less

At work in a vineyard at St-Émilion.

Château Fonplégade, St-Émilion.

Château Figeac, St-Émilion.

had accorded them *privileges, franchises et libres coutumes*!

St-Émilion wines are the biggest and fullest wines of the Bordeaux district, very often likened to those of Burgundy in this respect. Many vintages take a long time to mature. They are generous wines with beautiful, deep *robe*, the perfume being likened to truffles, if you happen to have eaten truffles in sufficient size to grasp the flavour. Sometimes the tannin is such that, locals claim, the wine will last thirty to forty years and still be excellent.

It is not surprising, therefore, that the St-Émilion wines have been given an official classification—but in 1955, exactly one hundred years after the Médoc rulings! The First Great Growths (Premier Grands Crus Classés) are headed by two superb wines on their own called Château Cheval-Blanc and Château Ausone. Local connoisseurs argue for hours over which is superior and at the moment Cheval-Blanc is in the lead. It takes its name from a White Horse inn that once stood here, surrounded by small farms. An avenue of splendid pines leads to the pleasant *château* and the vineyards stand on land that is heavy clay in one part and light gravel in another, plus a certain amount of iron particles. This variety, and the fact that the owners conserve a proportion of special old vines, maintains the quality and the delicate, soft body and bouquet.

Château Ausone claims to stand on the vineyards held by the Roman poet Ausonius, a much-travelled gentleman who also had vineyards on the German Mosel. The cellars are cut from the solid rock with pillars left to support the roof and here, too, some of the vines still producing are a hundred years old, sheltered from the north wind by rocks. It is a fine, generous wine, heavier than the Médocs. The same proprietors own Château Belair in the same classification, even older, and once the property of an Englishman, Robert de Knowles, whose French descendant changed his name to de Canolle.

Château Figeac is another fine St-Émilion, noted for the rich sap of its vines, and other names to consider are Clos Fourtet, Château Canon, Château Pavie and Château La Gaffelière. These are all well worth your drinking. There is also Château Canon-la-Gaffelière, graded slightly lower as Grand Cru Classé, which was the choice of two of England's leading Masters of Wine, Colin Anderson of Grants of St James's and David Peppercorn, then of I.D.V., when we lunched together. It has fruitiness and good bouquet. Another is Château La Clotte.

A vineyard in the Pomerol district.

The wines of Pomerol have not been classified but first place goes undoubtedly to Château Pétrus, which has a special flavour said to originate from the iron ores under the vineyard, as with Cheval-Blanc, which some liken to truffles. The *château* was long under the scrupulous attention of Madame Edmond Loubat, a very strict lady, and her traditions are followed by her family. The well-run Hotel Loubat at Libourne is named after her, for she was as famous down here as the Veuve Clicquot in Champagne, and you can dine there on *Lamproie de la Dordogne* made from local lampreys, which are similar to eels.

As with St-Émilion there are many vineyards at Pomerol. I have always enjoyed the fine Vieux-Chateau-Certain, despite its complicated name, Château Gazin, Château Nénin and, coming down to the *Deuxièmes Premiers Crus*, Clos René, often to be found on wine lists.

You can, of course, get wine simply labelled with the name of St-Émilion or Pomerol, and the words *appellation contrôlée*, drawn from these districts. In general Pomerol wines are smoother and fatter (softer and with less body) than the St-Émilions and so come between them and the Médoc wines.

Near this area are the wines of Fronsac, on the right bank of the Dordogne, coming to the public increasingly as other wine prices rise. These are robust wines, of attractive *robe*, under the *appellation* of either *Côtes de Canon-Fronsac* or *Côtes de Fronsac*, of which the first are the best with their fine colour, hint of spiciness in their bouquet, and full body. Their wine guild is 'Les Gentilshommes de Fronsac', a splendid name for splendid fellows, with some of whom I dined at the great Bordeaux Wine Festival of 1971, finding them and their wines excellent company.

The 1855 Classification of the wines of the Médoc

FIRST GROWTH
Château Lafite-Rothschild *Pauillac*
Château Margaux *Margaux*
Château Latour *Pauillac*
Château Haut-Brion *Pessac, Graves*

SECOND GROWTH
Château Mouton-Rothschild *Pauillac* *
Château Rausan Ségla *Margaux*
Château Rauzan-Gassies *Margaux*
Château Léoville-Lascases *Saint-Julien*
Château Léoville-Poyferré *Saint-Julien*
Château Léoville-Barton *Saint-Julien*
Château Durfort-Vivens *Margaux*
Château Gruaüd-Larose *Saint-Julien*
Château Lascombes *Margaux*
Château Brane-Cantenac *Cantenac*
Château Pichon-Longueville- Baron-de-Pichon *Pauillac*
Château Pichon-Longueville-Comtesse-de-Lalande *Pauillac*
Château Ducru-Beaucaillou *Saint-Julien*
Château Cos-d'Estournel *Saint-Estèphe*
Château Montrose *Saint-Estèphe*

THIRD GROWTH
Château Kirwan *Cantenac*
Château d'Issan *Cantenac*
Château Lagrange *Saint-Julien*
Château Langoa Barton *Saint-Julien*
Château Giscours *Labarde*
Château Malescot-Saint-Exupéry *Margaux*
Château Cantenac-Brown *Cantenac*
Château Boyd-Cantenac *Cantenac*
Château Palmer *Cantenac*
Château La Lagune *Ludon*
Château Desmirail *Margaux*
Château Calon-Ségur *Saint-Estèphe*
Château Ferrière *Margaux*
Château Marquis d'Alesme-Becker *Margaux*

FOURTH GROWTH
Château Saint-Pièrre *Saint-Julien*
Château Talbot *Saint-Julien*
Château Branaire-Ducru *Saint-Julien*
Château Duhart-Milon *Pauillac*
Château Pouget *Cantenac*
Château La Tour-Carnet *Saint-Laurent*
Château Rochet *Saint-Estèphe*
Château Beychevelle *Saint-Julien*
Château Le Prieuré *Cantenac*
Château Marquis-de-Terme *Margaux*

FIFTH GROWTH
Château Pontet-Canet *Pauillac*
Château Batailley *Pauillac*
Château Haut-Batailley *Pauillac*
Château Grand-Puy-Lacoste *Pauillac*
Château Grand-Puy-Ducasse *Pauillac*
Château Lynch-Bages *Pauillac*
Château Lynch-Moussas *Pauillac*
Château Dauzac *Labarde*
Château Mouton Baron Philippe (called Château Mouton-d'Armailhacq until 1956) *Pauillac*
Château du Tertre *Arsac*
Château Haut-Bages-Libéral *Pauillac*
Château Pédesclaux *Pauillac*
Château Belgrave *Saint-Laurent*
Château Camensac *Saint-Laurent*
Château Cos-Labory *Saint-Estèphe*
Château Clerc-Milon-Mondon *Pauillac*
Château Croizet-Bages *Pauillac*
Château Cantemerle *Macau*

* Château Mouton-Rothschild was promoted to first growth in 1973.

Vineyard scene at Corbières.

Vineyards at Banyuls in the Roussillon district.

Vineyards in autumn in the Roussillon district.

Languedoc Roussillon and South-west

Before leaving this part of France, one should remember again the much increased interest in the nearby V.D.Q.S. *(Vins délimités de qualité supérieure)* wines from the departments of Gard, Aude, Hérault and the Pyrenees, and covering Languedoc, Roussillon and such centres as Corbières, mentioned earlier. They have improved their methods of cultivation considerably.

One drinks the V.D.Q.S. wines with the best will in the world but nobody should be under the illusion that they can compare with the leaders of Bordeaux or Burgundy. I remember drinking one of these lesser white wines from the Sauvignon grape as an apéritif and finding it pleasant enough, perhaps personally influenced, too, by the sunshine and blue skies. At the luncheon following, my host, the amiable Terence Tofield of Percy Fox & Co., served a Beaujolais Blanc and the difference in body, quality and flavour showed up at once. Where the first was thin and slightly tart, even astringently so, the other was mellow, full and satisfying. Yet Beaujolais Blanc, although from the Chardonnay grape, is not a great example of white wine.

In this unhappy world of inflation and speculation it is at least something to know that these efforts to improve the cultivation and making of wine in the French V.D.Q.S. areas, where prices should prove more stable, are going on successfully.

Some of the red V.D.Q.S. have improved so much indeed that they have been raised to Appellation Contrôlée classification, as already described. Others are likely to follow and many are happily filling the gap in the French wine range left by the higher prices of Bordeaux and Burgundy.

The Loire

Few rivers have so many varied wines along their courses as does the Loire. It is a slow-flowing, silver river with golden sandbanks in summer from bend to bend and sometimes little enough water left to reflect the beautiful *châteaux* that look down on it. For nearly six hundred miles it winds from the mouth near Nantes, across country to Orleans, and then south to Nevers. Yet almost every type of wine is made here, dry white and sweet white, sparkling white, red wine and *rosé*.

They are not big wines, not mouth-fillers, but rather pleasant and delicate, the whites dry, crisp and fruity, a small amount from the Sauvignon grape that produces the great sweet wines of Sauternes but up here, on the Loire, offers something quite different, and much the largest amount from the Chenin Blanc grape. The best reds are from the Cabernet Franc grape, as at Chinon and Bourgueil. They have a splendid dark purple colour and smell of raspberries and Bourgueil, the heavier of the two, is a wine to cherish and appreciate.

Starting round Nantes one finds a V.D.Q.S. wine straight away in the Gros Plant du Pays Nantais, usually shortened to Gros Plant. It is very dry and usually drunk locally for it is an acquired taste and not more than moderate in quality. The grape is called Folle Blanche and usually has high acidity. But efforts continue to improve quality and it may be a wine of the future.

Gros Plant has lost ground to Muscadet, which has an *appellation contrôlée* designation and must be made to 9.5 degrees of alcohol. Some three-quarters of production is Muscadet de Sèvre et Maine, made from a grape called Melon de Bourgogne which produce a dry but fresh wine that is not acid. Locally the grape is often called Muscadet and it is probably one of the most pleasing of lesser wines, excellent with fish and oysters.

These are not big vineyards and they are still traditional, one custom being the making of wine *sur lies*, in other words from the lees or deposit in the original fermentation cask without any process of transferring the wine from barrel to barrel, the work known as racking which rids it of sediment. The bottling has to be done carefully but because the wine is off the lees it carries with it certain elements that are retained in the wine and make it naturally *pétillant*, or with a certain tingle that can only just be noticed. This comes out when it is chilled before a meal and though the appeal of *sur lies* is perhaps more for the wine knowledgeable—it was originally done, according to Yapp Brothers, the Loire shippers, to economise on cellar facilities and equipment—it has a difference of its own. The *lies* actually have a smell of yeast. Others claim it keeps the wine young and fruity.

As well as the appellation for Muscadet de Sèvre et Maine there is another for the wine of Muscadet des Coteaux de la Loire, which retains its youthful characteristics for a long time but is not quite so refined as the Sèvre et Maine.

Since this is an area of many growers, one is well advised to buy on the reputation of the shipper, though two better known growers whose Muscadet wines I have enjoyed are Château de la Cassemichere (for *Sèvre et Maine*) and the Comte de Malestroit's Château la Noë.

The next district of importance above the Muscadet area is Anjou, famous for its *rosé* wine, and here again the soil is flint and clay with a chalky region round Saumur, centre of some famous sparkling wines made by the *methode champenoise*, longer and more expensive than the tank method.

The cheaper *rosés* are made from the Groslot grape and some others, but the best come from Cabernet grapes and only wine made from these can be called Rosé de Cabernet or Cabernet d'Anjou. This latter has a fine colour and must have ten degrees of alcoholic strength. It should be drunk young, and is a fresher, lighter wine than Tavel from the Rhône, its famous rival, which has a fuller body.

Anjou has many historical links with England

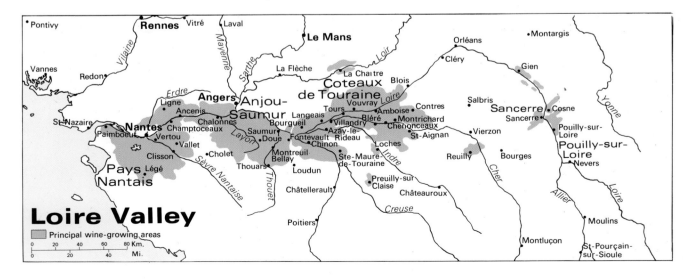

going back to the days when the Plantagenets were Counts of Anjou and not far away, at Fontevrault, you can see the tomb of Richard Coeur-de-Lion, with its magnificent carved figure, and those of others of his family.

There are some splendid sweet white wines in Anjou from the Chenin Blanc grape and they come here from the Coteaux du Layon, slopes round a little river called the Layon. They are full in body and the grapes are sometimes left until they reach the *pourriture noble* stage. There are also sweet white wines from the Coteaux de la Loire on the north side of the Loire itself, but they are not quite so good as those of the Layon area. Savennières is the centre of this section and is also gaining prominence for its dry white wines, rather full and some of them almost *demi-sec*. The wines of Baron Brincard are notable for their quality and his 1970 Château de la Bizolière I found particularly powerful yet fragrant, with a certain unusual attraction in the nose, when I tasted it with Yapp Brothers in the following year. Coulée de Serrant is another fine Savennières vineyard.

Incidentally the minimum alcoholic content of the Coteaux du Layon wines is thirteen degrees, unusually high for a white wine. It is sometimes fifteen degrees or more. Moreover it stays in bottle for many years and can improve in it. The superb example, in my mind, comes from Quarts de Chaume, with only half a dozen growers. I would advise anyone who appreciates sweet wines not to miss the opportunity of drinking Quarts de Chaume and I can think of no better accompaniment to a ripe pear. Remember, however, that they are strong wines too. A not dissimilar wine in the same area is from Bonnezeaux, slightly more scented.

Saumur is an impressive town as you approach it across the Loire and note the handsome *château* high above. The bridge and river were valiantly defended by young cadets from the French military school here who set an example in 1940 when the heavens were indeed falling for France. The sparkling wines that are produced there are stored in cellars in the white chalk cliffs. They are dry or *demi-sec* wines.

There are a number of communes entitled to *Appellation Saumur*, perhaps the best known being Dampierre, making mostly white wine but also some red and *rosé*. Coteaux de Saumur wines found favour with Edward VII who is still remembered there for his supposed interest in them. From Saumur one goes on to the district of Touraine and the first wines are among the most notable, being Bourgueil and Saint-Nicolas-de-Bourgueil, two reds of delicate distinction with flavour often likened to violets, though it does not seem so to me. They are certainly perfumed in an attractive way and Bourgueil has enough body to make it worth drinking with red meat, even roasts.

While Bourgueil lies north of the Loire, Chinon is

The town of Saumur.

A view of Chinon across the River Vienne.

to the south looking down on the River Vienne. Its great claim to fame, wine apart, is that Rabelais was born here about 1483 and until 1530 was still trying to settle down to the priesthood. During this time he looked after a local vineyard. He certainly praised the wines of Chinon and his recommendation stands today. They are somewhat lighter in body and colour than those of Bourgueil yet made from the same Cabernet Franc grape. There is also a white Chinon from Chenin Blanc and a *rosé*, both not very distinguished. The reds of Chinon and Bourgueil must have a minimum alcoholic content of 9.5 degrees which is not, of course, very strong.

We are now in Touraine, one of France's most romantic areas with a chain of lovely *châteaux* from

Villandry to Chenonceaux and majestic Chambord. Under these classic roofs were enacted many a drama of love and jealousy, murder and adultery. Most of the *châteaux* are open to the public and offer guided tours.

A white wine carries the name of Touraine but the most notable vineyards are those which produce Vouvray, centred on eight villages. This is a dry white wine—and often *demi-sec* too—that is at once pleasing and refreshing, splendidly matched with the spacious atmosphere of this part of the Loire. The driest whites are often made into sparkling wine, again by *methode champenoise*, which is the best. Aimé Boucher supply a well-known sparkling Vouvray, fit rival to the Ackerman '1811' sparkling Saumur from the other centre. Another well-known name for sparkling wines on the Loire is Bouvet-Ladubay.

The Vouvray white wines are made to eleven degrees alcohol but the sparkling types require only 9.5 degrees. From the Chenin Blanc grape, they are not wines of long life but I like them because in my experience they are sound, palate-cleansing drinks and never *too* dry, often indeed semi-sweet.

Although in the past Reuilly and Quincy have been described as little-known wines these two products of the Loire region are coming to better recognition. The soil here is chalky and we come into the kingdom of the Sauvignon grape, much less used than Chenin Blanc on the Loire but a notable vine in itself. It is the white wines that are favoured, both examples however being dry and inclined to acidity. The vines grow near the river Cher.

The Sauvignon is also used for the wines of Sancerre. The cross-country road to Sancerre from Tours has all the beauty that one finds on minor unspoiled roads in France. One of the first views of this old town is from the heights above the hill from which it rises, and it is a green hill, capped with grey stone houses in a sea of vines round its base. You drive slowly down the long road until you are actually below the town and must make a sharp ascent to reach the old ramparts and walls where life bustles along much as in any other French provincial centre. There is, however, the magic of the name, Sancerre. The land round here is limestone and again the wine may sometimes be rather acid, its white *robe* tinged with green, but I have usually enjoyed its clean, sharpish, flavour and you are never in any doubt that this is a dry wine! A leading vineyard is Chavignol, while Comte Lafond is another name to note in connection with Sancerre.

On the other bank of the Loire stands one of the greatest names of the whole river, that of Pouilly-sur-Loire, an attractive village with no less than three restaurants each boasting a Michelin star. They all offer fish dishes of one kind or another, not surprising when the river is so close. The famous

Chenonceaux, in the Coteaux de Touraine.

wine, Pouilly-Fumé, is an excellent accompaniment.

As you approach Pouilly there appears on either side a series of signs offering 'Degustation', or tasting, of wines by local growers. These are not necessarily free, though usually so if you buy a few bottles. But a half hour stop at such a tasting is always an interesting way of meeting local people and, if you have modest French, of finding out their views on wine and life. Close to the silver Loire, which runs within sight at the back of the houses, Pouilly is equally a charming place for a short stay though, since its hotels have a reputation and good cuisine, prices are a little higher than in some of the more rural areas.

Pouilly-Fumé is made from the Sauvignon grape, a crisp white wine of pale yellow colour without hints of green, and here lies a difference from Pouilly-Fuissé, the wine from the Chardonnay grape grown near Mâcon in Burgundy. Most wine books warn readers not to confuse the two but in my eyes the Fumé is white-yellow and the Fuissé pale-gold greenish. The grapes being different, the flavours are in fact different, Fumé has a musky, slightly spicy, flavour, while Fuissé has a hint of hazelnuts and is more vigorous. I must admit, however, that both are often called 'flinty'.

Another name for Pouilly-Fumé is Blanc Fumé

At work in a vineyard at Saumur.

A vineyard at Château Luynes in the Coteaux de Touraine.

de Pouilly; either *appellation* is permitted and a minimum of eleven degrees is required. Among noted producers are Château du Nozet of Ladoucette Frères, and Les Champs de Cri. Production is limited to some extent, but it is interesting that the terrain here is not unlike that of Chablis.

Pouilly produces a second wine under the *appellation* Pouilly-sur-Loire which is much the lesser and comes from the Chasselas grape. It is also dry but has neither the body nor character of the Fumé, possibly because the soil used has more clay in it, and a different grape is grown. If you order a carafe locally it is probably Chasselas.

One cannot leave the Loire without mentioning a wine still further south. This is Saint-Pourcain-sur-Sioule, produced in some twenty communes on the banks of the rivers Sioule and Allier. You will meet it often in this part of France, a V.D.Q.S. wine of some interest, served in the Middle Ages to the kings of France and now of lesser standing but with prospects of coming back into favour. It is usually a mixture of grapes, the Tressalier predominating in the white and the Pinot Noir and Gamay in the red and *rosé*. The whites have a pleasant fruity flavour, somewhat like apple in aroma, and the reds are strong and satisfying.

When I was *en route* near Bourges I lunched at a small roadside restaurant and found a large poster in the dining-room exhorting visitors 'Buvez un Saint-Pourcain, Blanc, *Rosé*, Rouge. Medaille d'Or Paris 1969, 1970, 1971. Prix d'Honneur St Pourcain 1970. Pagnon Elie, Proprietaire-Victiculteur.'

I had a bottle of his *rosé*, and quite good it was, rather pale in colour but fresh and palate-pleasing. Returning to England I found Monsieur Pagnon appearing in the wine-list of Yapp Brothers of Mere, already mentioned, at a price a little over £1 a bottle for his white. 'There are several hundred growers, most with very small vineyards, and Monsieur Pagnon is the only grower to devote his activities to full-time viticulture,' says the wine-list. 'His wines are bottled *sur lie* . . .'

So ends this tour of French wines, by no means complete but listing the outstanding examples and some of the lesser varieties that are coming to prominence. Acquaintance with the better French wines is very necessary in judging those of other countries for they set the standard, as is shown by the way many of their names have been adapted in other lands much to French annoyance: these include burgundy, sauternes, and chablis.

6
Germany

The division of Germany after the Second World War happily left the best wine regions in the west, whatever consequences this had for the nation as a whole. It is therefore possible to drive round the main areas, using the autobahns, in something like three days but not, of course, to study the vineyards and taste their brilliant products. In a two or three week holiday, however, a fair idea may be obtained of their extent and variety. The German vineyards are set in some of the most beautiful scenery in Europe and grow around two lovely and impressive rivers, the Mosel and the Rhine. In spite of pollution and increased traffic on them, this is an ideal vacation area for winelovers.

Both France and Italy make much more wine than is produced in Germany, where climatic and physical conditions demand hard work and resolution on the part of the growers. But neither France nor Italy can produce a white wine quite like the best German Riesling grapes. These vines grow dry and fresh along the Mosel and its tributaries, the Saar and Ruwer. Yet they are full and fruity by the Rhine, and richly sweet in Auslese form in the Palatinate. Thus the same grape is suited to fish and white meat as it grows in one area and to dessert and convivial drinking as it appears in another.

It is fortunate that German winegrowers possess the best attributes of their race: patience, perseverance, discipline and courage. All these are

Mayschob, a wine village on the Ahr river.

needed, for much of the time they fight a constant battle with the weather. When there is not ice or hail there is rain and wind and then, when the vintage is ready, the owner must guard it against the voracious local bird life, often covering the vines with vast lengths of expensive plastic netting or using automatic pop-guns to frighten the birds themselves.

The Mosel

The German growers scrupulously link three rivers together in the name of this area and the Weinwerbung Mosel-Saar-Ruwer promotes their splendid wines impartially. The chief river rises under the name of Moselle in France and passes by Luxembourg, where some pleasant though rather thin Riesling wines are made, and enters Germany. Trier is the first city of note and has already been described, a wine town of many centuries' existence.

Above Trier the Saar arrives on the scene, a river of remarkable achievement for it is mostly a cold, narrow canyon which does not curve sufficiently to protect the vines from the bitter weather that at times prevails. But though the wines are frequently acid, more so in bad years than others, they can reach a high standard of excellence for which credit is usually given to the topsoil slate that stores the sun's warmth. This happens, too, on the Middle Mosel, but there the river winds to place the best vineyards obligingly open to the sun.

Quite how the Saar achieves its magic is something of a conundrum. Perhaps it is due to the hard work of the winegrowers. The result is a wine of remarkable quality in good years, usually dry but also sweet and covering the whole range. The great Riesling grape, so adaptable to circumstances, is another reason in itself. Often the Saar wines are described as 'steely', but the word is used in a complimentary sense.

Sugar is added to the *must* before fermentation in bad years but it is done in accordance with the wine laws, and the fact is not hidden. The Saar men are naturally experts in their own locality.

The Saar flows into the Mosel at Konz and the vineyards stretch back some twenty-two miles from there. It is not surprising that they lie in a fairly short stretch for, higher up, the Saar reaches Saarbrücken amid a conglomeration of industrial premises with their attendant smoke and stench that has made the country wealthy but is the last place where one would expect grass, let alone vines to grow. Driving up the valley the scene changes before one's eyes from pastoral charm to smoking chimneys.

A firm that has long imported, in a pioneer way, the wines of the Saar and Ruwer, as well as the best Mosel and Rhine wines, is the House of Hallgarten, London. They have sought the finest and been content to offer it when it would have been easier

Harvesting in the Ahr vineyards.

to go for popular, better-known names, and their selection is astonishingly comprehensive. Other firms of standing who feature these wines are O. W. Loeb, Sichel, Deinhard, Saccone & Speed, and Hatch, Mansfield.

Ownership of the Saar has been contested politically in peace and by arms in war, yet, the breaks of battle apart, it has gone on producing its wines which, by a harsh coincidence, are at their best in those hot, dry summers that make the most suitable weather for war. Its most famous vineyard is Scharzhofberg, near Wiltingen. Here Egon Müller is the name to look for and his wines are eagerly sought by buyers. Both Ayl and Ockfen rank highly, and Ayler Kupp in the right year is superb, some of it owned by the Catholic seminary in Trier, which has some seventy acres in the Mosel area. One reason for the success of these wines is that the vineyards lie in a fairly sheltered area out of the wind and Ayler Kupp is a rather fascinating name in itself. Ayl is the village where Peter Lauer's inn was long ago recommended to me by Peter Longhurst of Robert James, Son & Co, the London wine importers. Kupp means a curved hill or summit. The Ayler Herrenberger vineyard is owned by Bischöfliches Konvikt, another Catholic body in Trier.

At Ockfen the best vineyard is Bockstein, with more body than Scharzhofberger but less finesse, so that the two are rivals at any vintage. Here Dr Fischer is a notable name and so is Gebert. At Oberemmel you find one of the most pleasant personalities in the German wine industry, Herr Otto Van Volxem, who has served as Staatsminister but has too much sense of humour surely for a politician. He has some fifteen acres at Wiltingen and Oberemmel, and produces excellent wines.

The river Ruwer joins the Mosel below Trier and the wines that grow on its banks, though again Riesling, are the lightest in the Mosel region. Like the Saar wines they may sometimes be too acid.

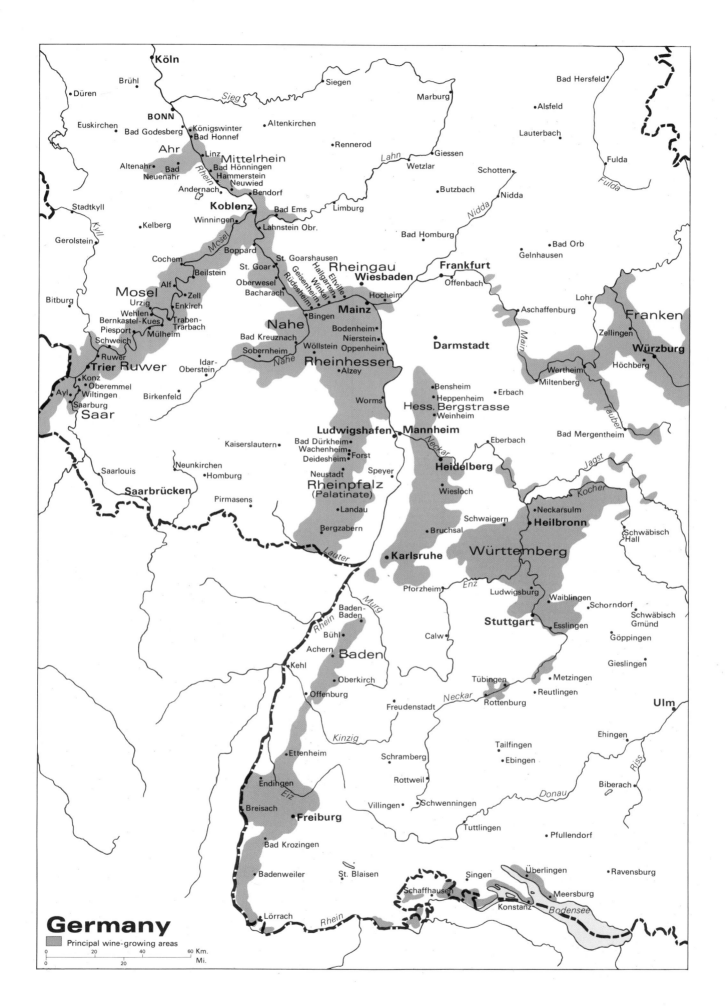

Germany

Principal wine-growing areas

0   20   40   60 Km.

0   20   Mi.

Although acidity is necessary in white wine to provide flavour, balance and longer life, if present in too large quantities it makes the wine tart and indigestible. This explains why, in bad years, a good deal of the Saar and Ruwer wine that is not up to standard is made into sparkling wine, in which process its deficiences can be quite happily adjusted.

The Ruwer is an even smaller and narrower river than the Saar, but it has not suffered the industrial fate of that river in its upper regions. Since the wines are light it follows that the alcoholic content is not high, but the vineyards are not so exposed as those of the Saar and seem to ripen more easily and with less struggle, something perhaps reflected in the notable bouquet which, while delicate, is quite outstanding. Although light, the Ruwer wines have considerable staying power and have been recommended for keeping up to eight or ten years, during which their bouquet might also be expected to improve with the wine. But this long keeping is not something I would really recommend myself, other than as an experiment or in a particularly fine year such as 1971.

The chief Ruwer vineyards lie in a stretch of under eight miles and begin some five miles from the junction with the Mosel at Eitelsbach and Mertesdorf. The first is famous for the great Karthäuserhofberg vineyard of some seventy acres, the property of the Hans Wilhelm Rautenstrauch family, coming to them in the early nineteenth century after long belonging to the Church. It has a remarkably handsome though very small label in green, red and gold which goes round the neck of the bottle instead of the waist, and incorporates a bishop's mitre as an indication of its former owners. Through marriage the estate is now under Herr Werner Tyrell, another great name in this area.

Its rival on the left bank is the Maximin-Gruenhaus vineyard, again a former Church property where the monks had made fine wine for nearly a century. They lost their property with the French Revolution and the subsequent French occupation. Again the wine boasts a handsome label in green, red and brown with copious vines and vine leaves and the *schloss* which once entertained an emperor off gold plate. This label goes round the waist of the bottle and incorporates the names of the von Stumm-Halberg and von Schubert families, past and present owners.

There are fascinating histories to record of both places but that is so of nearly all vineyards! It is certainly true of the town of Kasel, an attractive little place of white houses and low, green, vine-covered hills which produce some two hundred and fifty acres of wine, not only delicious in itself but cited as a cure for what Samuel Pepys called 'the stone' as far back as 1738. Doctors still recommend Kasel wines for health reasons, or so the locals avow. Rather sheltered, more wine is produced per acre than further up the Ruwer, and leading vineyards are Niesgen, Kernagel and Paulinsberg among a dozen of the best, and Church interests vie with private owners among some of these.

Waldrach lies further up the Ruwer where the land is more exposed but it has several notable vineyards including Krone, Hahnenberg, Laurentiusberg, Meisenberg and Hubertusberg. It shares the medicinal properties attributed to Kasel wines. There is also Avelsbach, in a valley some three miles to the south of the Ruwer and close to Trier. Here again are excellent wines with some of the vineyards owned by the Hohe Domkirche or cathedral of Trier—each with Dom in front of its name, hence Dom Avelsbacher and Dom Scharzhofberger—and the Hammerstein vineyard which is the property of the State Domain. These Church and State properties are not uncommon in Germany and are invariably well run, for German thoroughness coupled with a prestige body does not spare any necessary expense.

From this visit to the Saar and Ruwer tributaries of the Mosel the visitor coming from France sees at once that the vines are cultivated in a different way. Instead of the low, almost squat, 'bushes' of Burgundy these vines are tall and trained up poles higher than a man.

Avelsbach is an appropriately close setting for a return to Trier, discussed earlier in this book. We have seen how famous is the Hospice de Beaune in Burgundy, with its famous November auction, but there is a similar vineyard owner in Trier and another at Bernkastel. The Vereinigte Hospitien at Trier is a public hospital that has vineyards in five districts on the Saar and Mosel and others, including the Maximiner Pichter, actually in Trier. Some of these produce light and modest wines but its best possessions are in the Piesporter wine area where it has shares in Schubertslay, Goldtröpfchen and others.

Several of the Church wine interests share cellars in Trier which also has a college of viticulture. It is a city from which to start a holiday of wine tours in the Mosel region and each autumn in recent years the Weinwerbung Mosel-Saar-Ruwer of 86, Neustrasse, Trier, has held two-day courses in wine tasting for a reasonable fee. They are open to any visitors who apply in good time and some are conducted in English.

Trier is a splendid city and when you look out on the great Porta Negra, that remarkable Roman gate, and watch its weather-darkened sandstone glow pink and gold in the early morning sunrise, and visit the vineyards within its own boundaries, you will feel as a winelover that few other cities can offer such beauty close to their centre.

The journey south along the Mosel to the great vineyards is as thrilling an experience, if you have a little wine knowledge, as motoring down the Côte d'Or of France. First comes Trittenheim, with its light, attractive but lesser known wines, then

The Mosel valley near Traben-Trarbach.

Leiwen, home of the great Franz Reh organisation which sends its Prinz wines far abroad, and Dhron, proud of its Hofberg vineyard and the amusingly named Dhroner Eselsmilch, or asses' milk.

At Piesport the heart beats faster as you come to the Goldtröpfchen vineyard, 'little drops of gold' indeed, particularly for the growers, and sending wine to England since the Middle Ages. It is the first great name of the Middle Mosel, but one to be chosen with some care and attention to the grower and shipper, for unfortunately in recent times its popularity has led to some doubtful marketing by unscrupulous persons. As with every good wine the label is all, which explains once again why some understanding of a country's wine laws, already described, plus a regard for the label wording, is necessary to ensure that one gets what one pays for.

There is now something of a gap as one rounds the acute hairpin bend of the Mosel by Minheim, near which starts the slope on the opposite bank that ascends steadily till it reaches the majestic height opposite Brauneberg called the Juffer. This faces in turn Klostergarten beside the township itself. The Piesporter wines are inclined to verge on sweetish flavour with a distinctive, fragrant nose, very elegant. The Brauneberger wines are flowery, which is light and scented, but they are also rich so that your mouth fills when you drink them and they linger on the palate. To drink Brauneberger Juffer

is a great experience which I would rank above even the best Piesporter, perhaps because the Juffer slopes get such an overwhelming power of sunshine from their situation. The Paulinshofberg vineyards next to Juffer also produce fine wines, rather similar though lesser.

Another attractive but slightly lesser wine comes from the Sonnenlay vineyard at Mülheim where my friend Max Ferdinand Richter has his estates. His round, cheerful, middle-aged face smiles over his wines, of which he is naturally very proud. They have been in his family since 1680 and he is one of the largest producers on the Middle Mosel. The estates include vineyards in Trarbach, Wehlen, Graach, Mülheim and Brauneberg and enable him to make such high quality wines as Auslesen, Beerenauslesen and Eiswein. Max is the best type of pleasant, sophisticated German, intelligent, handsome and well-dressed, very different from the popular conception of a winegrower, yet his prices are sensibly reasonable. With him I sampled his 1971 Mülheimer Sonnenlay Riesling Spätlese, winner of a silver medal, with a splendid bouquet from a great year, and his famous 1970 Helenenkloster Feinste Spätlese Eiswein. This was called 'The Christmas Wine' because it was harvested on 23 December of that year when, as he told me, 'It was so cold I could harvest the grapes in their frozen state.' He sold it in 1972 at only £4.40 a bottle, a modest price then for a fine ice wine.

One could write many descriptive pages in the words of Thomas Wolfe's title 'Of Time and the River', but both flow too quickly where the Mosel is concerned. Now come two earth-shaking names, *mit gutem Klang* is the German phrase, of Graacher Himmelreich, what heaven it is! and Wehlener Sonnenuhr. The latter has the great sundial of its name perched among the vines and clearly visible from the road.

Himmelreich is grown high up on the slopes from the slate soil that gives it long life, individuality, and the liveliness for which it is famous, but there are several vineyards here, such as Domprobst, with similar fame. Wehlener Sonnenuhr is an even more notable name and many think it an even better wine than the world-renowned Bernkasteler Doktor. It would seem true to say that no other Mosels are ahead of Sonnenuhr, which is blessed with elegance and flavour and leaves a rich lingering in the mouth.

The home of the great Bernkasteler Doktor comes next, Bernkastel-Kues, beautifully situated on a bend of the Mosel with Kues on the left bank, the two joined by a broad bridge. The St Nikolaus Hospital described earlier is on the Kues side of the river and was founded in 1458. Behind it lie the slopes of its Kardinalsberg vineyard whose labels feature the name 'Kardinal Cusanus Stiftswein' after the founder, coupled with his coat of arms.

Rising above Bernkastel are the slopes of the Doktor vineyards, entered by a massive door set in a wall that you reach by ascending remarkably steep steps from the picturesque streets and market place below. Here the Thanisch estate used the name 'Bernkasteler Doktor und Graben' while Deinhard sometimes added to their portion the words 'Doktor und Badstube', but not always, and a third owner, the relatively small Lauerburg estate, used the name 'Doktor und Bratenhöfchen'. The Doktor wines are generally considered to have a smoky taste and I find something in this myself. It is probably from the slate in the soil, some local *gout de terroir*, as the French call it.

Dr H. Thanisch is a name to conjure with in Bernkastel and far afield, for the family that holds these vineyards has been there longer than anyone else. 'Graben' means ditch and refers to the drain that lies between the Doktor vineyards and its neighbours. There is a similar tradition to that of the Kasel wines over the Doktor's healing properties, and an Archbishop of Trier in 1363 is said to have been cured, when he lay dying in Bernkastel, by copious draughts of the wine. The Kardinalsberg vineyards are also excellent and if only Kardinal Kues had been similarly saved by his own wine when his fatal illness started (in far off Italy) then we might well attach as much importance to them as the world does to the Doktor. Having sampled both I would judge either an excellent

The great sundial on the hill, in the Wehlener Sonnenuhr vineyards.

restorative, giving the edge to the Doktor but thinking the Kardinalsberg much more reasonably priced.

The firm of Deinhard & Co Ltd are among leading London importers of German and other wines, and are linked with their relatives who centre on Koblenz. They supplied 1,200 litres of wine for Queen Victoria and Prince Albert when they stayed at Schloss Stolzenfels near Koblenz in 1845 and had been doing business with English customers since 1825. In the 1830s a Carl Deinhard settled in London and changed his name to Charles. In 1900 the firm bought their part of the Doktor vineyard, paying the astonishing price for those days of 100 marks per square metre, the equivalent of one vine. Hasslacher men have been in the firm since 1857 and today are responsible at the London end while the Deinhard company, with several subsidiaries, also prosper in Koblenz.

Beyond Bernkastel lies Wehlen, on the opposite bank, where a co-operative, the Winzergenossenschaft Zentralkellerei Mosel-Saar-Ruwer operates under a brisk friendly man in his early forties, Dr Rudolf Rinck.

Co-operatives flourish in Germany as in France and there are 3,500 members between the Luxembourg border and Koblenz. This success springs from a similar post-war situation in each country. Devastation in both Alsace and the Mosel valley led to the need for central cellars and vinification plants that all could share, since individuals lacked the capital to build their own.

We drank a 1971 Graacher Himmelreich Riesling

Landshut Castle, at Bernkastel.

Auslese, a Qualitätswein mit Prädikat as the new German wine labelling law requires, a wine of fine nose, rich and sweet as are all the 1971 Auslese wines. Dr Rinck followed it with a 1969 Zeltinger Schlossberg, an example of the old labelling and such phrases as 'Feine Auslese, Riesling-Natur, Original Abfüllung' on the label, words now forbidden. It was a fruity, spicy wine with again much sweetness.

A few miles from his office we looked at the huge cellars being built to hold at first forty million litres and then, by planned expansion, fifty million litres. There are stainless steel tanks of all sizes for the wine and in fact Wehlen exports more German wine to Britain than does the big Zentralkellerei at Breisach, its friendly co-operative rival.

There are private family firms at Wehlen also, among them those of Peter Prüm and a relative, Sebastian Alois Prüm, and a third firm Johann Josef Prüm. Not surprisingly Prüm is one of the most important wine names on the Mosel. In fact the Prüms hold the best parts of the Sonnenuhr vineyards as well as other fine sites. They have lived round Wehlen for over 800 years.

Further down the river lies Zeltingen with yet another sundial vineyard, much of it owned by J. J. Prüm so one is not surprised to find it produces a quality wine. Zeltingen, however, is a huge producer of wine, so obviously some of its other vineyards are putting production before quality.

Zeltingen has its share of good slate soil that makes for better vineyards and Schlossberg is a vineyard producing wine of body. There is also another Himmelreich vineyard here, though not as renowned as that of Graach already described. More famous, though with a third of the acreage, is its neighbour Ürzig in the centre of the next U-bend of the river, so that it is sheltered by the slopes around it, some of them acutely steep. The slate strata here is broken through by volcanic soil and red sandstone, a strange mixture indeed and found nowhere else along the Mosel. The result is a wine with a most interesting spicy flavour, very fruity and with powerful bouquet, although the actual body is not really greater than others, except that the aroma makes it seem so. It is a Mosel wine which I always look for with particular anticipation at tastings—sometimes the name is spelled Uerzig—and I am seldom disappointed. Though since I like 'biggish' wines of good bouquet it may be that Ürzig fits my personal preference and a taster who preferred delicate wines of finesse would feel less enthusiastic; a difference, in fact, not unlike that between partisans of Burgundy and Bordeaux. The two leading vineyards at Ürzig are Würzgarten and Goldwingert and again the Bischöfliches Priesterseminar of Trier owns portions of the first. They have earned it, for in 1066 Konrad, who was to be Archbishop of Trier, was hurled to his death from the Ürzig heights!

The next vineyard area going towards Koblenz is Erden, which is again a notable centre. The slopes are less severe here and the wines have some of the spice of Ürzig but not to the same extent or fame. Where the vines grow is sometimes called the Golden Mountain of the Mosel because of the area's fertility, and the slate is hard as at Bernkastel while *erde* is in fact German for earth. Foremost vineyards here include Prälat, though this is lesser known than Treppchen, named to describe the terraces and exported as a fine example of dry Mosel wine.

One follows the river past Kröv with its Nacktarsch vineyard, Wolf and Enkirch, another district with a very high production. In between the last two is the picturesque twin town of Traben-Trarbach lying on either side of the Mosel. It has a handsome bridge and pleasant restaurants while the whole town is redolent of the wine trade. Its wines are not in the top class but have something of the 'steely' quality found in the wines of the Mosel tributaries.

The last vineyards of the Middle Mosel arrive with Zell, which might be known for its superior wines if it had not, for better or worse, become irretrievably linked with Zeller Schwarze Katz (Black Cat), a popular wine name at home and abroad with the inevitable consequence that Zell has had to produce a seal of quality to authenticate the genuine article. It is a pleasant enough drink, though the cat on the label is terrifying, but it is the result of a gimmick and, like Beaujolais and Chablis, suspiciously liable to be 'stretched' in quantity unless great care is taken in the purchase. The price is not usually high so this also explains the demand. Perhaps in fifty years' time people will choose wines from their own knowledge and appreciation rather than the fancy appeal of such names, amusing of course as they are! In fact Zell deserves more fame for its historic Round Tower standing up among the vines and dating from the fifteenth century.

From now on the region is called Lower Mosel and though there are numerous vineyards the wine is not great and is drunk locally. One reason for this is the fact that the slate in the vineyards is now very hard and does not crumble and feed the vineyards as in the Middle Mosel, where the wine-grower has to cut slate again to replace the crumbling examples, a hard task on the steep slopes. Again, neither is the soil on the Lower Mosel of the same quality nor do the vineyards catch the sun in quite the same way. The best of the Mosel wines are left behind as the river, still bending but much less acutely, joins the Rhine at Deutsches Eck or German corner, where once stood a fine equestrian statue of King Wilhelm I until an American gunner shot it down in the Second World War.

All along the Mosel there are pleasant inns, many with terraces where you can eat and drink while looking out on the river. Places where I have enjoyed such interludes with Mosel wine include the Hotel Zum Anker at Alf, the Pölicher Held at Pölich, and the Burg Metternich terrace at Beilstein with its half-timbered houses like a miniature

The historic Round Tower at Zell.

Bernkastel and the setting for some German films.

With Robert Noll, who at that time was with the Franz Reh establishment at Leiwen, I drank a delightful 1971 Trittenheimer Apotheke Riesling Auslese. On his apologising for its being rather cold, our table companion, Herr Rudolf Bernhard, assured him that the British preferred their wines that way! We sipped the wine, admiring its bouquet, under the original painting by Hasenklever that is reproduced on many Franz Reh labels, 'The Winetasting'. It shows a buyer of ample proportions rolling a sample round his tongue with expressive facial contortions while the cellarmaster looks on hopefully for the verdict. It was purchased after a diligent search.

Herr Noll then opened two examples from the firm's Schatzkammer, or special cellar, a 1953 Leiwener Laurentiuslay Feinste Auslese and a 1957 Wehlener Sonnenuhr Auslese. I preferred the second of the two, but both seemed to me to have an aged flavour that I did not entirely enjoy, much as I appreciated the gesture of his opening the wines. Herr Noll was ready to admit that this was an acquired taste, and assured me that his wife preferred the 1971 Trittenheimer by a long way. However, as I didn't know whether or not Frau Noll was a connoisseur, I could not be sure that this was a compliment.

Gutenfels Castle at Kaub, in the Mittelrhein district.

The Rheingau

There is a convenient and delightful way of reaching the next wine region by taking a river steamer from Koblenz. The great white and gold boats travel to timetable and have handsome dining and wining saloons. The steep slopes on either bank are green with Riesling vines on high terraces. Among them stand ancient castles and other picturesque ruins while in the villages colourful wine festivals follow one another for half the year.

The Rheingau evokes wonderful memories for all who appreciate wine, and its products are given first place among German white wines. In 1971 the finest German wines for at least eighteen years were made on the slopes looking down on the strip of river between Rüdesheim and Eltville, while the names of the vineyards themselves are a roll-call of bottled history.

Just before Rüdesheim is Assmannshausen where some of the comparatively few red wines of Germany are grown from the Spätburgunder grape, a German variety of the Pinot Noir brought from Burgundy, never quite as successful as in its original earth where it gains greater body and bouquet than here, but very drinkable nonetheless.

Among the white wine grapes, seventy-five per cent are again Riesling, which stands up well to the winter cold in these parts, so warm and joyful in summer but rather bleak and forbidding once autumn is over. The resulting wines have body and long life and splendid flavour and aroma. One of the greatest wine colleges in the world stands at Geisenheim, a respected name to every grower in the land.

Rüdesheim wines are not among the greatest but maintain good standards in most years. In fact they are inclined to get too much sun, as the slopes are steep and drain quickly while the river, as with the Mosel, reflects great heat on them. There are many vineyards and those with Berg in the name usually come from the Rüdesheimer Berg area such as Berg Roseneck, Berg Rottland and Berg Schlossberg. A lot of wine is simply sold as Rüdesheimer Riesling and you can drink it to your heart's delight or your pocket's limit in such charming places as the Rüdesheimer Schloss in Drosselgasse, perhaps the most famous wine street, scarcely nine feet across, in the world. The local song hums tunefully about 'A little, little street in Rüdesheim' and this is the place.

It is crowded with excellent restaurants and *weinstuben,* several of them with typical German oompah bands. My weekend at Rüdesheim wine festival was noisy, crowded and good-humoured, a worthwhile memory in every way. In the evenings the crowds carry tiny battery-powered lanterns that look like thousands of glow-worms in the night, and the market place has dancing and stalls with huge barrels of Rhine wine.

In the hills above the Rhine a little farther east are two of Germany's greatest wines. The first is Schloss Johannisberg owned in turn by Bénédictine monks, Napoleon, the Emperor of Austria, and Metternich, in whose family it remains. Its wines are classified with coloured seals, pink, green, red and yellow in descending order, and it was a 1963 Grünlack which I drank in Drosselgasse, a pleasing wine though not a fine year. The castle is a splendid building in itself, and the cellars are open to the public during visiting hours. One has to remember that the word 'Schloss' is all important, for there is an ordinary Johannisberger at much lower prices. There is also a very superior grade of the Schloss wines made, depending upon the quality of the vintage each year.

A wine that I have enjoyed more often, and probably as much, is the neighbouring Schloss Vollrads, the property of the Graf Matuschka-Greiffenclau family, a wonderfully majestic name for a similar wine. Again there is a castle with a splendid tower. The family has been here for some 600 years and the wines have benefited, being splendidly perfumed, big and full and enduring in the mouth. I have usually drunk the blue capsule —again there is a colour range—and they are exceptionally distinctive and full of trembling flavours and suggestions. One can only echo old Omar Khayyam and wonder what on earth the vintners find to buy one half as precious as the wines they sell. There are other fine wines at Winkel, where Schloss Vollrads stands, among them the notable vineyards of Hasensprung and Jesuitengarten, appearing on labels as Winkeler Hasensprung Auslese etc.

The 1971 vintage of this latter is a particularly splendid wine though there can be considerable difference in price between one estate and another —as much as £1 a bottle in fact—and not all that difference in superiority. The lower priced came from Deinhard's share of the vineyard, admirably made. Next come the wines of Mittelheim, pleasant but not outstanding, and the same applies to Östrich. As well as Riesling they grow Sylvaner and Müller-Thurgau, the cross between Riesling and Sylvaner.

Hallgarten is the next village and will always have a pleasant ring about it for winelovers since it is from there that the well-known and popular London shipper Fritz Hallgarten, his son, Dr Peter Hallgarten, and the family take their name. The Hallgartens were wine merchants in Spain until forced to leave there in 1492 by the Inquisition. They settled near Winkel on the Rhine and then, some 450 years later, the coming of the

A view of the Rheingau from Schloss Johannisberg.

A vineyard at Schloss Johannisberg.

Nazis set Fritz on the move to England with his son, Dr Peter Hallgarten, who has now taken over the very successful wine importing business. Both father and son are authors of distinguished books on wines and liqueurs.

The village is high up on the slopes and its chief vineyards are Hallgarten Jungfer, where the local co-operative has a share, Schönhell and Hendelberg, both big and full, and Würzgarten. Soil peculiarities here help the wine to a distinctive bouquet. The same sort of soil extends to Hattenheim, down near the river, and noted for its Nussbrunnen and Mannberg vineyards. Here, too, are the Graf von Schönborn estates with wines of high quality such as the famous Wisselbrunnen, of which the 1959 Riesling Auslese Cabinet was still selling in fine condition in 1973.

Hattenheim for long had a quarrel with its famous neighbouring community of Erbach over the right to add the name Marcobrunn to its own. Now this is one of the most famous vineyards on the whole of the Rhine, part of it for a long time in the family of a prince of Prussia, and other parts zealously treasured by dedicated owners.

The men of Erbach finally won through and Erbacher Marcobrunner is one of the world's great wines, though in the higher price ranges.

Vineyards near Schloss Vollrads.

There is, however, Erbacher Michelmark Riesling Spätlese for 1970 and the Auslese for 1971, both from the local co-operative or Winzergenossenschaft, which give some idea of the spicy quality and body of these wines, particularly in Auslese style. The Graf von Schönborn estate has some of the best of the Marcobrunner vineyards. There is still a drinking well on the site of the boundary between Erbach and Hattenheim, closer in fact to Erbach and so taken to prove that village's right to the use of the Marcobrunnen name. A smart local, however, chalked a poem on the well that rather daunted the victors and roughly translated said 'Let Erbach keep the water so long as Hattenheim has the wine.'

Up in the hills there are Kiedrich and Kloster Eberbach, the first producing fine wines and the second with the great Steinberg vineyard that fairly blooms in good years and lies within a few yards of Kloster Eberbach, a former monastery of Augustinian and then Cistercian monks who planted vines in the twelfth century on this very land. Today the monastery is empty and used for storing the wine while the actual vinification is carried on nearby with very modern equipment. The Monastery is also used for the great Rheingau wine auctions. The old wooden wine presses of the Middle Ages can still be seen, as at Clos Vougeot in Burgundy. Steinberg belongs to the State Domain and is sold as such, for instance as Steinberger Riesling Kabinett, with the owners name given as Staatsweingüter. Permission to view the old monastery has to be obtained in advance but the moving silence of its white walls and typical tower in a majestic natural setting make it one of the outstanding sights of the Rhineland.

For many years Eltville was a palace of the Prince-Electors of Mainz, and the old buildings can still be seen near to the great vineyards of the the Freiherr Langworth von Simmern and the Graf zu Eltz estates.

The Fischer estates also date back to 1464 and include some of the Kalbspflicht vineyards also owned by Graf zu Eltz. Other noted names are Taubenberg and Sonnenberg. There are also Church and State holdings here and a number of excellent wines are made. Although one does not come across Eltville wines in Britain as often as could be wished, there is no doubt about their high standing in Germany.

Up in the slopes above Eltville is Rauenthal where the wines are expensive, only less costly than Schloss Johannisberg, perhaps because the vineyards produce rather less wine but of fine quality. I think there are other names that would satisfy me as happily as Rauenthal without paying the extra price, but even the Winzerverein wines are rather dearer than one would expect. However, they undoubtedly have a subtle, scented appeal with a spicy longlasting flavour—and, as with so many costly wines, a great name. Rothenberg, Wieshell and Siebenmorgen are among the better vineyards.

Hochheim is the eastern end of the Rheingau on the river Main, almost on its own but grouped with other Rheingau vineyards and important to the wine story because here is an estate known as the Viktoria-Berg, named after Queen Victoria who visited it. She became so entranced with the light, clean and rather earthy flavoured wine (from its sandy soil) that she often drank hock—as the name of the town became shortened—and more than once declared it her favourite wine.

A German, unless widely travelled, is unlikely to know what you mean by hock, but the name certainly made the wine in England, aided by King Edward VII's preference—when he wasn't drinking champagne—for hock and seltzer, wine fizzed up with soda water. The leading vineyard is the unusually named Domdechaney, with full and fruity wines, and another is Rauchloch, which means 'smoke-hole' and indeed those who do not find the wines earthy are inclined to describe them as smoky.

Rheinhessen

This is the area on the south bank of the Rhine which runs almost parallel with the Rheingau as far as Mainz, where it curves deeply along the inner side of the Rhine till it reaches the Palatinate or Rheinpfalz.

In the Rheingau, the noblest area of Rhine wines, three-quarters of the grapes are Riesling, about ten per cent are Müller-Thurgau, and ten per cent Sylvaner. In Rheinhessen the proportions are very different with Sylvaner at forty per cent, Müller-Thurgau slightly less, and Riesling at only nine per cent. In addition there are other grapes such as Portugieser, Rulander and Scheurebe, the latter another cross.

There is scarcely any comparison between Rheinhessen and Rheingau. The wines are typical of their grapes, simple, sweet, but not too sweet, and of moderate bouquet. They do not last more than some nine years at best and are made in quite astonishing variety. It is not even a very attractive part of the world. The towns are rather grey and grim, and inland the countryside, while rolling in parts, is not distinguished any more than the people, pleasant but stolid, fair-haired and countrified. Indeed they are much like their ancestors who, shipped to America to fight for the British cause against the rebels, fell to enjoying a German Christmas at Trenton the night before Washington arrived and took a thousand drunk prisoners as the result.

There are exceptions among the wines but the case of Liebfraumilch makes the point. Many people order a bottle of Liebfraumilch, particularly if it bears a well-advertised branded name, and think they are getting a good German wine. Depending on the shipper and the label, they may get a reasonably blended wine, but will have very little idea of where it was grown or what grape was used, except that the wines should have been grown in four defined wine areas.

The new German wine law makes some amends over Liebfraumilch and lays down that it must be a Qualitätswein, and not a Tafelwein, the lowest grade. The wine must come from the Rheingau, Rheinhessen, the Nahe or the Rheinpfalz, and it must have more than sixty degrees Oechsle, the grading of sweetness. Again, the wine used must be typical of the grapes employed and have their taste, and the greater part must be made from Riesling, Sylvaner or Müller-Thurgau grapes. On the other hand the names of the vines may not be used or coupled with the word Liebfraumilch. Although the middle grade of Qualitätswein is granted to Liebfraumilch, there are sufficient other restrictions to show that it is far from reaching the high identification standards of other German wines.

Bingen is a noisy little town with the railway running right through it along the river bank. One might paraphrase Dr Johnson and say that the best prospect a traveller at Bingen sees is the car ferry to Rüdesheim except that Rüdesheim has another railway! There is some good wine made in Bingen, however, and at the St Ursula cellars looking down on the river I not only sampled Goldener Oktober, the Liebfraumilch that is very popular in Britain, but the excellent medium-sweet 1969 Binger Scharlachberg Riesling Auslese from Villa Sachsen, the élite part of the St Ursula estates, a wine I have enjoyed several times through the kindness of Heinz Frank, the technical director.

Heinz Frank is still young, an example of the modern German, and we tasted the 1964 Scharlachberg with fine bouquet but showing its age a little and he explained how, Riesling being the grape with the most acidity, this develops in the wine-making process and shows in the bouquet.

Vineyards at Nierstein.

The 1967 still showed some of its youth and the 1969 he forecast would be at its peak in 1973 and, with its acidity, would last until 1980.

We were sitting in the Anker hotel drinking a bottle of the 1969 Binger Kirchberg Riesling Spätlese of Villa Sachsen, and looking across the Rhine at the high green hills above Assmannshausen, with the Niederwalddenkmal, the great black stone figure of Germania built to gaze proudly over this beautiful scene and commemorate the foundation of the Second German Reich in 1871. And as I had last visited it when the Third German Reich was in the full power of its thousand-year-reign that disappeared in German dust after twelve, I saw it as a piece of ancient history earning its preservation as a reflection of the times it was built in. I said as much to Heinz but he shook his head.

'I would like to see it pulled down,' he replied with unusual fervour in his voice, and I realised that while the aggressive, boastful statue represented, for me, something in the far past with no power to touch us, for Heinz Frank it was a symbol of something in the German spirit that he deplored.

Then he told me an amusing story, the sort of thing I love to hear from winetasters about so-called 'experts'. He smiled as he spoke. 'I took a bottle of Goldener Oktober and I put it in a splendid old bottle with a great label on it and a wonderful year. We had a group of men who really know their Rhine wines and I told them I was going to give them a remarkable experience. Then I produced the bottle and half-filled their glasses. They sniffed and tasted and looked at me, at the ceiling and back into their glasses. Then they got up and clasped my hand, patted my back, said what a great treat I had given them. And it was just my good but simple Goldener Oktober in a bottle with an impressive label. There is a sort of moral there, a lesson from life I think. In the end I did not tell them of my little trick because I could see it would have upset them too much. They still talk of that night!'

A cellarmaster at work; the first thing he tests is the colour.

Well, there may be a moral and if anything it is to form your own judgment of a wine and stick to it. You may be right or wrong, but don't be overwhelmed by the label!

Another notable name is that of Hermann Kendermann of Bingen and Wiesbaden. As well as many fine examples of the best Rhine and Mosel they supply reliable German-bottled wines of reasonable price under region names. These represent good, pleasant drinking, not great wines or years but sound enough.

Other leading Bingen vineyards besides those already mentioned are Rochusberg, grown among slate, Ohligberg and Schwätzerchen. Once again people talk of a 'smoky' taste, and some blame the railway and the river steamers though it probably comes from something in the soil. Next comes Ingelheim, where red wine is made from the Spätburgunder grape and can be recommended except that there are so many better whites to enjoy! Indeed there are quite a number of wine towns here such as Ockenheim with its Müller-Thurgau grapes and Elsheim, where they hold a wine festival, but the next real names of note are Bodenheim, with its medium wines of spicy bouquet, and Nackenheim which grows Riesling and Sylvaner. Nackenheim paddles its feet in the waters of the Rhine and though it has only a small area of vineyards the quality is exceptional. The leading vineyard is Rothenberg, taking its name from the red clay soil, growing wines that perhaps reflect its fire in their depth and delicate perfume. You don't often find these wines in Britain as they are limited in quantity. What you do find are plenty of Nierstein and Oppenheim wines, each producing much more than little Nackenheim, and each with a well publicised name known the world over.

Nierstein produces the best wines in Rheinhessen, fresh, elegant, filling the mouth and making for great contentment, the best being from the Riesling grape. There used to be many, many vineyard names—50,000 at one time it is said—but the new German wine law has at last brought some semblance of order to the various areas.

Personally I regret the disappearance of so many local names, merged in larger areas. But I recognise that for those who have neither the time nor the inclination to study or visit them, the reduction in vineyard designations and the stabilisation of production areas will simplify matters for the majority of consumers.

The minimum alcohol content for Tafelwein is 8.5 degrees and it comes from one of four main areas or *Weinbaugebiete*. These are Rhein und Mosel, Main, Neckar and Oberrhein. Tafelwein is mostly drunk in Germany and the labels can carry village, but not vineyard, names.

The two upper grades of Qualitätswein and Qualitätswein mit Prädikat come from eleven districts or *Anbaugebiete*. These are Ahr, Baden, Franken, Hessiche-Bergstrasse, Mittelrhein, Mosel-Saar-Ruwer, Nahe, Rheingau, Rheinhessen, Rheinpfalz and Württemberg. The labels also carry information on village and vineyard and grape. The Prüfungsnummer on the label shows that the wine has passed the official tasting and testing.

For example Rheinhessen is an Anbaugebiet broken down into three Bereiche which are Bingen, Nierstein and Wonnegau. Rheingau is broken down into two Bereiche which are Johannisberg and Hochheim, while Mosel-Saar-Ruwer has the four separate Bereiche of Zell, Bernkastel, Saar-Ruwer and Obermosel.

Most of these names are already familiar to wine drinkers and it is simply a matter of understanding their new application and the extent of the area that they cover. The label may still seem to carry a lot of involved information but it is directed towards more definite areas.

Among such Nierstein names are Gutes Domtal, Rehbach and Spiegelberg, all good.

Oppenheim wines can be very good in hot years but otherwise are not usually as good as Niersteiners, though many like their full, less aggressive flavour. Sackträger and Zuckerberg are leading vineyards.

While there are numerous other towns centred on wine, none of them has achieved the fame of those described and it is only when one comes to Worms that one pauses. This is not for the local wine but because it was here that the local Chamber of Commerce decided before the First World War that Liebfraumilch could be used as a name for any wines of Rheinhessen. As a result the name came to mean a blend of almost any German white

Rhine wines until the new German wine law corrected the situation somewhat. Liebfraumilch is still sometimes mentally associated with the Liebfrauenkirche, the Church of Our Lady at Worms. The Chamber of Commerce's decision so long ago certainly made many fortunes which the German delegates never envisaged!

Rheinpfalz

This is the name by which the Germans know The Palatinate, an area for which I have a particular affection. It is some distance inland from the Rhine, but down its spine runs the Mittelhaardt mountains, a splendid dark blue and black range against the bright blue Palatinate skies of summer.

There is, too, an abundance of joy in living here that, combined with a lingering simplicity and friendliness, makes for an atmosphere of contentment. From north to south runs the charming road called The Weinstrasse, narrow and winding but seldom hilly, looking on either hand on a sea of golden-green grapes, the vines supported on long wires anchored to stout blocks of stone.

One finds this atmosphere at the Bad Dürkheim Wine Fair in September, still called Wurst Markt and still selling sausages. The vast fairground is filled with booths selling wine by the *schoppen*, a half-litre jug, and the crowds sit at wooden tables on benches drinking, talking and singing. There are fun fairs and stalls selling everything from souvenir dolls and postcards to roast chicken, waffles and sweets.

The great pre-fair event is the tasting of the fair wines and this, by courtesy of the Burgermeister, Herr George Kalbfuss, I was able to share. We sipped the 1969 wines with, first, a simply named Dürkheimer Riesling, good nose, a little acid; then a Dürkheimer Hochmess, from the Ruländer and Sylvaner grapes, sweetish and pleasant; next a Dürkheimer Nonnengarten; then a Leistädter Hertfeld, a soft Sylvaner slipped in from a neighbouring area; a Dürkheimer Spielberg Riesling, very elegant; a fine Dürkheimer Steinberg and then a Dürkheimer Feuerberg, seeing which listed I expected an example of Dürkheim's famous red wine from the Portugieser grape but found instead that it was the white wine of the same name, from Riesling and Traminer grapes, with crisp, fresh flavour.

Yes, half a million visitors drink 400,000 pints of good German wine and many of them eat in the 'Dürkheim Fass', the huge barrel painted black and red that overlooks the fairground and is actually a restaurant. It is run by Herr Richard Thomas, the Küchenmeister, who offers you thirty-two different wines by glass or bottle and insists on your having the correctly shaped glass for each wine; 'Respect, please, the form of the glasses'.

There are good times to be enjoyed in Bad

Vineyards at Bad Dürkheim.

Dürkheim at the casino or on the fairground and there are pleasant musical evenings where you taste wine as well in such beautiful old cellars as those of the gentle and kindly Herr Fitz-Ritter of the Weingut K. Fitz-Ritter. He sells many fine wines, among them his own Dürkheimer Rittergarten, fruity and refreshing. In an upper room, far into the night, my wife and I heard splendid singing of old German songs and many amusing verses from Herr Helmut Metzger, the local poet.

For a long time Bad Dürkheim envied Rüdesheim's cable car system that takes visitors to the heights of the Niederwald. Now they have one of their own, the Gondelbahn, which swings guests up to the Devil's Stone, a neighbouring cliff where a restaurant has been built in the shade of the trees. They have everything in Bad Dürkheim, or soon get it, and the helpful information office can send you details. There is no better town for starting to learn about the Palatinate wines.

A little further along the Weinstrasse you come to Forst, home of the famous Forster Jesuitengarten Riesling, a full, elegant wine of noble sweetness, some examples more medium-dry than sweet. A great name here is that of Dr Ludwig Bassermann-Jordan, whose family have cultivated the vine for two hundred years and still live in a splendid mansion at Deidesheim built two centuries ago. Dr Bassermann-Jordan is slightly austere, as befits a man with a degree in philosophy, but he has a good heart for when I called and told him of my long ambition to see his famous Jesuitengarten vineyard he immediately offered to take me there that afternoon.

We drove to Forst and up a narrow road to the left, drawing occasionally to the side to let lorries pass that bring up basalt from nearby quarries for the vineyards. As we stood among the vines looking down on the world-famous little church from which the vineyard takes its name, Dr Bassermann-Jordan paused and, true *vigneron* that he is, caught a vine tendril and curled it round the support, an automatic but professional gesture.

Among his other Forst holdings are such great

names as Kirchenstück, Pechstein, Ungeheuer and Ziegler. At Deidesheim he has holdings among other vineyards *mit klang* such as Hohenmorgen, Grainhübel and Leinhöhle with more at Ruppertsberg.

Between Forst and Deidesheim is a little town that is livelier than the first and less lovely than the second. Wachenheim would be famous in any case as the home of Weingut Bürklin-Wolf, a name that is to be found wherever great Palatinate wines are listed. Dr. Albert Bürklin and his lovely and elegant wife Jutta live, like their friendly rival Bassermann-Jordan, in a splendid mansion, also two hundred years old, at the southern end of the town. Its white walls glisten under the blue skies, and the hot sun that warms the vines reflects also on the swimming-pool, on the tennis-court and the smooth, English-style lawns that Frau Bürklin, a Wimbledon tennis fan, greatly treasures.

There are no wines in their cellar, however, because it has been converted into an indoor swimming pool so that Dr Bürklin can swim daily under his doctor's orders in the winter. He is a man of courage and courtesy and a really great wine-maker whose counsels are sought at the highest levels both in Germany and the Common Market. His wife has similar knowledge.

What is more Dr Bürklin is a born teacher. An hour or so of conversation with him in the historic drawing-room of his house taught me more about Palatinate wines than many books. I say historic because Jutta Bürklin pointed out a distorted, shaded area of the parquet where Napoleon's soldiers had lit a fire for cooking in the French invasion a hundred and fifty years ago.

Together they own the charming Zur Kanne inn at Deidesheim, which has welcomed travellers in its restaurant and *weinstube*—tasting room—for nearly eight-hundred years and under their care has won a Michelin star for its cuisine, many of the dishes being local recipes.

Deidesheim is one of the prettiest wine villages in the world and Zur Kanne stands, with its black and gold paint and delightful old hanging sign, just opposite the Gothic church and the eighteenth-century town hall from the steps of which a goat is auctioned each Whitsun as part of an old tradition. Although small, Deidesheim has several big, modern hotels which in no way spoil the appearance of the colourful, flower-decked streets.

The Bürklin-Wolf estates, controlled now by the Bürklin family alone, are a roll-call of honour among the great wines of the world. They include at Wachenheim such names as Wachenheimer Mandelgarten, Goldbächel, Rechbächel and Langebächel. At Forst they have vineyards of Kirchenstück, Ungeheuer, Pechstein and Ziegler and at Deidesheim there are Deidesheimer Hohenmorgen, Kalkofen and Reiss. They also have holdings at Ruppertsberg of Hoheburg, Reiterpfad, Nussbien, Schlossberg and others. In every case the wines are recognised as outstanding in their class and the greatest care is taken in their making. There is another noted estate in Deidesheim, that of Reichsrat von Buhl, a company run under management but of high quality with interests in local hotels.

Another hobby of the Bürklins is a castle half-way up the hills on the right-hand-side driving south. It is called simply The Berg and from its ruined battlements there flies a flag to show when the tasting rooms sited there are open to visitors. This saves disappointment after a slightly tiring walk up the hill!

The eighteenth-century town hall at Deidesheim.

A wood carving to be seen by the roadside on entering Deidesheim.

The wine village of Frankweiler in the Rheinpfalz.

There are, of course, many other owners of vineyards in the area. The towns themselves have holdings while there are a number of co-operatives, the first in the Palatinate being founded as far back as 1898 in Bad Dürkheim. Pride in wine is everywhere and I remember finding a huge sign about four feet square at the entrance to little Maikammer. Boldly in big letters, it announced: 'Maikammer—Residence of the Palatinate Wine Queen!'

The Palatinate wines are in general mellow, whereas the Mosel tend to have a touch of acid—'noble acidity' is how the local growers describe it—and the Rheingau wines have body, particular bouquet, and special elegance. Whereas the men of Mosel often have to add sugar to their wine as permitted by the regulations, the Middle Palatinate growers get so much sunshine and so moderate a rainfall that they have no need for this and their best sweet wines can stand comparison with any in the world. Riesling is fifteen per cent of the grapes and Sylvaner and Müller-Thurgau make up over half of them.

The Nahe

This river runs into the Rhine at Bingen and when you drive beside it inland looks dull and depressing. Further up, however, it produces particularly likeable wines, often of very pleasant medium sweetness. The grapes are Riesling, Sylvaner and Müller-Thurgau, each in about thirty per cent proportions.

In my opinion Schloss Böckelheim on the Nahe produces some of the most satisfying German wines,

Horneck Castle, in the Württemburg district.

the greatest names apart. The price is more reasonable than most and the wines are smooth and have a hint of sweetness that makes them ideal for a warm day because they are interesting without being lush. I well remember a journey down the Rhine with a bottle of Schloss Böckelheim Riesling on the table in front of me gently trembling to the rhythmic beat of the giant paddle-wheels while a splended panorama of old castles and famous vineyards unfolded before me on either side. The cool, sweet wine was an ideal silent companion.

The Germans have the word 'Spitzenweine' for great wines and one would include the Schloss Böckelheimer Kupfergrube from the State Domain in this, though whether its charm is due to minerals in the copper mine, to which the name refers, is another matter. The State keeps the vineyards in perfect order and the answer is in the glass. There are other wines such as the simply named Schloss Böckelheimer Riesling, at little over half the price.

the latter wine, often from the Reichsgraf von Plettenberg estate, being increasingly seen on English wine-lists.

Baden

Overshadowed by the great Rhine names in the past, this interesting area, one of the eleven new German wine law Weinbaugebiet, is now coming to some prominence as a wine-exporting region. In the past most Baden wines were drunk in Germany, but with competition from Italian wines on their home territory under Common Market agreements, the men of Baden want to place some of their eggs in other baskets. In recent years both International Vintners & Distillers, owners of the Peter Dominic shops, and Bass Charrington Vintners, with the Galleon chain and other outlets, have sold Baden wines.

Co-operatives in Baden claim to control over eighty per cent of production and the huge Zentralkellerei Badischer Winzergenossenschaft has forty-five per cent of the co-operative wines.

The cellars at Breisach are certainly impressive, with their narrow, stainless steel vertical tanks, three or four floors high, painted in spotless primrose. They have a capacity of 12,000 to 80,000 litres and a total storage of over 50 million litres covering 150 different wines and including trockenbeerenauslese. One of the specialities is their St Ehrentrudis Weissherbst from the Spätburgunder grape, made as a *rosé*. Because the grape is a notable one, however, the wine has more quality and alcoholic strength than other *rosés*. I have enjoyed it with Herr Strub, the Director of the Zentralkellerei, and it is certainly a most attractive, refreshing drink of some body, reaching eleven to twelve degrees of alcohol.

The Zentralkellerei has since further extended its capacity because Baden, and particularly the Kaiserstuhl area, has redesigned large areas of vineyards, as has also been done on the Mosel and the Rhine, with lower terraces easier to work and new vines. These are now coming to fruition and the local cellars have had to find new storage space.

By no means all the growers favour co-operatives and some claim that such mass treatment produces standard wines, although Herr Strub has medals to show otherwise. The Anbaugêbiete Baden is cut into no less than seven Bereiche, and one of these is Bereich Kaisertuhl/Tuniberg. This latter is again divided into two 'Grosslagen', Vulkanfelsen and Attilafelsen, the first sub-dividing into forty-three Einzellagen and the second into eight Einzellagen. Which makes you wonder whether the labelling under the new wine law will really be any simpler!

The Kaiserstuhl Kellerei, mentioned earlier in this book, is run by the Friederich Kiefer company of which my friends Siegfried and Hanna Körner are guiding spirits with other relatives. The redesigning of the vineyards for the extra produce

Lower down the river, on the right bank, is Bad Kreuznach founded by the Romans, in recent years a US army centre with one-way streets and massed traffic lights that have destroyed its charm. Near here, however, is the Gutleuthof Carl Andres estate and on it stayed Marshal Blücher before marching off to join Wellington at Waterloo. Perhaps the charm of its wines explains his tardy arrival on the battlefield! Most of the wines come from Riesling grapes and the Kreuznacher Mollenbrunnen, a fine dry wine I have enjoyed, grows in red earth which gives it a full character and also makes the companion Hinkelstein similarly full. Roxheimer Mühlenberg and Birkenberg are two other fruity wines. The cellars are hewn out of solid rock and maintain a constant temperature of 50°F. in winter and summer, very helpful to the family's hundred-and-seventy-year-old tradition.

Still further down the river stands Winzenheim with such vineyards as Honigberg and Rosenheck,

At work in a vineyard in the Baden district.

meant they had to increase their capacity from half a million litres to two million and build new cellars to install more tanks for the future growth.

This required courage and confidence, based on good relations with the growers who promised to support their efforts. But there was still a great expense to face by a relatively small company and a huge upheaval of their land while the tanks were put in place, not to mention worries over building delays as the inexorable harvest crept nearer and nearer. Today they face a bigger, better future however, whatever the temporary problems entailed. And their wines, with the Einzellagen of Lerchenberg and Herrenbuck under the Bereich Kaiserstuhl/Tuniberg on the label, will go even farther afield. Very good they are, too, and the 1971 Riesling Sylvaner Eichstetter Lerchenberg and the 1971 Weisser Burgunder Eichstetter Lerchenberg, both Qualitätswein mit Prädikat, are fine examples of what they produce. Among 1971 Auslese of note was a Rülander Eichstetter Herrenbuck while there was a fine Spätburgunder Weissherbst Spätlese, Eichstetter Herrenbuck, unusual for being late-picked.

South of the volcanic land of the Kaiserstuhl, rising like a commanding hump close to the auto-bahn, comes Markgräflerland, a region that, with the continuing care being given the vines, should in the future make a better name than it has in the past. The grape here is mainly the Gutedel, an import originally from Switzerland, a white wine of light, delicate bouquet with a certain tartness.

Baden grapes are varied, about a third being Müller-Thurgau, then Gutedel and Rülander making up another third, with Riesling and Sylvaner being each about five per cent. Spätburgunder, the red grape, is a quarter of the total against the other seventy-five per cent white wines. Weissburgunder and Traminer are also planted, both doing well on the Kaiserstuhl.

Spätburgunder also does well for reds on the river Ahr and there are white wines from the Riesling and Müller-Thurgau, but this district is so far north that cultivation is difficult and the wines little known outside Germany.

Franconia (Franken)

There is one more German wine to mention for its individuality. This is the Steinwein of Franconia, grown around Würzburg by the river Main. Strictly speaking this name should only be applied to the products of the Stein vineyards. It means stone wine, and indeed is a hard, dry wine that is an acquired taste. When I met some winelovers of Würzburg they were confident I would not have heard of their wine and equally astonished when I assured them it was not difficult to buy in Britain.

Franconian wines appear in the squat, unusually shaped *bocksbeutel* and are mostly from the Sylvaner grape, which does well here, a small amount of Riesling, and the usual crosses between the two. The bottle itself is the wine's best agent, and for those who like really dry white wines the answer is probably inside it.

Carved wooden casks in a cellar at Würzburg.

7
Italy

Italy's claim to be the world's largest wine producer is seen on every side as one travels up and down its vast length. No other country is so covered with vineyards. In the north the Adige Valley, with its twenty different wines growing at the foot of the rose-pink Dolomites, makes a splendid beginning.

And in the extreme south the sun-soaked island of Sicily is famous not only for Marsala, that fortified, aromatic dessert wine of many delights first brought to England in the eighteenth century, but for a number of table wines that include such increasingly known names as Corvo and Etna.

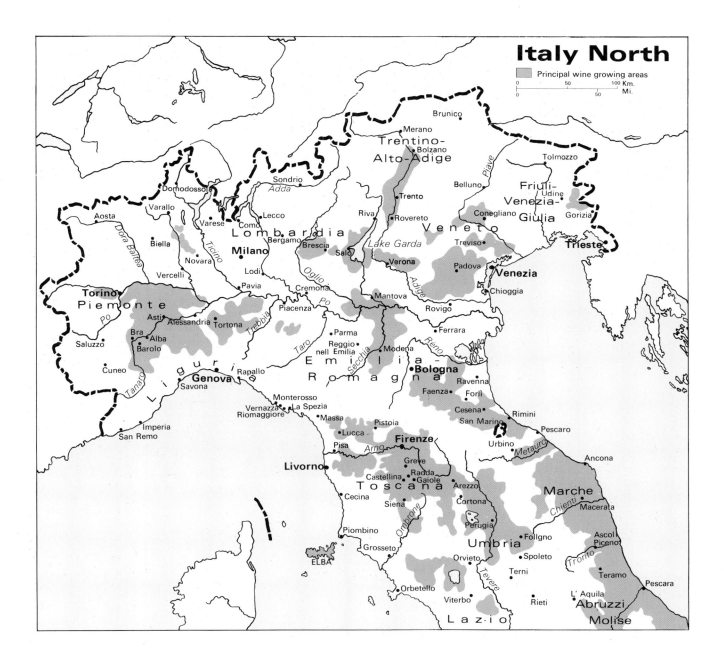

All these wines will in due course benefit from the new Italian wine laws already explained, and their gradual enforcement on a semi-voluntary basis is speeding up the higher standards that were admittedly necessary. In 1972, Italy's wine exports totalled 308 million gallons, an increase of eighty million gallons over 1971, and significantly 175 million gallons of that 1972 figure went to France. Equally important is the Italian aim to keep prices down so as not to hinder their present successful export drive.

French prices are currently so high that the French themselves are glad to buy Italian wine and it seems probable that Italy may become Europe's main provider of sensible table wines at moderate prices. There is still room, however, for improvement in quality among some of the wines that do not come up to the standard of Chianti, Barolo, Barbaresco and Valpolicella, which have rightly earned the respect of consumers everywhere. The fact that these four names have achieved world-wide acceptance is proof that Italian wine, properly made, can rank in a high order of merit, even though in the past some less scrupulous producers have not hesitated to abuse these names. At one time almost any red wine in a straw cover was passed off by rogues as Chianti.

Well, the straw-covered flask, or *fiasco*, is now disappearing for the simple reason that it adds too many lire to the price of each bottle. Some producers have descended to plastic imitations instead of the hand-woven originals made by women as a cottage industry, but most people would find a plain bottle preferable to a plastic-covered one.

Tuscany (Toscana)

The genuine Chianti comes from some of the oldest Florentine families whose estates have been cultivated since the Middle Ages and who have never had reason to lower their standards. Barone Ricasoli, who died in 1880, perfected the modern blend of grapes. Chianti is a part of Tuscany and the wine of that name is now always a red wine, the white being called simply White Tuscan.

Chianti springs from a splendid region where old castles still frown down from hilltops while fortified farms recall the days when men retreated from the fields to defend their homes. As far back as 1924 the producers in the Chianti area formed a *consorzio* to control production and make sure their wines conformed to the necessary characteristics of Chianti Classico. They chose as a seal for their bottles a black rooster on a gold background, similar to the emblem used in the fourteenth century by the Chianti League.

By 1932 a decree had been obtained which set out the areas of the seven zones entitled to the name Chianti. The term Classico was reserved for the historic area which includes such towns as Greve, Gaiole, Radda, Castellina and certain others. The

A wine press dated 1791, in the Tuscany region.

Castello della Sala, the family home of the Antinori family.

six other zones produce Chianti Montalbano, Chianti Rufina and Chianti from the Florentine hills, the Siena hills, the Arezzo hills and the Pisa district.

These regulations have been strengthened, and today Chianti must be made from stipulated grapes including Sangiovese, black Canaiolo,

Tuscan Trebbiano and Malvasia del Chianti. The maximum yield for Chianti Classico is 115 quintals of grapes per hectare producing a total of 81 hectolitres of wine with an alcoholic strength of not less than 12°. For ordinary Chianti the comparable figures are 125 quintals of grapes per hectare producing 88 hectolitres of wine at 11.5°.*

The blending of the grapes listed above provides the particular flavour and appeal of any Chianti, with the Sangiovese grape making up some seventy-five per cent of the proportion, which varies with different houses. The best wines are aged in a claret-type bottle. Despite the romantic appeal of the *fiasco*, it therefore holds a relatively lesser wine. One has only to drink these classic older wines to realise how superior they are, much as a Classified Growth of Bordeaux rises above an ordinary Médoc. The *fiasco* wines are meant to be drunk in their youth.

Chianti may not be made available for drinking before the first day of March following the grape vintage, and after two years can be called Vecchio (old) and, after three, may carry the word Riserva, or reserve. So if you drink a Chianti Classico Riserva you should be getting a big, full wine of real bouquet and flavour, deep and dark purple in your glass, not unlike a good Burgundy and probably smoother than a Châteauneuf-du-Pape, though with some of the latter's qualities.

A view of Florence from Piazzale Michelangiolo.

Among leading houses is Ruffino (not to be confused with the area name of Rufina), whose Ducale Riserva I rank among the most pleasing Chiantis I have drunk. They also make a light and brilliant Rosatello, a *rosé* wine using the powerful Sangiovese grapes. Melini is another great house, dating from 1705, with Stravecchio Melini heading a number of Chiantis among them Chianti Classico and Chianti Riserva. Antinori has Villa Antinori and is a leading house in the Classico area while Chianti Brolio Riserva represents the great Ricasoli family. Bigi, Cecchi and Giannini are other names to look for and all these Chiantis are now shipped abroad in quantity.

Stretching over the region round Florence, that supremely beautiful centre of Italian culture, the Chianti area is worth exploring and it runs south as far as Siena where there is a notable wine museum, Enoteca Italica Permanente, including a wine tasting bureau offering more than four hundred and twenty varieties!

As well as Chianti, already described, there are several other leading names here. From the Isle of Elba comes a sweet dessert wine with aromatic flavour called Aleatico di Portoferraio, up to fifteen degrees in alcoholic strength. Perhaps Napoleon brooded over it instead of his favourite Chambertin. Brunello di Montalcino is a dry red wine with some bouquet, Brunello being a relation

* 1 quintal = 100 kilograms.

of the Sangiovese grape which has such a large share in Chianti. It matures well and can have a remarkably long life in bottle, up to thirty or more years. Among white wines there are Candia and Montecarlo, both hill wines, the latter from the Trebbiano grape, and the notable Vino Santo, of golden amber shade, a rich dessert wine, sweetish, made from pressing Trebbiano or Malvasia grapes.

Piedmont

Chianti has been given first place in this chapter because it undoubtedly represents Italian wines in outside eyes and is splendid in itself. To consider Italian wines geographically, however, one starts with Piedmont, very close to France. Wines in Italy may be named after an area, a town or a grape. Piedmont is particularly famous as the home of Asti, the town on which centres the famous Asti Spumante, the Italian sparkling wine from the Moscato or muscat grape that is grown so extensively in Piedmont.

Asti Spumante is known the world over and only those with a stubborn predilection for dry wine will find fault with its natural sweetness that can, however, be so overwhelming as to earn the description from one wine authority of 'sickly sweet'. The answer is to drink it at an appropriate time, perhaps with fruit or simply as a relaxation. Production of quality wine is ensured by an inspectorate representing the growers, and bottles judged as acceptable carry a coloured seal showing San Secondo, the town's patron saint, on a horse and the name of the Consorzio.

It is made almost entirely by the *cuve close*, or closed tank, method which allows the vital fermentation to take place on a huge scale. This was the invention of the Frenchman Charmat, and saves the great expense involved in time and labour by the champagne method of fermentation in the actual bottle. German sparkling wines use this tank method overwhelmingly today and Deinhard in Koblenz has huge glass-lined tanks for this purpose that hold 40,000 litres, about 53,000 bottles. The supporters of *cuve close* not only point out the saving in money but claim it aids hygiene because contact with the air is avoided and absolute sterility achieved.

Near Asti there is some use of *methode champenoise* for a dry sparkling wine made from other grapes, and I have enjoyed examples from Cinzano, which uses the French champagne grapes, but I would not go so far as to say they approach real Champagne.

Leading Italian firms making their own particular Asti Spumante include Martini, Gancia, Fontanafredda and Cinzano. There is also a lesser sparkling wine called Moscato d'Asti, invariably rather sweeter but not quite as sophisticated.

Piedmont's real claim to wine fame comes from the production of two splendid reds. They are

Man and beast, a timeless vineyard scene from Piedmont.

Production of dry, sparkling Gancia Riserva by the methode champenoise.

Barolo and Barbaresco in that order, big, noble wines that mature slowly, very robust, both with an intense and unusual flavour, sometimes described as pungent. The grape they share is Nebbiolo but the wines are somewhat different in that Barolo is the greatest red wine of Italy, even above Chianti, while Barbaresco matures sooner and has not the same potential, good as it is. Barolo is almost black in colour, and lies maturing in barrel for five years or more in the best examples. It is an interesting test to drink a fine Barolo against a fine Burgundy or Bordeaux. The French wines somehow exemplify the meaning of those elusive words 'breeding' and 'finesse'. Perhaps the two Italians compare more with the better Rhône wines but they are certainly suited to the food of Piedmont, prepared for hungry men, the dishes often highly seasoned and consisting, perhaps, of chamois meat, venison, or substantial roasts. With such food a big, hearty wine is essential and weaklings would be quite lost against the food flavours.

Near here is Alba, famous for its white truffles which contrast with the black truffles of Perigord. It is noted for a restaurant that specialises in them and is linked with that attractive apéritif, Punt e Mes. This is made by the Carpano company and is a splendidly aromatic compilation of herbs and vermouth. Although I fervently believe that a dry sherry, such as Pando or Tio Pepe, is the most

A vineyard scene in Barolo.

suitable drink for the palate before a fine meal with fine wines, I find too many occasions when I am seduced by the insidious, alluring charm of Punt e Mes instead.

Barbera is another interesting wine named after its grape. It is dry and while having body, is not so big as Barolo. The alcohol contents of these wines are interesting. Barolo is thirteen to sixteen degrees, Barbera twelve to fifteen degrees and Barbaresco thirteen degrees.

Gattinara has a striking ruby colour and because of the amount of tannin is somewhat harsh when young, but as it ages the colour and taste changes. The Italians regard this as a particularly invigorating wine and recommend it for illness, but it is a good drink even when you are in the best of health! A lighter wine, it also comes from Nebbiolo grapes. Incidentally there are more Barbera grapes in Piedmont than Nebbiolo, but the latter is the 'noble' grape and also produces a light red wine which is called simply Nebbiolo. There are dry and sweet versions of this, the latter being pinkish and sometimes sparkling.

Grignolino is yet another light red wine with a pleasing, nutty flavour and attractive bouquet that can be drunk with most dishes while it is young. It has the advantage of substantial maturity when aged and then goes well with big roasts.

Liguria

South of Piedmont is Liguria, a coastal strip running behind Genoa, with a notable white wine in Cinque Terre. Much as I dislike the deplorable habit of choosing wine by the sound of its name, Cinque Terre has an unusual attraction in being a French name in Italy. The five lands referred to are the villages of Corniglia, Biassa, Monterosso, Vernazza and Riomaggiore set among cliffs near the sea with vineyards inaccessible to all but the local expert. There is an interesting account of them by Cyril Ray in his useful book *The Wines of Italy*. The wines are made both dry and sweet, the first excellent with fish and the second with dessert. The dry wines have an aromatic bouquet and reach twelve to fourteen degrees of alcoholic content. The local name for these wines is Sciacchetra.

There are interesting white wines in this district such as Coronata, a pale straw-yellow with refreshing flavour and bouquet, and the somewhat similar Polcevera, with a nutty flavour. Both are served with fish.

Lombardy

From Lombardy come a large number of wines, though not in the mountain regions nor in the area round the river Po where rice flourishes more than anything else. Two names, however, stand out and are being exported. The first is Sassella, rather unusual in that, as it ages, it turns from a star-bright ruby to a deeper red with orange tints. The bouquet is likened to roses. With Grumello and Inferno, fascinating names but similar to Sassella and all made from the Nebbiolo grape, it provides the best wine of the Valtellina region. Sassella grapes and one or two others are blended with the Nebbiolo but in small proportion.

Frecciarossa comes from a family vineyard where Giorgio Odero follows his father's tradition of producing exceptional wine, bottled on his own estate. The *demi-sec* is amber-yellow with a penetrating and unusual bouquet, a dessert wine. There is also a dry white, very pale in colour, served

Monterosso, showing vineyards on the steep hills.

The village of Vernazza.

with *hors d'oeuvres* and fish. Both these are twelve to thirteen degrees. The red Frecciarossa is kept for years in both cask and bottle and is particularly well thought of. There is also a *rosé*, again sharing something of the individual bouquet of these wines.

Trentino-Alto Adige

Another northern region is Alto Adige, close to Austria of which it was once part. The wines are usually described as of German style but in my opinion they differ in flavour, though Riesling and Traminer grapes are used. The Riesling, in particular, tends to be thinner and sometimes acid. Pinot Bianco, another white wine, has a similar sharp flavour. Indeed most of the white wines have this tartness. In all fairness, however, I must say that some shippers regard this as an area with a future for the growth of dry white wines, though marred by stubborn retention of traditional methods that do not make the most of the grapes.

Certainly it has beauties of its own in the snow-capped mountains and countryside. Much of the wine goes to Austria and Switzerland, and winewise it seems this region has scarcely been assimilated into Italy. Among reds, Santa Maddalena is the best from Alto Adige, and has been compared to Barolo and Barbaresco, though not really up to their standards. Teroldego is the red wine of Trentino, a dry wine with a bouquet like almonds and somewhat sharp when young but becoming smoother as it matures.

Veneto

Three wines come from here that have won fame wherever they are exported. They are Soave, Valpolicella and Bardolino, names that run together as readily as a comedy trio. Each has its own Classico area. Soave is an excellent dry white wine, very pale yellow with greenish lights, crisp, refreshing and slightly acid. It is made mainly from the Garganega grape and should be drunk young. It is one more example of a popular name that tempts the unscrupulous.

Valpolicella comes from north of Verona and has won appreciation in Britain, the United States and other countries. If Barola is the great 'big' Italian wine then Valpolicella has claims to be the middleweight though a little light for my own taste. It has a ruby colour and the Italians drink it with all meals. Like Bardolino, it is made from a blend of several grapes including Corvina and Negrara. There are two grades—ordinary and superior dry —the second somewhat darker in colour and more velvety. Both have a bouquet somewhat like almonds.

Bardolino is another red and perhaps the light-weight here, for it has slightly less alcoholic content and is of light body and colour. It is very popular in the area, however, going with everything from pigeon to stewed rabbit. It should be drunk

A vineyard in the Trentino region.

The Bardolino vineyards of the House of Bolla in Veneto.

Cultivation in a Soave vineyard where horses are still popular in upland wine areas.

young, when it is fresh and clean and has some of the open appeal of Lake Garda, round which it grows. These three are outstanding but there are many more wines in Veneto which, in time, may improve their production methods and so find wider markets.

Round Treviso and on the Piave one finds quality red wines in Raboso and Cabernet and excellent whites in Prosecco and Verduzzo. Other good wines also named from their grapes are Merlot, Tocai and Pinot Bianco.

Emilia-Romagna

This is a noble wine area, a vast expanse with Bologna as its centre, and wines that, although less famous than some already mentioned, are more to my personal taste. You can find vines in all sorts of places here, which is not as useful as finding them in carefully prepared vineyards but does show the natural instinct of the people to grow grapes and make wine wherever possible. The humble *spaghetti bolognese* known wherever Italian restaurants are found, from London to Australia, is of this region but there is also great interest in good food, for example, *filetti di tacchino,* made of turkey or chicken breast with slices of ham covered in fondant cheese and baked in the oven, a dish fit for any country to boast.

The leading red wine is Lambrusco di Sorbara, a fine dry dark red with violets in the bouquet, fruity and refreshing with a natural sparkle, 'One of the most straightforward, sincere, and delicious of Italy' is how an Italian authority describes it. The sparkle is, of course, the natural mystery and found in few other places, the Loire being among them where it is called *pétillant*. It goes well with *Tortellini*, those squares of paste stuffed with chopped veal, egg, and spice, or even better with that wonderful dish *lasagne al forno* in which thin layers of macaroni dough alternate with meat and cheese. But this is no cook book!

There are at least four Lambrusco wines to my knowledge, all good and made from the grape of that name. They are called after different areas and I am told there are several others. The Sorbara has the highest alcoholic content at 11.5 degrees.

Sangiovese is a stronger wine, dark red and dry, full-bodied, with a powerful bouquet. Its grape gives the wine its name and is used also in Chianti. The right age to drink it is four or five years old. Also grown in the region is Trebbianino, both dry and sweet white wine, and Albana di Romagna, yellow-gold in colour, stronger alcoholically than Trebbianino and more mellow even in the dry type.

Umbria

A neighbouring region to Tuscany, Umbria produces the excellent white Orvieto, a wine that was once sweet though the dry version is the favourite form today. Transparent, pale yellow and rounded, yet with a certain individual tang, it rivals Soave. The older generation of Italians maintain that real Orvieto should be semi-sweet, but certainly the newer, dry version is a most refreshing drink and is also higher in alcohol. Orvieto Secco is dry while Orvieto Amabile is not quite so dry. The sweet is Orvieto Abboccato for which the grapes are allowed to rot slightly after picking. Umbria, alas, is inclined to be a region of careless winegrowers, where olive trees again mingle their grey shades among the green vines, but

The town of Ascoli Piceno in the Marche region.

discipline is slowly being introduced. At least one red reaches England, however, and this is the ruby colour Rubesco Torgiano made by the Lungarotti family, matured for four years in oak casks and for two in bottles.

The Marches

This is a hilly area, rather unspoiled, rural countryside with much vine cultivation but only one outstanding name among wines and that is Verdicchio, another wine sold in Britain, sometimes in unusual flasks. The full name is Verdicchio dei Castelli di Jesi. It can be dry or semi-sweet and being twelve to fourteen degrees has the advantage of travelling well. It is a full, mouth-lingering wine that, in the dry form with slightly tart finish, goes well with *hors d'oeuvres* or fish dishes. Winner of the Italian wine Oscar of 1970 it is sold in London in an attractive amphora bottle by Hedges & Butler among others.

Latium (Lazio)

From Emilia-Romagna, round the rim of Umbria, this big region runs back to the Mediterranean and has long been famous for its Frascati pale gold wine, which I well remember drinking in Gatti's, that splendid wine bar *cum* Italian restaurant in the Strand, in pre-war days. Gatti's has disappeared along with Romano's and Frascati's itself in High Holborn, but the wine stays on, more popular than ever.

The district that Frascati comes from is called Castelli Romani which has some fine grapes, among them several already met elsewhere such as Malvasia and Trebbiano. The soil, the grapes and the warmer climate produce here extraordinarily pleasing white wines, dry or sweet, more usually dry. Frascati Superiore is the best, strong and uncompromising and yet of quite high alcoholic content, above twelve degrees. It is often sold in straw-covered flasks similar to those for Chianti.

Some way north of Frascati is made a wine that has won a place in history by its name Est! Est!! Est!!! Bishop Fugger made a trip to Rome from Germany 800 years ago and sent his servant ahead to mark the inns serving the best wines by scrawling 'Est' and 'Non Est' on the lintels as he found them good or bad. It was, of course, at Montefiascone that he met perfection in the semi-sweet wine with a yellow tinge, and the story has it that the Bishop, too, was so pleased that he settled in the town for the rest of his days.

Latium has a number of other very pleasing wines. The sweet version of Frascati, for instance is called Cannellino di Frascati, a delightful golden yellow colour and from twelve to fourteen

degrees in strength. Lulled by its sweet but slightly tart finish I once indulged with a companion in a second bottle as we ate those wonderful, big Italian peaches, so rich and fruity in themselves. Sitting outside our *albergo*, only partially shaded from the sun, we never reached our *espresso* coffee and retired—drowsily, we assured ourselves, but that may have been a convenient expression—to bed.

There is also Falerno, made from Falanghina grapes, a rather dry white, which is made from the same grape in Campania, but which of the two is the true Falernian wine of the old Romans I know not. Both go well with fish and there is a red version.

Abruzzi and Molise
This is an enthralling part of the Italian scene because of its mountains and rivers, with charming valleys between the ranges. Agricultural land is therefore treasured and one area is famous for its

Italy South

Principal wine-growing areas

0   50   100 Km.

0   50   Mi.

potatoes. Because there are many sheep, cheese is a speciality, among others being *ricotta*, a cottage variety. The grapes are grown near the sea, where you also find such dishes as *brodetto*, a fish stew which includes garlic, onion, and bay leaves. It goes admirably with Trebbiano d'Abruzzo, a wine taking its name from the grape that we have met before. Here it gives the wine a rather full, gold colour, tastes dry and has a notable bouquet.

Apulia (Puglia)

If ever a wine region of southern Italy had a future it is here, in the spur and heel of the Italian 'boot'. It deserves such success, for there is still much poverty and the superstition that goes with what can only be called peasant life. The wines are big and strong, coarse perhaps but with potential that can be realised some time in the future with more skill and capital.

The people have cultivated the vine for generations in much the same way throughout the area, with low stems and intricate trelliswork close to the ground, an attractive scene. What is more, huge orange groves are to be found in the area and the oranges are sold at the roadside, like strawberries in England, while the golden fruit hangs glistening from the modest, leafy trees all along the way.

A lot of wine is sent in big tankers to France and Northern Italy where it has been traditionally used to 'reinforce' other wines by blending. But many of the wines are good to drink in their own right, deep purple in colour, strong in alcohol and going up to seventeen or even nineteen degrees, the latter called the 'black' wine as indeed it looks. There are also table grapes like the attractive Italia.

One of the leading growers is the Marchese di Sbano who has more than 800 acres of the best local grapes such as the red Malvasia that makes a fine dessert wine with an alcoholic strength of eighteen degrees and a piquant bouquet. In recent times the purchase of new equipment, the sinking of Artesian wells and the introduction of new strains of disease-resistant vines has revolutionised the wine industry. The old 'bush' grapes are being uprooted, the land ploughed and left fallow for a year, and the vineyards replanted with taller growing vines which are easier to spray and pick, and permit tractors to be used between them. In Puglia there are now 400,000 acres devoted solely to vines, with each district bearing the name of its wines such as Martina Franca, Locorotondo, Alberobello, Lecce, and Taranto. The latter are the best known, being made in the small town of Lizzano which won the *Oscar del Vino* for the best Puglia wines of 1968–1970. They are produced by the local co-operative, the 'Cantina e Oleificio Sociale', and I am indebted to John and Phoebe Quarrington, English residents in Pulsano and

A vineyard near Peschici in the Puglia region.

friends of the Marquese and Marquesa Sbano for these local details.

Other attractive Lizzano wines are the full-bodied red Primativo del Tarantino, Negramaro di Lizzano (gold and silver medal winners) and Tarentum, another gold medal winner at the Fair of Mediterranean Countries. *Rosés* include Sangiovese, pleasant quaffing wine with a slightly bitter but agreeable taste, and Negramaro del Tarantino. As well as Malvasia there is another dessert wine called Moscato, from the Moscato d'Amburgo grape, with a delicate, sweet flavour. I have enjoyed all the foregoing and can recommend them.

At least one English buyer has told me of his favourable impressions of Lizzano wines and it may yet be that, with the ever-increasing demand for Italian wines, they will find their place on the market in Britain.

Basilicata

If Apulia makes more wine than anywhere else in Italy, its neighbour makes almost the least. You will find its red wine Aglianico del Vulture listed on Italian wine maps, a splendid name indeed from the vineyards on the slopes of Monte Vulture. Its flavour reflects the volcanic soil on which it grows, though the volcano is now extinct. It comes from the Aglianico grape, as one might guess from the name, and this produces a bold wine of body and flavour. Though other wines are made here, chiefly white, they are not comparable to the red. The same grape also makes a sparkling wine. The region grows the golden Malvasia wine so often met in the south and Muscat or Moscato is also drunk here as well as other white wines like Asprinio, the latter rather too light to be of much account except for a certain natural sparkle.

Campania

This is another large area including both Naples and the Isle of Capri, 'where I found her' as the song says. The wines are generous, 'fiery and full of the flavour of the volcanic earth' is how one authority comments on them, and include Falerno, already mentioned, and here linked with Horace, Virgil, Pliny, Catullus and other Romans who praised it. From Capri comes both white and red wine under that name, the white particularly well thought of with its dry flavour. Sorrento, another theme for song, has Colli Sorrentini while Ischia offers Biancolella d'Ischia, a straw-coloured white that is one of the best on the island and goes well with local fish. There is a purple wine called Vesuvio which actually grows on the lower slopes of the mountain and even has a faint burnt taste!

Lacrimae Christi is the most famous wine name in Campania, however, and the genius who thought up the name 'tears of Christ' for this wine with its gold tinge and dry but flowery flavour from Greco and Fiano grapes, did much for his fellow countrymen. The tears were shed by Christ over the sins of Naples, according to legend, and turned into vines as they fell on the wicked soil.

There are also red and *rosé* versions, the *rosé* being a delicate wine and the red rather smooth and improving with age.

Calabria

One thinks here of the late Norman Douglas, who enjoyed most of the pleasures of this world, sinful and otherwise, despite modest means and wrote some of the best books for armchair travel. He was a notable part of the D. H. Lawrence, Compton Mackenzie era, now long passed, with its love of southern Italy. There are more 'tears' here with Lacrimae di Castrovillari, and then Pellaro, medium-dry with a perfumed bouquet, and Savuto, velvety and of good bouquet. All are rather light-coloured reds to go with roast meat of every kind. Among dessert wines are Moscato di Cosenza and Greco di Gerace. The first is aromatic and the second more delicate, but both are pleasantly sweet. Unfortunately there is not much of the Greco available, or its fame would be wider.

Sicily

The vine grows abundantly here, rivalling the oranges and lemons, and one product alone has made Sicily world famous. Marsala is the chief dessert wine of Italy. It is dark brown, flavoured by a remembrance of burnt sugar. The base is the white wine of the area, fortified with grape brandy and then improved further with sweet, concentrated grape juice. It was ordered by Nelson for his fleet, but at one time fell from favour due to the competition of Sherry and Madeira. Within the Common Market, however, its prospects of wider sales are improving.

A view of Palermo.

A British discovery of the Woodhouse family in 1773, the English names of Woodhouse and Ingham are still on Marsala labels with Sicilian rivals in Rallo, Pellegrino and Florio.

Among the red and white wines, Corvo Bianco, Duca di Salaparuta, made on estates near Palermo, has achieved considerable popularity. It is pale, straw-yellow and very dry, but its bouquet is elegant and the alcoholic content goes up to thirteen degrees. The red is velvety and medium dry. The slopes on Mount Etna that face the sea produce from carefully blended grapes wines such as Etna and Ragabo, not great wines, but good enough as white, red and *rosé*. And the Malvasia grape, met so often in the south, appears here as Malvasia di Lipari, a dessert wine with a pleasing aroma, very rich and perhaps as good in this area as anywhere else.

A sweet white wine is Moscato dello Zucco, a Muscatel really to be served with dessert and reaching sixteen alcoholic degrees. There is also Moscato of Pantelleria, Syracuse and other centres. Rosso Pellegrino is a particularly attractive Sicilian aperitif.

The traveller in Sicily will find many district wines with local names, often rather thin, but estates are being reorganised to make fine wines and new methods of marketing are being adopted. Small growers are being persuaded to give up mixed farming and to replant with quality grapes which will bring them better prices, while the regional authorities are providing technical assistance; normal enough in other countries but particularly beneficial in Italy and very necessary in the south. Most styles of wine can be made and, since Sicily is Italy's second largest wine-producing area, the potential is immense. This is so throughout the whole south, as a verse on an Apulian wall points out:

'He who drinks water rusts out,
He who drinks milk goes sour,
He who eats grapes lives to be a hundred,
He who drinks wine never dies,
But he who *grows* grapes dies of hunger.'

8

Spain and Portugal

Spain

Although one thinks automatically of sherry when Spain is named, this is an accident of circumstance. In fact Spain could be the world's largest wine producer if its four million acres of vine-growing land counted alone. Much of it, however, due to the tremendously hot sun, does not produce the amount of wine that would be available in a more temperate climate.

Yet there are areas such as the Rioja valley, some sixty miles inland from San Sebastian on the northern coast, and lying between Vitoria and Zaragoza, that produce very fine wine known to all winelovers. Again, in the La Mancha area southeast of Madrid, there is much wine of lesser quality but of some distinction made and sold under the name of Valdepenas, the chief town. From Cata-

lonia, setting for the Costa Brava, comes a great deal of red and white wine, and Tarragona is a notable producer of both and also a sweet, fortified red wine called simply Tarragona, once popular in Britain as a rival to port. Valencia, further down the Mediterranean coast provides rather bigger red wines.

But although the quantity is modest in the world picture sherry as a name stands high. It is only in recent times that the general public has come to realise how much other wine is made in Spain. Here the advertisements for Don Cortez, the cheap but satisfactory branded, blended Spanish wine that sells so extensively in several varieties through Grants of St James's, are partly responsible. Other companies also import Spanish wine for their brands, among them International Distillers and Vintners with La Vista, mostly from Tarra-

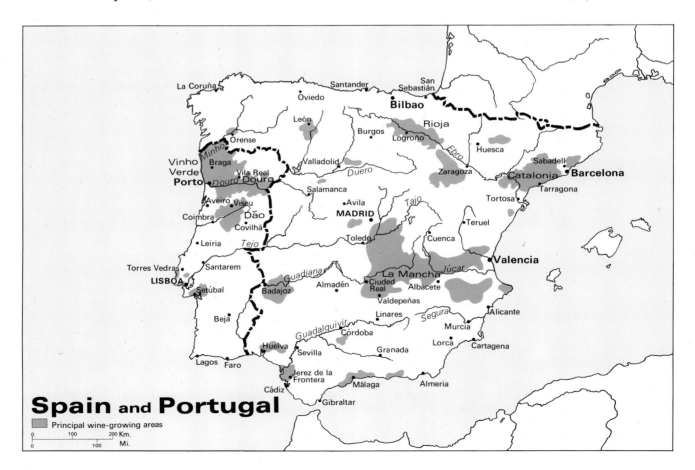

Spain and Portugal

■ Principal wine-growing areas

0   100   200 Km.

0   100   Mi.

A typical vineyard house in the sherry-producing area near Jerez de la Frontera.

The undulating hills near Jerez de la Frontera, showing the white chalky 'albariza' soil.

gona, and Stowells of Chelsea with Corrida. Charles Kinloch were among the pioneers of Spanish table-wine importers during the mid-fifties.

Sherry, however, comes from a relatively small district among the hills near Jerez de la Frontera, to give Jerez its full, romantic name.

It is a town that lives for its main export, which had been sent to England long before Shakespeare gave to Falstaff the praise of sherris-sack. In most hotels the bars carry representative sherries of every great shipper but in the streets there is the bustle of modern traffic. Indeed Jerez has only one problem today—where to find more sherry. The world demand, led by Britain, shows no sign of falling-off, and while there is ample land that might be turned into further vineyards it is not easy to persuade the owners to sell at reasonable prices. After all, it takes about five years before good wine is produced from a new vineyard and that is a long time to wait.

Not unexpectedly, the best land, called *albariza*, contains a very high percentage of chalk, which is what one finds in many good white-wine countries. But although sherry begins its life as a dry white wine from the Palomino grape, with the Pedro Ximinez being used for sweetening, it is the subsequent treatment that turns it into a rich experience. The harvest is in September and the pressing is done by modern machinery, naked feet being no longer the fashion here for sherry or, in Portugal, for port.

The sherry process traditionally uses big casks, each holding 108 gallons, made of American white oak—that same white oak, incidentally, was a factor in the American Revolution when Britain demanded it to make masts for her warships—and it is these stacked casks that make the *soleras* so impressive. Today, much of the must is fermented in large concrete vats.

At the end of the year the experts taste and inspect the wine. Where there is thicker flor yeast on the surface of the wine this indicates that it is more suited to become either a Fino or an Amontillado. Where there is no flor and a less pronounced bouquet, it is made into Oloroso. There are other factors to take into account in these decisions. The prospective Fino or Amontillado is lighter, with the best bouquet, whereas the future Oloroso is a full, heavy wine.

The selected types are drawn off into different casks and fortified with grape brandy, perhaps fifteen degrees Gay Lussac in the case of the Finos and up to eighteen degrees for the Oloroso. Before this addition, the wine is absolutely dry, all the sugar having been used up in the tumultuous fermentation that is more spectacular than usual. The casks are then left to mature, being inspected from time to time and various marks made in chalk on each cask to denote its development. The drier wines continue to make flor, the sweeter and fuller-bodied do not and this decides their treatment.

Although nature thus takes its course, there is the usual professionalism in the caring for the wine. The makers can only influence the development to a certain extent, however, and must wait to see what will finally result. When the development is completed, the casks take their place in the appropriate *soleras*. Casks that finally disappoint are distilled into brandy.

A solera is a group of casks. A solera system consists of several rows of casks of the same style of wine but of different ages. There are sometimes up to four tiers. In theory the lower casks are refilled from the higher ones. In practice it is more complicated. Finos develop better nearer the ground. Olorosos develop better in the warmer upper tiers. Up to half the wine in the ground level tier is drawn off during the year and the casks so half-emptied are filled up from the tier above. This consists of somewhat younger wine of the same style and these casks, in turn, are replenished from the still younger wine in the casks above them. There is thus no actual vintage year with sherry, the final drink being a blend of different years drawn from the oldest casks. Whilst they are in the oak, dessert sherries tend to darken and to increase in alcohol content, so that when they are to be put in bottle it is necessary to blend them further with sweetening and colouring additions to a standard sweetness and colour to meet the customer's taste, and need for continuity of style and quality.

The *bodegas* that house the *soleras* are high, vaulted buildings, quite airy and unlike the normal underground cellars where wine is kept. Air, it seems, is helpful to the flor, whereas normally it is fatal for good wine. The *bodegas* are in semi-darkness and are sometimes built to face the sea breezes, as are the Manzanilla bodegas in Sanlucar.

With other wines it is necessary constantly to top up the casks as the level falls through evaporation, but with sherry there is no need to keep the butt filled in this way. What would turn normal wine to vinegar only helps sherry to flourish, and one of the driest sherries, Manzanilla, is said to reflect the Atlantic sea winds in its flavour since it is made and stored at the mouth of the Guadalquivir river. For some reason it is associated with bullfighters, though a dry sherry seems hardly the best liquid for a dry mouth as the trumpets herald the entry of the bull at the *corrida*.

Manzanilla and Fino are dry sherries, very pale and straw-coloured. Amontillado comes next, light amber in colour and with a distinctive nutty flavour, dry to medium in taste. Oloroso is darker still, the best examples having a notable bouquet, and invariably sweet when sold abroad as dessert wines, though it is possible to make them slightly off-dry. Cream sherry is an even sweeter, smoother Oloroso, and brown sherry is fullest and sweetest of all, quite dark brown in colour.

There is thus a full range of taste, Fino being recognised as the best apéritif, since its dry flavour does not affect the palate for the red and white wines to come, while an Oloroso could leave a rich, cloying taste behind. There are many great shippers such as Harveys of Bristol, Pedro Domecq, Avery of Bristol, Croft, Williams & Humbert (now called Sherry House), Findlater, Mackie Todd, Gonzalez Byass, Duff Gordon and Sandeman. As well as the first grade range, many shippers now import sherries blended to make a cheaper range, perhaps two-thirds the price of the best. These are quite drinkable but, as with Champagne, the best is always the best provided you can afford it.

There are also sherry-like wines called Montilla and Moriles made near the town of Montilla in Cordoba, from which district El Cordobes, the bullfighter, takes his name. In fact the word Amontillado was chosen originally for sherries showing some of the qualities of Montilla wine. Montilla may not be sold as sherry, however, since

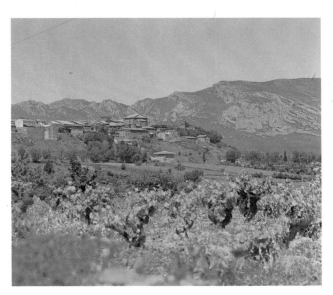

Laguardia in the Rioja region.

Quixotic sixteenth-century windmills at Campo de Criptana, in the La Mancha region.

it is made outside the delineated sherry zone. It uses the Pedro Ximinez grape which gives a dry wine here and is made similarly to sherry.

Where table wine is concerned, however, the splendid Rioja wines from Old Castile are the best in Spain. There are three areas, High, Low and Alava, while the name Rioja comes from the River Oja and is pronounced Ree-oh-ha. There is red and white, the first being the best and matured in oak casks, in some cases for a number of years. Two of the leaders are Marques de Riscal, light and elegant, and Marques de Murrieta, more fruity and softer. The Marques de Riscal wines rest in casks in great vaulted cellars called by the firm The Cathedral of Wine. Here they stay for at least four years. It tastes not unlike Bordeaux and the bottle is covered with an attractive gold wire mesh, sealed in place. The white Rioja is similar to a dry white Burgundy, but there are also sweet varieties.

Another leading producer of Rioja wines is Bodegas Bilbainas of Haro, using the Ederra label as well as bottling special estate wines such as Vina Pomal and Vina Zaco. Rioja wines appear increasingly in British wine-lists to compete with the dearer French wines and leading importers are Clode & Baker of Aylesbury, some of whose wines are sold by Dolamore of London. Standards are maintained by the 'Consejo Regulador of Rioja', the official body which provides certificates of origin and stamps the labels of the wines marketed in bottle. Vintage years, however, do not always have the significance or authority of French wines.

Round Valdepenas, Valley of the Rocks, there is a large production of red and white wine, much of it going to Madrid as carafe wine from this old region of Don Quixote. It is drunk young, like Beaujolais, but has not quite the same general quality, being on the thin side to my taste with some acid. Others, however, find the wines pleasing, and local efforts aim to improve standards of name and quality.

Around Barcelona there are two names to note— Alella and Panades. The first produces agreeable white wine which comes in brown hock bottles, like German wine, *demi-sec* from the Garnacha grape. There is also a red made from Black Garnacha, a relation of the Grenache grape that does so well in the Rhone valley of France, and which is used also in Rioja. Villafranca del Panades is a centre for a very clear white wine which is also produced in a sparkling version as Xampan. A somewhat similar wine is Perelada which featured in a legal case over the use in Britain of the name 'Champagne', which is now forbidden to Spanish and indeed any other wines made outside the French Champagne area. I find Perelada quite acceptable as a sparkling wine.

One must not leave Spain without considering Malaga, rival in favour to Marsala and Madeira and, like them, somewhat diminished in popular interest, having lost out to sherry. There is the same sort of rivalry between the sherry and Malaga areas as exists between Bordeaux and Burgundy. Malaga, however, is purely a dessert wine, tasting like a particularly sweet one. It is fortified, but to a lesser extent than sherry, and gets its sweetness from the grape blend, in which Pedro Ximenez plays a large part. Yet, drinking its rich flavour it is hard to believe that it is not 'assisted' heavily in some way. It is a pity Malaga has gone out of fashion, because fashion creates a demand which can often reduce prices for quantity shipment.

The future of Spanish wines depends to some extent on the Common Market regulations. Sherry, Madeira and port have received certain price considerations from the EEC but other wines are liable to be affected by reference prices which will favour those wines produced within the Common Market area.

Portugal

The similarity in history between port and sherry lies in the historic wine links between Britain and the two countries concerned and the long popularity of these drinks that has continued over two hundred years.

Madeira is only out of fashion in so far as its long shipment from the Atlantic adds to the cost, and it is Portugal's successful answer to Malaga. Although it is no real rival to either sherry or port it is a very interesting drink. The island of Madeira was discovered by the Portuguese in 1419 and is only forty miles long by fifteen miles wide. Zarco, who first landed there, found the land densely covered by trees so thickly interwoven that it was impossible to hack a way through. His simple solution was to set a light to them and soon the whole island was ablaze with a fire that, it is said, lasted for years. When the flames finally died out, however, the island was covered with ash which, mixing with the volcanic soil, made a fertile earth for the settlers who duly arrived to plant Malvoisie (Malvazia) grapes and grow sugar cane. Malvazia is the same grape that does so well in Italy and which also made the English Malmsey, a butt of which was used to drown the unfortunate Duke of Clarence, who clearly was no great drinker.

Other types of grape, all white, are Bual, Verdelho and Sercial each, with Malmsey, giving its name to a type of Madeira. Sercial is a dryish wine, light in colour and body, often drunk as an apéritif and once fashionable with soup. Verdelho is an in-between wine, darker than Sercial and with more body, medium in flavour but tending to dryness. Bual is a dessert wine, sweet and not so big as Malmsey which is very rich, dark coloured, powerful and which soon goes to the head; a wine to be drunk as an accompaniment to fruit cake as was the custom of our ancestors.

The problem over Madeira is when to drink it. Being a fortified wine it is not suitable as a table wine; only Sercial might serve here and not very successfully. As dessert wines, which the others are,

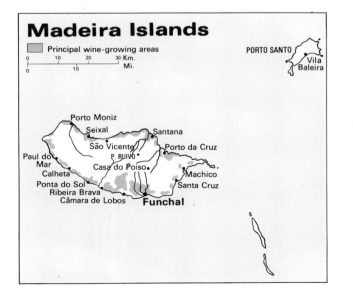

they come up against port and cognac and armagnac, not to mention liqueurs. Pricewise some are dearer than standard ports, although others, notably Shortridge Lawton Madeiras are cheaper than standard ports and also less expensive than many sherries. The Madeira shippers of London are as charming and pleasant a body of men as one could wish to meet, and I have dined and wined with many of them more than once. Fortunately they also ship other wines as well and are encouraged to persevere with Madeira.

Land is valuable on Madeira so the island slopes are terraced with neat patches of vineyard around the coast. Inland the land rises some six thousand feet to its famous peak. The wine is fermented in oak barrels for three weeks and then is given the *estufa* treatment for at least three months, something that wine nowhere else undergoes. The *estufa* is a large store with central heating, the equivalent of a hot-house. This process was set up after the discovery that the wines improved on tropical voyages when the heat of the sun and the rolling of the ship helped to mellow and mature them. At one time barrels were placed in the *estufa*, and these are still used for the best wines, but concrete vats are now normally employed. The temperature is slowly raised to some 115°F and as gradually reduced. From the *estufa* the wine goes into clean vats where it rests for a year or two.

The fortifying of the wine is done with cane sugar spirit, distilled on the island, and the final process may be by the *solera* system and further blending, or blended from 'lots' like port. One result is that a good Madeira may well be very drinkable at 100 years of age.

The London Madeira Wine Association aims to promote the product, which certainly deserves to continue at the table, if only for the care and attention that goes into its making and the very original process employed. But for the reasons stated it will always face problems.

Another Portuguese product, Port—a much more famous one—endured a similar period in the doldrums up to the mid-1960s. Port, like sherry, benefited from the work of the English families who established themselves in Oporto and Jerez respectively in the seventeenth century to ship these splendid, gentlemanly and profitable wines to their native land.

The same history was true of Madeira. Following the Jacobite rebellion of 1745 a man called Rutherford found it expedient to leave his native Jedburgh in a hurry before the avenging English. He made for Madeira where his name appears in 1760 and his son, T. Rutherford, shipped the family's first cargo of Madeira wine in 1814, the year before Waterloo. Today the wines of Rutherford & Miles of Madeira are imported by Rutherford Osborne & Perkin Ltd of London, the Managing Director of which is the genial David Rutherford, a direct descendant of the reckless supporter of Bonnie Prince Charlie. In fact David inherited his ancestor's impetuosity and in his youth departed in haste from one wine merchant's staff after he had arrived on a white horse and ridden round the boardroom table.

Both Irish and English figured in the early Jerez history and as late as 1877 a clerk called Alexander Williams founded Williams & Humbert with his father-in-law's funds. Duff Gordon & Company

A mural showing the transportation of grape juice to Funchal by boat, from the more inaccessible island vineyards.

was started by the British consul in Cadiz in the mid-eighteenth century, Sir Thomas Duff. One of that firm's employees, John William Burdon, left to build up the still well-known name of Burdon's sherries.

The Oporto story is even longer-established with Anglo-Portuguese treaties dating from 1308, although it was not until 1670 that wines from the Douro arrived in quantity while the Methuen Treaty of 1703 gave them real preference. The French Revolution and its effect on the export of wines to Britain gave Portugal a further chance to extend its shipments. It had been found that the Portuguese wines travelled better if a small amount of brandy was added to them before export, and this appears to have led to the idea of fortifying the wine. This arrested the fermentation and left the wine naturally sweet in a way that appealed to British tastes; in short, port, more or less as we know it, had arrived.

British merchants had been in Oporto, that lovely old town of climbing stone walls looking down on the river and its shipping, the whole scene hot, colourful and fascinating, since early in the sixteenth century. Indeed, when Philip II of Spain took the throne in 1580 he hurried to expel all English merchants, and this was well before the Armada of 1588. The English were back in 1640 as soon as Portugal regained independence, so they obviously felt there was something worth garnering there.

One of the handsomest old buildings of Oporto is known as The Factory House, the headquarters of the British merchants, which was built between 1785 and 1791. Its splendid proportions, noble dining-rooms and library and extensive offices make it a model of its period. The merchants had other premises before the charming building was finally planned, but it was The Factory House that henceforth provided a meeting place for port-wine merchants to do their business as well as a social centre for the balls and parties enjoyed by their families.

Names still leading in the port trade are to be found in the records of firms like Brompton Croft Ltd. The firm of Croft can claim to have been 'purveyors of port' since the reign of Charles II and it was a John Croft who, in 1788, declared, 'An Englishman of a certain standing cannot do without a glass of port after a good dinner, in the same way that a slice of Cheshire cheese is also served as an aid to digestion'.

The great names in the port trade read like a drum roll: Calem, Gould Campbell, Cockburn, Croft, Delaforce, Dow, Graham, Fonesca Guimaraens, Quinta do Noval, Robertson, Sandeman, Taylor and Warre (oldest of them all). Close-knit and inter-married, the wine families of Oporto have maintained the firmest links with England and their London offices. They are people of two countries,

An ox-cart as used for transportation of grapes in the remote areas of the Douro.

equally at home in either, both in language and residence, perfect examples of Britain's oldest alliance. The 'Factory' owes its foundation and magnificence to Consul John Whitehead (1762–1802). Whitehead was a bachelor, but his sister Elizabeth married a William Warre, first of the family in the firm. A portrait still hangs today on the main staircase of the Factory House of William Warre's grandson Lt. General Sir William Warre who fought under Wellington in the Peninsula.

As with most wines the port harvest begins towards the end of September, but although a Sandeman book printed as late as 1964 still describes the treading of the grapes in the *lagars* or stone troughs, those days are almost past. This is not for any fanciful reason of hygiene but because few Douro men are now available. They are working elsewhere and wages, in any case, are now so high that local growers prefer to sell their produce to the big companies who employ centrifugal presses which separate the stalks and crush the grapes so scientifically that they do not even damage the pips.

There are technical differences in the process, but the fermentation is stopped when the desired degree of sweetness in the wine is reached, being measured by saccharometer. The longer the fermentation continued in the process of turning the sugar into alcohol, the drier would be the result. The wine is drawn off into large vats and mixed with a measured amount of pure grape brandy which immediately halts fermentation and the result is port of both the required sweetness and the required alcoholic strength, a delicate balance in fact between the two.

All this is carried out at the *Quintas*, the wine estates, and early in the following year the wine is transferred by road tanker, down the Douro to the 'lodges' in Vila Nova da Gaia, opposite Oporto. Here in the special entrepôt area the port is matured, usually in large vats, but also in casks or pipes. As with sherry, this blending is an essential part of the process, and is skilled work undertaken by experts to maintain the tastes and standards of their house. There may be wines of three to four different years, varying in age from three to seven years, in the final product of a ruby port. An example like Sandeman's Partners' Port, which is a rich ruby, is the result of blending the finest wines from the best vintage years aged in cask.

It is an interesting feature that while ruby port loses its colour as it ages, sherry becomes darker. Another contrast is that sherry does not really improve in the bottle, whereas certain port, especially vintage port, certainly does, particularly in the great examples. In recent times port vintages have been less full-bodied than in the past, so they mature in seven to ten years in the bottle but continue to improve for a long time after that.

Many people associate port with a vintage year, but vintage port is not by any means made every year. There are several reasons for this. A vintage port comes from a year of specially fine wine in the eyes of the shipper, and he must be then prepared to set aside some of his best stock to mature in wood for two years. This means he has to be in short supply of the best wine which he would otherwise keep for his regular blends. After being in cask the vintage port is bottled for two to two and a half years, in Oporto, then it spends ten or more years in bottle, during which it throws a crust or sediment. It is to avoid breaking and mingling this crust with the port that one undertakes the delicate but not fearsome operation of decanting the wine. However it is very important when decanting a bottle that one does not stop pouring and then attempt to restart. Such an act invariably defeats the object of the whole operation!

All this work with vintage port means of course that much time and money is involved both for storage space and for labour. That is one reason why a vintage wine is expensive and all the more credit to the generous port shippers who are so ready to share their splendid examples, kept over the years, with their friends from time to time. There are also relatively few years in which climatic conditions are favourable to produce a perfectly balanced wine. When these conditions do occur the resulting wine is naturally expensive.

In 1972, I had the pleasure of joining the firms of Sandeman and Cockburn, at different times and settings, in sampling vintages chosen and stored over the past hundred years.

The House of Sandeman was founded in London in 1790 by a Scot, George Sandeman, who shipped a vintage port of that year. The twenty vintage ports I sampled began with an 1870, though here

Barrels of port on the quayside at Vila Nova da Gaia opposite Oporto.

Port vats in a Gaia lodge.

the brandy had eaten up the fruit of the wine itself but left it nonetheless drinkable. I drank the port of my birth year and enjoyed, too, the 1927 where the combination of ripe grapes and perfect weather made one of the great ports of all time. It certainly tasted so to me, splendid and without flaw, a noble work. But what a lot of history, war and violence while it has lain in its cask! The 1960 that I sampled was just ready for drinking and by the time this book is published the 1963 should be proving another notable vintage.

It did not take the firm of Cockburn long to rise to the bait of the Sandeman occasion and soon afterwards they presented sixteen vintage ports from 1878 to 1970, the latter, of course, still too young to drink. When I asked Wyndham Fletcher, the Managing Director of Cockburn Smithes, why he could not equal Sandeman's twenty he smiled in a rather superior way and remarked, 'We are more selective than some of our competitors and we did not declare a vintage between 1912 and 1927!'

The differences in port are worth remembering. Vintage ports are chosen from the best wines of an exceptionally good year and are not blended with wines of any other year, as already explained. Late Bottled Port is bottled when mature, after a maximum of six years in the wood. It is chosen

Terraced vineyards at Pinhão in the Alto Douro.

from good years and though it lacks the superb quality of a great Vintage Port, it can be very good.

Then there is Tawny Port, a blend of several years, kept long in the wood and gaining a lighter, tawny colour, almost brown, in turn more expensive than Ruby Port, which is also a blend but of young wines, refreshing and fruity and kept in the wood for a lesser time so that its colour is less affected. White Port is made from white grapes and efforts have been made to sell it as an apéritif but with only modest success. My choice to combine the requirements of pocket and pleasure would be either Late Bottled or Tawny.

Up to recent years port was somewhat in the background, having been pushed out of fashion by brandy and some liqueurs. This was a pity for port is a unique pleasure, its sweet, full flavour and fragrance an ample repayment for the drinker, and its twenty degrees of fortification able to stir him to all kinds of endeavour, useful and otherwise. As with many French wines, the modern trend in port is to shipping in bottle so that eventually one should more and more see the original names of the Douro rather than some of those adopted by bottlers over here.

Although port long dominated the publicity for Portuguese wines, this was rather unfair. The Vinhos Verdes are at last coming into their own

and though this name translates as 'green wines' the reference is to the youth of the wines and not to their colour, which is a clear, almost untinged, white. They come from the region north of Oporto called Minho and though they are by no means big wines and, indeed, have modest alcoholic strength, they are a most refreshing drink. Often these wines have a very slight prickle, due to malolactic or secondary fermentation. There is a faintly tart flavour which seems to add to their attraction, particularly apparent in their native land though I have also enjoyed them in England where I think they benefit from slight chilling. I certainly much prefer them to Mateus *Rosé,* that pink and popular seller whose sweetness is not at all to my taste. The same firm ships both, and Vinho Verdes also come from several others. There is red as well as *rosé* and white, but the white is the best, such as Aveleda.

It is not generally realised that the Portuguese drink nearly as much wine per head as the French, the greater part, as in France, being *vin ordinaire* but there are superior wines subject to *appellation* by Government regulation. Portugal, like Spain, is a country that in future may well supply more and more wine for increasing world demand. The Vinho Verdes are well established as exports, so much so that, in order to maintain their reputation for the prickle already referred to, certain artificial

The home of Mateus Rosé at Vila Real.

aids are sometimes used and there are unfortunate tendencies to sweeten them. The true Vinho Verde needs no such assistance and artificial sweetness spoils its fresh, stimulating but light flavour. The Casal Garcia, original bottling, is an example.

Portugal's greatest red table wine comes from the Dao area centring on Viseu, a town among the hills and pine woods on the river of that name south-east of Oporto. But it gets exported only too seldom since a lot of the production is used for branded names and such wine as reaches England can be too young. Grapes used include Tourigo, Alvarelhao and the splendidly named Bastardo, all also used in making port. To enjoy the real Dao red wine, which is big and fruity and mouth-filling but lacks the finesse of the best French wines, one must find an example that has matured in bottle, something not easily done outside its native land.

Another red that is interesting and sometimes very good is Colares, using a grape called Ramisco grown in an area close to the sea near Lisbon on sandy soil above clay. This is a rather remarkable mixture for vineyards but it makes one of the few areas in Europe impervious to the attacks of *phylloxera*, the dreaded insect described in an earlier chapter. The wine is rather lighter than Dao wine and the vineyards are becoming smaller as 'civilisation' advances around them. Not everyone enjoys its distinctive flavour or *gout de terroir* which has some of the salt of the sea about it.

However one cannot leave red Portuguese wines without paying homage to an immortal name,

Torres Vedras, a small town with a Moorish citadel and a place in English history. The Portuguese and the English had stood out alone in Europe against Napoleon's continental system. Invasion followed and Lt. General Sir Arthur Wellesley landed with his army in early August 1808 at the mouth of the River Mondego and in due course built the invincible lines of Torres Vedras between the Tagus and the sea. Aided by Brown Bess, the musket, and the robust red wines of Torres Vedras itself, which you can still happily drink today like your forefathers of 160 years ago, the forces stood firm until they could emerge from behind the lines and trounce Massena at Busaco in 1810. Portugal, like Belgium, deserves well of Britain if history is anything to go by.

There are other wines, too. North of Lisbon produces Bucelas, white and pleasant from the Arinto grape, and Portugal is the source of that well-known table wine, Justina, a range from the province of Estremadura including red, sweet white, and dry white. Docura is another light red wine, slightly sweet, marketed by the same company, I.D.V. And there is also the noble and more expensive Moscatel de Setubal, a great golden muscat, rich and impressive as dessert wine. It is made somewhat unusually, the fortification with spirit serving to stop the fermentation and so leave much sweetness. It has something akin to that other great rich but, in comparison with top Sauternes, little known wine, Beaumes-de-Venise which is made near Avignon.

9

North America

California

It seems hardly feasible that growers in California should find it profitable to export wines for sale in Europe. It would appear to be a case of shipping coals to Newcastle, and faced by increasing home demand this policy may yet change there. But two winegrowing groups stand out in this advance on Europe. They are the Christian Brothers of the Napa Valley, the religious body already described, and the firm of Paul Masson near Saratoga in Santa Clara County. The products of both are stocked in leading London stores and restaurants and this success can only be due to the painstaking care that goes into the cultivation of the vines that came originally from Europe and now return there in bottle.

Of the many vineyards in California, those of the Christian Brothers are certainly the most remarkable. The Order's main object is to provide education for children in their schools and 20,000 Brothers teach in eighty countries. Their vineyards take second place to this but have won more than two hundred gold medals and a thousand other prizes in the last fifteen years. As well as wines they make some very good brandy, a large proportion in fact of those brandies produced in America. Nor do they lead such spartan lives as in some religious orders. Their surroundings are more comfortable and their table welcoming, with, of course, the wines they grow. All brothers have taken vows of poverty, chastity and obedience and lead consecrated lives.

California

Principal wine-growing areas

0   50   100   150 Km.

0   50   Mi.

Looking back over the long links of wine with religious houses, it is hard to find any so successful as this, and the Christian Brothers have wisely made use of commercial advice in marketing and publicising their wines so their story is efficiently presented. The marketing and publicising of their wines and brandy is handled by the exclusive world-wide distributor, Fromm & Sichel Inc.

The Brothers started to make wines for the sacrament in 1882 and first sold wine commercially in 1887. From the Mont La Salle Vineyards they produce a range of generic, or type-of-wine names, as well as varietal, or grape variety names. Thus in the first case they use the word sherry in association with their own titles, something strictly controlled in Europe, and in the second, grape names like Chenin Blanc—one of their most famous products—and Sylvaner Riesling.

Near Napa they have 200 acres producing table wines and at St Helena are 700 acres of vineyards for table and sparkling wines. Near Reedley is the Mount Tivy Winery with 1,000 acres devoted to dessert wines, vermouth and the Christian Brothers' brandy. Oak casks are used for ageing the wine, red wines taking four to five years and white wines two to three years. The wines are bottled under the Brothers' supervision and are never shipped in bulk for bottling under any other label. Laboratory controls are carefully maintained. An historical collection covering all aspects of wine includes 2,000 books, many of them rare and dating from 1550 onwards, while prints and drawings include the work of Chagall and Picasso, this collection is now housed in the Wine Museum in San Francisco.

The Christian Brothers 'Select Napa Valley Chenin Blanc' is a light but fruity white wine with attractive bouquet and a hint of sweetness from the Chenin Blanc grape. They claim that this flourishes more lusciously in their Californian vineyards than by its native Loire. Certainly the examples I have enjoyed are equally charming though possibly less individual since vintage years are regarded of less importance, Californian sunshine and weather being much more consistent than in Europe. The Christian Brothers, indeed, tend rather to label certain bottles with the *cuvée* number than give the year of production.

Another notable wine is the very sweet Château La Salle, gold in colour with a honey taste. Served chilled it is a dessert or after dinner wine and the Christian Brothers also recommend it with a spoonful of sherbet topped with a maraschino cherry, though this is not to my taste! Neither do I agree with another suggestion of serving it on-the-rocks, with ice cubes bobbing in the glass!

Among their red wines, Zinfandel comes from the name of one of the most popular red wine grapes in California. It has a pleasing body and good nose with unusual spicy but attractive flavour, suitable for accompanying steaks and

A worker inspects the verdant vineyards at a winery in northern California.

Casks in an aging-room in one of California's newer wineries.

exacted up to twenty tons of grapes from an acre, he was content to grow two tons or less on the mountain slopes and to plant slow-ripening varieties with better flavour.

Paul's great moment came in 1900 when he returned to Paris with examples of his wines and won a distinguished award for their quality. He died in 1940, saddened by his country's trials in the war against Hitler, but knowing that he had won world-wide fame. Today Paul Masson wines are exported to thirty-five countries and the original vineyards have been extended to San Ysidro in the foothills of the Coast Range and the Pinnacles in the northern part of the Salinas Valley.

The current list covers more than forty wines, six of them sparkling and one of these Very Cold Duck, a blend of sparkling white and sparkling burgundy. Under its simpler name of Cold Duck, this wine blend originated in Germany and is popular in both Canada and America for party occasions though it has not yet achieved similar recognition in Britain, partly because of the competition.

Paul Masson Emerald Dry is a superb example of white Californian wines at their best. It has a flowery bouquet but a dry finish, and is crisp and refreshing. Its delicate appeal and green-gold colour makes it a good accompaniment to fish, shellfish, white meats and chicken. The Paul Masson wines are imported in Britain by Cock, Russell Vintners of London and Emerald Dry is one of the most popular. Paul Masson red wines include Cabernet Sauvignon, from the classic Cabernet grape grown in California, a wine of good bouquet with robust flavour that I have found particularly pleasant drinking. The Pinot Noir, from the Burgundy grape, is a full, big wine with the smooth, velvety balance that one expects.

As stated the Christian Brothers and the Paul Masson wines are found in leading wine stores and restaurants in Britain where the proprietors are increasingly willing to offer fine wines from countries outside France and Germany. This is still slightly adventurous, but is bound to become rewarding as prices of the last two keep rising, provided always that the Common Market regulations enable the newcomers to sell at reasonable prices.

There are, of course, other notable vineyards in California and the remarkable thing about vine growing there is that vines similar to those grown throughout Europe are produced in a comparatively small area. The growers do not hesitate to use generic names although the place of origin is always stated by law on the bottle, indicating that the contents are that "type" of wine. Port, Sherry, Champagne, Burgundy, Vermouth, Sauternes and Riesling are among them, all resembling closely enough the original sourses and yet being not quite the same. In fact the wines of California are

roasts. Other red wines include Pinot Saint George, the grape brought originally from the Nuits-Saint-Georges district of Burgundy, doing best in the Napa Valley, and Cabernet Sauvignon, from the Bordeaux grape. This last is a dry red that takes a number of years to mature in oak casks and then in bottle. The result is excellent.

The Paul Masson company has direct links with France. The original Paul was born close to his family vineyards near Beaune in 1859 and emigrated to California at the age of nineteen. He was entranced by the climate where the grapes come to full maturity each year and suffer far less from weather hazards. Romance came to him with the vines when he fell in love with Louise LeFranc, daughter of a local grower, and together they built a home and developed the great cellars of his firm in the Santa Cruz Mountains. Paul was clearly a man of imagination, for he chose the splendid name of 'The Vineyard in the Sky' for his home. The vineyards he acquired included some cultivated since 1852, now the oldest in California, and he looked after them so well that during Prohibition he was given a government licence to continue making wine, including sparkling wine.

One of his secrets he no doubt learned in Burgundy, for whereas other growers in the hot valleys sufficient in their own right and could win a place in any market without recourse to the titles of other lands. This, however, is the way in which the industry has grown up and continues to expand.

Vines were first planted by a Franciscan, Father Junipero Serra, at Mission San Diego in 1769 and he is believed to have used a Spanish grape that became known as the Mission grape. The Mexican government confiscated the friars' properties in 1840 but proved inept at winemaking. There were, however, other growers. Joseph Chapman had planted vines near Los Angeles in 1824 and in 1831 Jean Louis Vignes, son of a Bordeaux wine family, planted a vineyard in what is now the centre of Los Angeles.

Vignes, an earlier Masson, brought French wine knowledge to the rich soil and realised that the Mission grape would never make fine wine. During the 1830 period onwards he sent to France for cuttings and these were carefully packed and shipped to Boston. From there they went to sea again and reached California via Cape Horn. Vignes was thankful to find them in good condition after the long journey and they flourished in his vineyard. Indeed, he did so well that within two years of his arrival he was said to produce the best wine in California, and that from the Mission grape he had been forced to use. He also sent home for his relatives, at least eight of whom made the adventurous journey—for those days—to California.

When he was 80 years old, in 1851, Vignes (whose name means vines) offered his estate for sale and described it as a vineyard with 40,000 vines of which 32,000 were bearing grapes and able to yield 1,000 barrels of wine per year, 'the quality of which is well-known to be superior'. His nephew, Jean Louis Sansevain eventually bought the property for 42,000 dollars.

It was the coming of the gold rush that set vine-growing on its feet. The American population of California grew from five hundred to several hundred thousand in a few years, most of them Forty-Niners who had failed to find gold and now turned to the land. The man who first found gold was James Marshall but he did not make enough from his discovery and lived off his vineyard at Coloma.

One of the arrivals in 1849 was a Hungarian nobleman who was greatly to influence the future of Californian wines. He was Agoston Haraszthy, still called the Father of Modern Californian Viticulture, a splendid but well-deserved title. He did not come to find gold but mainly because he thought that the climate might improve his health. After a stay in San Diego he moved north and planted experimental vines. In due course he came to the same conclusion as Jean Louis Vignes and in 1861 set off for Europe to buy vines. His journey

A homestead surrounded by vineyards in northern California.

through France, Germany, Switzerland, Spain, Italy and England lasted five months and he bought 100,000 cuttings of some three hundred varieties. Although he paid the cost and the freight from his own funds he had been promised reimbursement by the California Legislature. These gentlemen proved as unrealiable as English and American politicians have usually done down the ages, our own times not excluded. The promise was broken on his return and he never got a cent of the money back from the State. Poor Haraszthy planted his vines to keep them alive and found they crowded his estate out. While still arguing with the Legislature over his money, he had to cultivate them as best he could.

Struggling to keep his head above water, he had to start selling the vines to other growers, often in lots of ten or twenty. To sell 100 at a time was a large order. In all this confusion the identity labels on the vines were often lost or smeared by handling so that the names disappeared for ever. Yet, tragic as this turn of events was for Haraszthy, it proved wonderfully fruitful for California. From these 100,000 superb European vines, so introduced and scattered about the wine areas of California, grew the great wine industry of today.

It is believed that the *phylloxera* insect which devastated the great vineyards of France came to that country from the United States on an imported vine. California suffered from it nearly as much. In 1874 a vineyard in Sonoma County, near the old Haraszthy home by sad coincidence, was discovered to be riddled with the pest. Within another five years vineyards in Napa, Yolo, El Dorado and Placer counties had been ruined.

By a miracle of nature it was the tough, strong roots of the native American vines growing in the eastern and central parts of the country that provided the solution, not only for California but for the rest of the world. These American vines did not produce wine of consequence, but they had grown resistant to the pest, endemic in parts of these areas, over the years. The easten rootstock was transplanted in California and Europe and grafting of the wine-providing *Vitis Vinifera* proved successful, as described in an earlier chapter. Wine was saved for mankind! Although Europe gives credit to Charles Valentine Riley for much of the research, California has her own hero in Eugene Waldemar Hilgard, an agricultural chemist who early on recognised the threat of *phylloxera* and helped in restoring the vineyards. He also proved a farsighted guide in the processes of vinification suitable to California, where the warm climatic conditions required somewhat different methods, among them a concept of cool fermentation and new thinking on the use of yeast cultures.

Hilgard, in fact, came from a great European wine country, being born in Germany in 1833 and he had his own ideas on wine. In 1899 he was writing in the *San Francisco Examiner* of William Randolph Hearst on the wisdom of moderate drinking and saying that if the standard of cuisine was improved more wines would be drunk with meals and temperance encouraged!

Prohibition in the 1920s practically closed down winemaking though some vineyards were permitted to continue. The re-opening in 1934 not only meant that the growers had to start almost from scratch but a whole generation of the population knew little about wine, despite the knowledge they might have acquired of bath-tub gin and wood alcohol. However this new start also enabled the State to lay down quality standards for Californian wines that have helped the success of today.

There are some three hundred 'wineries', to use the peculiar word that has found a place in the American language for cellars, operating in nine wine districts, the products of which are studied by the famous Department of Viticulture and Oenology at the University of California, in Davis.

American wine production amounts to about three hundred million gallons a year of which some eighty per cent comes from California while New York State makes ten per cent. Despite both Federal and State taxes per case, consumption is expected to have risen by fifty per cent in 1975, compared with 1972. Wine consumption in the U.S. in 1973 was 347 million U.S. gallons.

Imports have a relatively insignificant share of the market and eighty-seven per cent of wines drunk are produced within the USA. France, Germany, Italy and Spain are the chief outside suppliers, invariably with their better wines, but increasingly satisfactory wines from Argentine and Chile are finding and exploiting new markets in USA.

While the two Californian sources already discussed are perhaps best known in Europe, there are other notable names to be found in the almost

Pickers emptying lug boxes into large containers for transport to the crushers.

600 mile-long strip from Mendocino in the North to Cucamonga, near Los Angeles, in the south.

Among other Napa Valley vineyards are those of Inglenook at Rutherford, a house particularly respected for the emphasis it lays on quality. Its publicity, too, concentrates on educating the public towards wine in general as well as their own products. With their best Cabernet Sauvignon they point out that this wine can mature up to twenty years and a good one 'has an incredibly long life expectancy. The longer you can keep your paws off it, the better it gets,' they state, a welcome change from the drink up quick and buy another bottle school of advertising. In fact one of their brochures on wine choosing and tasting does not mention a single one of their own wines, with the exception of a drawing of a bottle of their Gamay Beaujolais. This, however, I consider taking modesty too far.

Inglenook Vineyards and Italian Swiss Colony are both part of United Vintners, recently acquired by Heublein Inc, the distillers, but as long as the Inglenook Vineyards are run on the lines of the above example I have no fears for their future. They deserve support. Their founder was Captain Gustav Niebaum and when he died in 1908 he was succeeded by his nephew, John Daniel and later by John Daniel Jr who was responsible for its success in modern times. A further example of their correct outlook is the fact that the emphasis and the emphasis of most California producers is on grape varieties, and their bottles bear these names rather than the generic titles of French areas popular in other firms. The vineyards are not particularly large but they are very carefully run, divided almost equally between red and white wines.

There is still room for the adventurous in California and Rodney Strong, a Broadway choreographer, left the Great White Way for the Golden

State and became the owner several years later of 1,100 acres of the Windsor Vineyards of Tiburon Vintners in Sonoma County, not far from Napa Valley. Now he proudly signs his letters 'Rodney D. Strong, Winemaker'. He is yet another who believes in the varietal grape names and puts quality before quantity. So great is the demand for his carefully produced wines that he does not make them available in stores or to the retail trade in general. These premium wines are in short supply and the limited amount made each year is reserved for customers who buy direct and receive regular news of the wines available by post. With typical American selling vision he has a mail order project of gift wines with personal labels.

In the last few years, Sonoma Vineyards have changed their distribution methods to correspond with their expansion. They now have three different labels; 'Sonoma Vineyards' is the name for their wines which are now widely distributed in the U.S. 'Windsor Vineyards' is their brand name for wines which are sold in California directly or through the mail, and it is the name of the wines which can carry personalized labels. 'Tiburon Vintners' is the third brand name for their wines in economical gallon and half-gallon sizes with national distribution or for some fifths sold directly by the winery.

The quality of his wines he attributes to the fact that his vineyards are in different local areas to take advantage of the Californian climate most suited to each type of grape. His Chardonnay and White (Johannisberg) Riesling, which ripen early, are cultivated on the cool hillsides near the coast while the Pinot Noir, ripening in mid-season, is grown in a more sheltered area. The Cabernet Sauvignon is planted seven miles inland at Alexander Valley where it finds more heat for its late maturing qualities.

'We particularly shun the introduction of chemicals to the wine as is commonly done to insure shelf life and resilience for thousands of miles of shipping,' he explains. 'We make every endeavour to present you with a wine in its authoritatively natural state and a definitive example of its type. . . . We will always be more concerned with quality than quantity.'

In the town of Sonoma are the Buena Vista Vineyards originally planted by Agoston Haraszthy, the cellars of whom were sadly damaged by the San Francisco earthquake of 1906, about 37 years after his death. The restoration has maintained the high traditions of the founder and his sons who succeeded him and today Buena Vista is held in very high regard and is also a State Historical Landmark. The town is also the location for the well-known Sebastiani Vineyards.

In the Livermore Valley further south and to the east an outstanding name is that of the Concannon Vineyard founded in 1883 by James Concannon in

A typical California vineyard after the harvest season.

Almeda County, also the home of Weibel Vineyards which produce excellent sparkling wines by the champagne method. Rudolf Weibel came there after experience in the Champagne area of France and with Swiss wines. Wente Brothers located across the road from Concannon were also founded in 1883 and are another firm to lay their emphasis on the grape names and specialise particularly in white wines and the best grapes such as Chardonnay and Semillon. Their Sauternes are particularly valued.

Still further south in the Santa Clara Valley are vineyards like those of Almadén who also make sparkling wine by the champagne method and sherry type wine by the Spanish *solera* methods, using the correct Palomino grape. They also use the Portuguese Tinta grape from the Douro Valley for their port type wines. Their reputation, despite the vast operations, ranks with the highest and this is particularly encouraging.

The founder here in 1852 was Charles LeFranc, a Frenchman who worked with Etienne Thée of Bordeaux to produce the best that they could from the land. Once again the emphasis is happily on the varietal grape names and the proprietors emphasis that 'fine wines can only be made from a few select, superior varieties of grape. For white wines, the two incomparable wines are the Pinot Chardonnay and the Johannisberg Riesling; for red wines, the Cabernet Sauvignon and the Pinot Noir. For *vin rosé*, the Grenache.' Almadén Grenache *Rosé* is a splendid product, famous throughout the United States and regarded as comparable to the Tavel *Rosé* of France, which uses the same Rhône valley grape.

The Almadén Vineyards in such romantic places as Santa Clara, San Benito, Monterey and elsewhere now total more than 8,100 acres planted with over four million vines, and particular care is taken in the final tasting by a panel of experts. The

A vineyard beneath the hills in California.

company also offers several estate-bottled vintage wines specially selected from their cellars.

Another Santa Clara name is Mirassou Vineyards founded by Pierre Pellier with grape cuttings brought from Bordeaux in 1854. He was succeeded by his son-in-law, Pierre Mirassou and in 1961 the fifth and present generation extended the vineyards into Monterey County. Here again the emphasis is on the varietal wines with high ideals—'It is our desire to follow in the tradition that has set Mirassou apart, family owned and operated with an uncompromising commitment to excellence' is their pledge.

The Mirassou wines are described with particular care, the label carrying the year, growth area, grape name and alcoholic content which, in the case of their 1969 Gamay Beaujolais was twelve per cent. For the 1970 Gewürztraminer 'H', for instance, customers were supplied with details of bottling date, number of bottles produced (10,325), alcohol (11.70 per cent by volume), sugar content, total acid and period recommended for improving in bottle (three to four years).

Visitors are welcomed as in other Californian vineyards, but at Mirassou there is a wine garden where private groups can hold tastings, receptions and luncheons with seating for 125 visitors who eat among the great casks of maturing wine in the 'Cask Room'. Mirassou also uses a mechanical harvester/crusher and has vines for varietal grapes on their own roots where *phylloxera* has not appeared in their modern Soledad vineyards.

There are other notable names in California, among them Charles Krug Winery in the Napa Valley started in 1861 and a training ground for some of the early growers. It is now owned by C. Mondavi & Sons who have expanded the vineyards and done much for wine. The Beaulieu Vineyard is also highly regarded. It was founded in 1900 by yet another Frenchman, Georges de Latour, with cuttings from France. Inland at Modesto in the San Joaquin Valley are the hundred

stainless steel tanks holding the wine of the E. & J. Gallo Winery. Julio and Ernest Gallo, both in their sixties, are a remarkable pair. Sons of an Italian immigrant from Piedmont they began their vineyards after Prohibition on 6,000 dollars they had saved. Within ten years they were doing well, partly due to a team of forceful salesmen they employed plus a strong appreciation of marketing, though they did not seek publicity for themselves. The Gallo brothers were one of the first companies in the new US trade of pop wines, sweet and bubbly, for the young adult market. Although some people look down their noses at their ultra-modern, business-like, selling orientated approach, the Gallo brothers produce and sell a lot of wine. They may not make the best, but the public likes what they do make.

The most southerly area is Cucamonga, inland from Los Angeles, where small quantities of wine are produced in a warm climate. They are not in general of the same standard as farther north, but reflect a pleasant regional character and are much appreciated by wine drinkers.

Looking to the future, one can see wonderful opportunities for California as American demand increases. French and German wines are now so highly priced that the local product must have all the popular market advantages. The Californian problem lies partly in its climate which tends to produce a standard type of wine. There is no Bordeaux versus Burgundy contest here and only occasionally wine that comes up to the best French standards but the middle wines are of good quality.

For a European brought up to drink to French conceptions of excellence comparison must therefore present difficulties. Though fierce sunshine can be a problem, the climate of California is generally so equable that the vines do not have to struggle for life as does the Chardonnay of Chablis or the Riesling of the Mosel. In this struggle against wind, rain, hail, snow and ice, drought and poor sunshine, this thrusting down into hard, sometimes thin, soil by the roots searching for life and nourishment, the vine grows strong, becomes individual. Much the same as the sheltered life usually produces an unimpressive human being, so the sheltered vine, receiving its warmth and mild rain each in due season, can lack distinction.

The Californian vine, too, is in danger of receiving too much attention. When the peasant goes out at one door and the white-coated-scientist strides in at the other he may bring technology and analysis but he quite possibly has booted out sympathy, understanding and instinct. Although the steel vat and the computer are on the march in France and Germany, there are still traditionalists there whose instincts tell them that the oak casks and the old methods produce great and individual wines. Hasten slowly is a motto with particular application in vineyards, and although Germany has many outstanding wine technologists they have yet to produce one great red wine. Some things are possible, some are not.

But this does not mean that there is anything wrong with the better Californian wines. Despite the European ancestry of their grapes, they are simply different. They are softer and less strident, but they have fine qualities, particularly among the whites where competition is not so exciting against European wines as it is with the French reds. The sparkling wines, too, have notable appeal.

Nor should it be taken for granted that the weather in California is always predictable. The 1970 season brought devastating cold and frost, 'heart-breaking' was how one grower described it. Yet although it reduced quantity, the wine that survived was, in his words, 'superlative—a vintage year', through this very concentration.

Even more upsetting was the weather in 1972 when frost in the spring and an overwhelming heat-wave in August made the harvest the smallest for thirty years. Prices have risen accordingly. If such weather changes continue, the growers may well be driven to put the vintage year increasingly on the label. This would be a good thing for the consumer, for the US wine laws only insist that a varietal wine must contain at least fifty-one per cent of the grape it is named after. Such a law, of course, is an open invitation to blending, and all credit to those growers who have refused to take advantage of it in that way. But if a vintage year is inscribed on the label then ninety-five per cent of the wine must, under the same laws, come from the year mentioned which at least goes in some measure to ensure a certain validity.

In Europe winelovers would think very carefully before buying a non-vintage label unless it is Champagne, Sherry or Port. On the other hand the expanding wine market and the increasing consumption might be expected to bring in a new public that is less careful than the old one. All indications, however, are not in this direction.

Interest in wine is proving to be accompanied by interest in caring for wine, for drinking it at the temperature where it will show its best qualities, and for keeping it in the way that it will mature most satisfactorily. A scholastically better educated general public is also a public more educated in purchasing and enjoyment.

The work of the oenologists at the University of California, the Wine Advisory Board of San Francisco and the California Wine Institute are playing an important part in improving Californian wine and encouraging those who really care for it, both among growers and consumers. California deserves its place among the six immortals of future world wine production.

New York State

Taking a lesser but not unimportant rôle in wine production are such other US areas as New York State which comes second with less than ten per cent of American wines, a large proportion being sparkling. The natives often consider them superior to the Californian sparkling wines but connoisseurs do not agree. The Catawba grape is used for them, but there is a considerable amount of still white table wine made from the Delaware grape among others.

Finger Lakes lie between Rochester and Ithaca exactly like the fingers of a hand, and there are a number of vineyards in the region producing sparkling wine and some still wine as well. The growers use both hybrid and native grapes but most of the sparkling wine comes from Catawba and Delaware. The better sparkling wines are fermented in the bottle as in the champagne method. The Pleasant Valley is one of the leading centres and Lake Canandaigua is another with a notable firm at Naples specialising in native wines.

The usual complaint about Eastern States wines is that they have a 'foxy' smell and taste due to the hybrid grapes that even the most skilful wine-

Finger Lakes

☐ Principal wine-growing areas

Lake Keuka at Hammondsport, with vineyards in the distance.

making cannot overcome. They are thus at a disadvantage compared with the Californian product, though regional loyalties dispute this. Some firms in the area defeat the 'foxy' flavour by blending their local grapes with wine from California and this succeeds to a considerable extent, particularly with sparkling wines.

The nearest region to New York itself is the Hudson River Valley, where both dessert and wine grapes are grown some 80 miles from Broadway. Concord and Delaware grapes are used for making table wine but there is also production of red and *rosé* wines using crossbreed grapes. Catawba grapes are also employed.

In the area between Lake Chautauqua and the southern side of Lake Erie there is another considerable vineyard region devoted to Concord grapes. In some ways Concord might have hoped to be the leading American native black grape but unfortunately it does not make wine of any distinction. It is a sturdy grape that produces wine in quantity and can survive in varied climates and different soils but for little purpose where quality is concerned. It suffers from the 'foxy' drawbacks already mentioned and is blended with other wines sometimes for use as Kosher wine. Despite its faults it sells in considerable quantities, possibly

A basket of 'Concord' grapes, grown in New York State.

because of its ready availability.

Along Lake Erie in the Ohio section there are considerable vineyards growing the Catawba grape and various others. Both red and white still wines are made and quality sparkling wines are produced. Again there is an amount of blending with Californian wines for much the same reasons as elsewhere. Wines of quality have, however, been increasingly produced and the best of these have their stout advocates.

In the south of Michigan near Lake Michigan are grown Concord, Catawba, Delaware and other grapes, with Concord predominating. Both sparkling and table wines are made but again there is a general lack of distinction in the end product.

At one time good wine seemed likely to flourish in Virginia but the necessary impetus has been lacking. New Jersey is another area with declining prospects. Because of its climate, California has proved a splendid setting for the European grapes of *Vitis vinifera*, and that State has been amply and generously repaid. But in other States the weather conditions have usually been too much for European vines while the native examples have lacked the necessary qualities to produce wines of fine bouquet and subtle nuances. The stalwart winegrowers persistently cultivating American native grapes deserve to succeed and may eventually do so, but the problems are very real.

In the long years when French wines were cheap there was no need for the winelover to look much further afield, except out of his broad interest in wine. France, as has been said before, can supply all that one would wish for in quality wine, but this very fact has retarded the development of other countries whose opportunity comes with rising French prices. Yet here again France's dominating influence on the EEC wine and agricultural laws will continue to make things difficult for possible wine competitors outside the Common Market, and the extent to which such countries can make agreements, as Cyprus has done, remains to be seen in the years ahead.

It is still true that when one door shuts another opens and the world appetite for wine now stretches from the USA to Japan. So countries which hitherto have had to grow their wine for supply in branded, blended wines, or for consumption behind the political iron curtain, are likely to find in the future new and immense markets in areas they never anticipated.

10

The Rest of Europe

Hungary

On the European front Hungary has long fought valiantly to make her very deserving wines better known. The best have great appeal and merit, but their producers have been caught in a dilemma of whether to use the unpronounceable (to others) Hungarian names or to adopt simpler titles. It has yet to be solved by Monimpex, the government body that controls wine exports. In fact the chosen title for Egri Bikavér, that splendid wine of full bouquet, deep crimson colour and mouth-filling warmth and flavour, was Bull's Blood, immediately calculated to turn every woman, and most men, away from its selection. Yet it stands comparison with Gigondas or other Rhône wines and is more robust than most Italians.

All its qualities spring from the mighty Kadarka grape, the fount of the best Hungarian reds of which Egri Bikavér is the leader, grown on the soft volcanic soil at Eger, that town of many cellars guarding precious barrels. Other grapes are blended with it, as in the Rhône wines. The best examples are aged in cask and bottle, and it was Egri Bikavér that sustained the men of Eger when they repulsed a lengthy Turkish siege of their town. Copious draughts were brought to them, tradition says, by their womenfolk. It is excellent with roasts and duck.

Some of Hungary's finest white wines grow on the slopes of extinct volcanoes looking down on the lovely waters of Lake Balaton. So from Mount Badacsonyi comes Badacsonyi Szurkebarat, a delightful dry, full-bodied but fragrant wine for poultry or white meat, sometimes called Greyfriars of Badacsonyi. It is made from the Pinot Gris grape known as Rulander in Germany. Another attractive wine is Balatoni Riesling, medium-sweet but balanced enough to please most tastes. A third white wine is from the Wälschriesling grape, a relative of the Riesling. Badacsonyi Keknyelu is a wine of fine bouquet, aromatic, and really a dessert wine. There is also Balatoni Furmint, medium-sweet as one might expect since it is from the grape that, with more complicated treatment, makes the great rich, golden Tokaj, one of the noblest dessert wines in the world. Furmint was brought by Walloon settlers in the thirteenth century and is Hungary's most famous white wine grape.

Mori Ezerjo is named after another yellow-white grape grown to the north-east of Lake Balaton at Mor, where there is much sand which has made the vines safe from *phylloxera,* as we saw with the red Colares wine grown near Lisbon. This is a wine I have greatly enjoyed. It is very dry and of interesting bouquet and goes well with fish. For those who like a sweet wine there is Debroi Harslevelu, comparable to the lesser sweet French wines round Bordeaux. There are a number of red wines beside Egri Bikavér and there is also Nemes Kadar, a very attractive offering of strength and appeal for a *rosé.*

Hungarian sparkling wines are particularly well-made and are exported under the name of Hungaria, both *demi-sec* and extra-dry, the latter being to my mind especially good value and quite worthy of its place in the market. Prices of all the above wines are still reasonable and if the Hungarians maintain this approach they should reap the reward.

One cannot leave Hungary without writing on Tokaj, and here again the prices asked for this carefully-made dessert wine are still reasonable. The Furmint grapes are used, but as they mature irregularly two types of wine are made. One is Tokaj Szamorodni in which the grapes are pressed together. The other is Tokaj Aszu, comparable

Vineyards on the shore of Lake Balaton.

An eighteenth-century map showing the wine regions around Tokaj.

with Château d'Yquem as an after dinner offering. The picking of some of the grapes is delayed into autumn until *pourriture noble* appears, when they are gathered in *puttonys* or buckets. The number of buckets of these late grapes added to the wine made from those maturing earlier is shown on the label as three, four or five *puttonys*. The more *puttonys*, the greater the richness of this golden dessert wine.

The top version of the wine is called Tokaj Aszu Essencia, and this had not been exported since the Second World War until Berry Brothers and Rudd of St James's Street, London, obtained the first 3,000 bottles of the 1964 vintage allowed to leave Hungary. This I tasted in 1972 in the firm's lovely old cellars dating back to the eighteenth century, with a frontage painted in black and gold that makes the building one of the handsomest in London. Dark, gold-brown, almost cloying, the Essencia was a superb experience and at £11 a half-litre bottle reflected its rarity, though much higher prices would be expected at auction. Its aromatic undertones and bouquet of many nuances made outstanding a wine that otherwise had something of a tremendous cream sherry in the flavour. Although traditionally recommended as sexually stimulating, I regret to say that I did not notice any exciting reaction but the sample was not, at this price, perhaps large enough for that purpose.

Austria

Everyone likes the Austrians because they are a jolly, carefree people with a great gift of survival, and that goes also for their wines. One has not lived unless the pleasures of Grinzing have been discovered in the Vienna suburbs, where the wine-houses hang a leafy bundle of twigs outside to indicate that the latest vintage is ready, the local *heurigen* wine, dry and sometimes a little sharp, which, however, tastes like nectar when drunk in the right company in the open air. It may, or may not, be grown by the proprietor but he will put before you lavish helpings of cheese and sausages as you sit at garden tables and someone plays a zither—could it be the Third Man?

Austria has a number of wines though none of them is great, but since the vineyards are close to the capital the Viennese drink as much wine as they do coffee, a great deal of it from the Grüner Veltliner grape which makes a medium dry white wine of considerable charm and freshness. It is certainly a great drinking wine, much as is Beaujolais among reds in France, and is characteristic of the Weinviertel area where so much is planted. It travels well and is now quite widely available in Britain through such shippers as Hatch, Mansfield.

On the opposite side of Vienna, to the south, lie tragic Mayerling, making wine from the Veltliner grape, and Gumpoldskirchen, whose name as a wine town is probably better known to the outside world than any other in Austria. Its wine is certainly fragrant and fruity and even produces Auslese, so let us give credit to the soil though the catchy name is a help too. On the label Gumpoldskirchen is linked with the grape used.

In Wachau, to the west, you will drink good wine at Durnstein where the faithful Blondel found Richard the Lionheart in prison, but the name of note here is the Lenz Moser Company whose cellars centre on Rohrendorf.

Indeed Dr Lenz Moser has given his name to a system of planting high vines well apart from each other, instead of the more common, rather crowded, rows. The firm sends a large amount of Schluck abroad, a wine made from the Sylvaner grape and

Vineyards at Gumpoldskirchen, Austria.

sometimes *spritzig*, or slightly prickly. In addition to modest wines, Lenz Moser produces the very fine Apetloner Rheinriesling Feine Auslese from time to time. I remember the pleasure of tasting the rich 1969 vintage, full and luscious as an Auslese should be.

The Prince Metternich estates dating back to 1170 are recognised as among the best in Austria. All the wines are estate-bottled and include Schloss Grafenegg, named after the family home near Krems, from the Veltliner grape, an excellent dry white wine. Another notable wine is produced at the town of Rust in Bergenland where the climate is very warm. It is called Ruster Ausbruch and has something in common with Hungary's Tokaj, though it is not made to the same intense standards. The Furmint grape is used with others and the grapes are picked later and make a sweet dessert wine of some character. The area round Rust is another of the few that escaped the *phylloxera* because of sandy soil and there is even a wine called Sandweine.

Although the grapes mentioned, plus Müller-Thurgau and Sylvaner, are the chief varieties, there are a number of local names linked with Veltliner and others such as Neuburger, Zierfandler and Weissburgunder. There is some red wine production using the Blauburgunder, and in Styria they make an interesting *rosé* wine called Schilcherwein from the local Wildbacher grape.

Austria is clearly a country with a wine future, both for quality wines that will keep improving with increasing technical skill and as a source of cheaper wines for widescale use.

Yugoslavia

One of the problems for Yugoslavia in the immediate future is her relationship with the EEC.

Much of her refreshing white wine has sold well in Britain as Yugoslav Riesling or Lutomer Riesling, from the district of that name in the north-east of the country. The steady, warm climate does not produce wines of the best German quality but they are certainly pleasing and, although marketing is done by the State and its agencies, there is still a lot of individuality in the vineyards. There is a considerable variety of grape from Riesling and Sylvaner to Chardonnay, Traminer, Sauvignon and Furmint, under Yugoslav names, the grape variety being carried on the label.

The Common Market system of safeguarding EEC wines by imposing higher prices on outside competitors seeking to enter, will hit Yugoslavia hard unless negotiations can reduce the effect. One possibility is that the wines will not be able to use the German names of their grapes, and this will be a test of their acceptability to the public without the titles they have borne so long. All this, however, is still being decided.

With an average annual production of 5,546,000 hectolitres* of wine, and eleventh place among world producers, the matter is important for Yugoslavia. In Slovenia is the home of 'Tiger Milk', carrying the tiger head on the label, a sweetish wine from the Ranina grape near Kapela. It is usually slightly dearer than the drier Rieslings such as

Horgos. Dalmatia has many very acceptable red wines, often high in alcohol, as holidaymakers visiting there soon find out, and the whites are also wines of some strength and to be drunk with according care. Teltscher Brothers and Clode & Baker are leading British importers.

Perhaps Yugoslavia is best known in the alcohol world for Slivovitz, that plum brandy which is the national drink of Serbia and supporter of all Yugoslavs in moments of stress. But when Yugoslavia has solved its problems, which include some easier naming of its wines, it will play an important part in meeting world demand for good wine.

Bulgaria

In recent years these wines have become more widely known abroad as Vinimpex, the Government organisation, extended its activities. In Britain they are represented by Cock, Russell Vintners whose list includes several known by their grapes. Among these, Cabernet is a red of high quality while Gamza is the most popular red in Bulgaria, slightly lighter than the Cabernet.

Among the white wines is Misket, a medium dry of crisp, fresh flavour and Sylvaner, medium sweet with a pleasant bouquet. The same firm also markets two branded wines of which Boyar is a

A vineyard scene on the island of Hvar, Yugoslavia.

robust red and Sofiya, a white wine.

The winemaking here is more strictly controlled than in some of its neighbours, and the future appeal of Bulgarian wines will depend upon the way this control is used. Bulgaria has always grown the vine, but the effects of the last two wars and political change have not helped the situation which, however, is now improving.

Switzerland

Visitors know very well the attractive qualities of Swiss wines, most of which are consumed by the Swiss themselves. The Cantons of Neuchâtel, Vaud and Valais are the largest producers and winegrowing is an important occupation along the shores of Lake Geneva.

In Valais the Fendant grape, known as Gutedel in Germany and Chasselas in Alsace, produces a rather light white wine of attractive bouquet, dry and not too full.

There is also a white wine made from the Swiss Müller-Thurgau grapes called Johannisberg, which should not be confused with the great German vineyards of Schloss Johannisberg on the Rhine. A pleasing red wine is Dole, produced from a blend of Pinot Noir and Gamay grapes, rather soft but with fair body. It is regarded as the best Swiss product among reds, but when I was last in that country I was very taken with a pleasing red wine labelled under the name of Chemin de Fer, much better than one would expect a 'railway' wine to be and similar to claret. I have not been able to find any further examples however.

Behind the famous Château of Chillon on Lake Geneva the traveller by river steamer may see high terraces planted with vines and cultivation is particularly hard work, as on the steeper slopes of the Rhine and Mosel. The white wines of Neuchâtel are perhaps among the most attractive. The soil is chalk and they benefit as do most whites in such vineyards, though a little on the light side. When bottled young they often retain a pleasant sparkle.

Fèchy village and vineyards in Canton Vaud, Switzerland.

Greece

The Greeks had a god of wine, Dionysius, when the rest of the world was scarcely civilised and that country has been producing interesting and varied wines ever since from a remarkably large number of different vines. Unfortunately, for most western palates, many of the wines are resinated and this petrol-like flavour is an acquired taste. I have been assured that, drunk under blue skies in a sailing boat gently rocking on blue seas, it is ideal, but I have not so far had the opportunity of sipping it under those conditions. Some of the best wines are exported by Achaia-Clauss of Patras, who have large, modern premises, and Norton and Langridge of London are their helpful agents.

If you are offered Retsina you will have a white wine to which a quantity of resin or pine essence was originally added as a preservative before the modern cork and bottle were invented. The Greeks have been drinking it so long that it has become the national drink, an honour it shares with Ouzo, a lively apéritif doubly distilled from anis with a mixture of aromatic herbs and a high alcoholic content. It is somewhat dry with a delicate flavour.

There are, however, two very pleasant wines called Demestica, one white and one red, both

Château of Chillon, on Lake Geneva, Switzerland.

140

being light and dry and very good accompaniments to the delights of Greek food such as *moussaka*. Another white from Achaia Clauss is the dry Santa Helena with a particularly good bouquet, like almonds, while Castel Danielis is a distinguished red, rather better and heavier than the Demestica red.

The Achaia-Clauss company dates back to 1845 when a German from Bavaria, Gustav Clauss, came to work in Patras. On a nearby hill he built a small hut and bought a local vineyard, and his wine proved so popular that the firm was founded in 1861. The garden looks across the sea and marble plaques record distinguished visitors of the past who admired the view. In 1920 it was bought by V. Antonopoulos of Patras and became a Greek company, today managed by his sons.

Another Greek wine importer is Capital Wine and Travers, who list wines from many countries including Turkey and China, in their cellars. Among the Greek wines are Mavrodaphne, the sweet red dessert wine of Patras, and Samos, from the islands of Samos, made from the Muscat grape, also sweet.

The leading wine firms apart, the Greeks are rather easy-going in their attitude towards wine. They have much to offer, but greater stringency in

standards and the use of modern wine technology are needed to make the best of their products.

Turkey

This is a country which sent wine to western Europe right up to the First World War, somewhat strange for a land where the religion forbade the drinking of wine. When Islam was no longer the official religion, interest arose again in vine-growing and some of the Turkish wines that reach Britain are, to my taste, well worth the journey. Capital Wine and Travers import three, of which Buzbag, the dry red wine bottled in Turkey, has a fine body, deep red robe and interesting bouquet. I have enjoyed the red Trakya 1970, somewhat lighter, and there is a medium dry white Trakya as well. Villa Doluca is a white, on the dry side, having a distinctively unusual but pleasing bouquet, with fine nuances.

The State authorities have gone to considerable trouble to improve vinification methods and to introduce modern techniques and machinery, and their wines go to Germany and Scandinavia as well as to Britain. As with some of the other countries reviewed here, Turkey has important prospects as a wine exporter. At present there is a rather large variety of grapes, but concentration on the best of these, as shown in some of the wines mentioned above, should bring further recognition.

Cyprus

One associates Sir Walter Raleigh with the discovery of tobacco and with the Tower of London, but hardly with Cyprus. Yet in his days in high favour with Queen Elizabeth I, he obtained the monopoly of Cyprus wines entering England. Today Cyprus wines, and more particularly Cyprus sherry, have a large share of the market and claim to be Britain's third largest supplier after Spain and France.

This has all come about in a decade for in 1960 Cyprus exported 750,000 gallons to the UK whereas in 1971 it had reached 4,525,000 gallons. In fact Cyprus has only made a real effort to capture some of the world market since 1957, inspired by earlier British encouragement to improve her vineyards.

The secret of its success lies in a rationalisation of the industry, modern equipment, a willingness to employ expert guidance, and careful research into other countries' requirements. Most of the vineyards are in small plots. Like California, Cyprus claims that its vintage hardly varies from year to year because of the even climate and the unfailing amount of sunshine. The main areas are Limassol and Paphos, using mostly the local Mavron grapes for red wine and Xynisteri for white.

Othello is a dry red, light in the mouth but of attractive colour, that is blended from Mavron and Opthalmo grapes, and Afames is another red. Among white wines are Aphrodite, on the dry side,

A grape harvest at Platres, Cyprus.

A vineyard at Rishon-le-Zion, Israel.

made near that lovely lady's birthplace and distinctly aromatic, while St Panteleimon is a rich dessert wine, often served in Cyprus with cakes. A very pleasant semi-sparkling white wine with an interesting pale gold colour is Bellapais, the first *pétillant* wine to be made in Cyprus. Bass Charrington Vintners' sweet branded wine called Carousel is made from Cyprus wine.

Perhaps Commandaria, a full, sweet dessert wine, is individually the best known of the country's products. It claims to be 2,800 years old, the most ancient in the world, and referred to by Greek poets. The Knights Templar gave the wine its present name and it was probably from Commandaria that Sir Walter Raleigh made his profits when it was brought to Britain.

The wine is prepared in the mountain villages using a blend of Mavron and Xynisteri (the mixture of white and red grapes is not uncommon in this part of the world). It is given a long maturing period and may then be subject to further blending to ensure the right flavour.

The Cyprus sherries exported to Britain fall into three categories according to their strength. They range from Pale Dry to Medium and Cream. From the terms of the agreement between Cyprus and the EEC for two years from 1973 it appears that eighty-five per cent of the previous exports can be maintained without too heavy a price increase.

The two years' grace will be important to Cyprus for in this period she has the opportunity to make her products comply with EEC requirements. From the number of other countries, including several of those described, which have reached agreement with the EEC it is clear that the future for wines outside the Common Market may not be as difficult as was once feared.

Israel

The wines of Israel are now sold in more than forty countries from Great Britain and the United States to Italy, Japan and Mexico, which is not surprising since nearly every book of the Bible mentions wine and grapes many times. The Talmud, too, lays down laws for making wine and mentions scores by name.

Vine-growing has gone on in Israel for nearly a hundred years and was the first form of agriculture developed in the Jewish settlements. Vines were brought from France by Baron Edmond de Rothschild who built the first modern wine cellars at Rishon-le-Zion and Zichron Yaacov towards the end of the nineteenth century. They grow in the south round Beer Sheva, in Shefela where Samson fought his battles and fell in love with Delilah the Philistine, to the north of the Plain of Sharon, and in Upper Galilee.

The quality of the wines and spirits produced is controlled by the Israel Wine Institute at Rehovot, which also carries out research in its own laboratories while a pilot vineyard explores marketing possibilities.

One of the largest of the several companies is Carmel Oriental Ltd which operates the original vineyards set up by Baron de Rothschild on the edge of Mount Carmel. It is the trade name for the winegrowers' co-operative. Among its red wines are Cabernet Sauvignon and Carignan, and among whites are Sauvignon Blanc and Semillon, dry and semi-dry respectively. Hebrew names, however, are increasingly used.

Other companies include Eliaz Winecellars with its Binyamina red and white, and Caesarea and Muscat dessert wines, and Tnuva Winecellars with Arad red and white and its Independence dessert wine.

Vines have been imported from a number of other countries besides France and, with local strains, cover a very wide range of wines. The dessert wines, like the brandy, are matured in oak casks. Many of the wines are bought abroad for Jewish ritual purposes, but the wines of Israel are of good standard and interesting in their own right. The industry has greatly increased since the establishment of Israel in 1948. Producing something approaching three-quarters of Israel's wines, the Carmel Wine Company has offices in both London and New York.

11

Australia and . . . Other Countries

Australia

Vines have been in Australia almost as long as western man, for when the First Fleet sailed there in 1788 with its cargo of mixed desirables Captain Arthur Phillip, who was in command, took with him cuttings of vines that he had gathered *en route*, some of them at the Cape of Good Hope. This famous first Governor had no sooner reached New South Wales than he was hopefully planting his vines in what is now the heart of Sydney. When they did not do too well he made another planting effort at Parramatta, some fifteen miles away, which was more successful. Parramatta is still a name in wine history for it was from this valley that Gregory Blaxland sent a small amount of red wine from his grapes to London in 1822. The Royal Society of Arts promptly awarded him a silver medal and when he repeated the venture in 1828 he was given a gold, the wine being described as similar to claret.

So Australia can fairly claim to have been exporting wine to Britain for 150 years, for others followed Blaxland's venture and there is something rather touching in this determination to show the people in London what the founding fathers of Australia were producing and how well they were doing it.

It was fortunate for the growth of the wine industry that the early efforts were made in New South Wales. Time has shown that, with Victoria, this was one of the best parts of the continent. Today the Hunter River Valley, the Murrumbidgee Valley, and the Corowa vineyard area are all great names there. South Australia is now just as famous a producer, and in the area close to the territory border there are Coonawarra, Langhorne Creek and Barossa Valley among leading names. Tahbilk and Great Western are noted names in Victoria. But apart from a small district at Roma, 300 miles west of Brisbane in Queensland, and round Perth, Western Australia, the wine is made mostly in the south-east.

A remarkable young man arrived in Australia in 1824. He was James Busby of Edinburgh and his father, a civil engineer, had come there to plan the Sydney water supply. Strangely for a Scot, young Busby had long abhorred whisky and loved wine. Possibly he had heard about the award of a silver medal to Blaxland, for he had already decided Australia was an ideal country for cultivating the vine before he left Britain. Indeed he rushed

Vineyards in the Barossa Valley.

to France and passed several months there studying viticulture and questioning *vignerons*. On the voyage to Australia he set all this down as a book, *A Treatise on the Cultivation of the Vine and the Art of Making Wine*. Within three months of reaching Sydney he had received a grant of 2,000 acres in the Hunter River Valley where he put his theories into practice.

He did this successfully enough and called the vineyards Kirton, after his birthplace near Edinburgh. It was to produce vintages for exactly a hundred years until 1924, and there is still a Chablis-type wine called Kirton made in Australia, though not from his site. James went to work as a schoolteacher for a time in these early days and arrived on the Parramatta River. Naturally he planted a vineyard and began writing another book.

From all this experience he decided that better vines were needed, and in 1830 he returned to Europe for a four months' tour of France, Germany and Spain and in due course returned to Australia with more than three hundred and fifty varieties. In this way he pre-dated Agoston Haraszthy's journey round Europe in 1861 on behalf of the Californian experiments.

It is particularly interesting that these two men, both expert growers at opposite ends of the earth, decided that local grape varieties were not good enough and only the best vine of Europe, the *Vitis vinifera*, could really make great wine.

Hitherto the grapes used in Australia had not given very notable results. Busby had found that the grapes brought originally from South Africa gave the wine a 'nauseous and earthy taste' which must have shocked him after the French clarets, popular in Scotland, on which he had cultivated his fondness for wine. The Verdelho grape, used in Portugal for making white port and also in Madeira, had done comparatively well in Australia, but now, as Busby's work progressed, the continent's growers had first-class vines that happily took to the native soil. Today the leading Australian vineyards are descended from vines first planted at Kirton, and it is a sad thought that nothing was done to save this historic vineyard as a national landmark.

The soil of the Hunter Valley is so happily varied that it can produce a range of wines. There is clay and gravel and volcanic soil and also lighter earth while the climate, with cold winters and reasonably hot summers, is not unlike that of Burgundy. Here grow red wines made from the Hermitage and Syrah grapes, those stalwarts of the Rhône Valley in France, and among whites, Semillon, Verdelho and Ugni Blanc, the latter used to make the dry white wines of Cassis in France, and called Trebbiano in Italy.

For many years the Australian vineyards were family affairs with such names as Penfold, Lindeman, Seppelt, McWilliam and Angove as leaders.

A winery at Waikerie in the Murray Valley.

In the last few years a number of companies have gone public or sold out to bigger interests, such as Tulloch and McLaren Vale Wine Estates bought by Reed, the English paper combine, and the C. H. Morris properties acquired by Reckitt and Colman in Rutherglen, Victoria. Allied Breweries of London has obtained the famous Seaview winery at McLaren Vale in conjunction with an Australian brewery.

Wine consumption has risen from two million gallons in 1956 to twenty-four million in 1970, all in keeping with the increase in other parts of the world. Dry red wines account for nearly half of the market and dry white for about a quarter, but although the Australian Wine Centre in London has been a pioneer for its country sales have been declining in Britain and are likely to fall further under Common Market conditions.

The Australian problem has largely been one of shipping costs, which must be reflected in price, and considering this factor the charges have been reasonable in the past. The red table wines are now often labelled under the name of the grape, although French descriptions are also frequently given to indicate the type of wine.

Today's wines are of good quality, certainly to my mind on the same level as those of California and Italy. In some cases, better. The old image of

Winery emblem at Château Tahbilk.

Australian burgundy tonic wine is being deservedly left behind. It has been a handicap in the past.

I have enjoyed a number of Australian wines and I recommend them and only hope that the EEC price regulations will not make them too expensive. Australians, however, have no cause to fear the wine future. Japan is rapidly awakening to the charm of wine and Australia has boldly challenged California on its own doorstep for the American market. The Barossa Valley Co-operative is exporting its Cabernet Sauvignon and Johannisberg Riesling to a big US supermarket chain and other Australian companies are to follow.

Among Australian wines I have recently tasted with pleasure are McWilliam's Dry Friar from Great Western, an attractive sherry-type. Their Private Bin Riesling has crisp, refreshing qualities, and the fine wines they produce have long been famous, especially those from Mount Pleasant in the Hunter River Valley. In charge here for many years was Maurice O'Shea, who studied wine in France and raised quality standards on his return home. Another pleasing white is Tahbilk Estate Marsanne, with sufficient attractions to justify its claimed likeness to Chablis. Here again a great Australian grower, Eric Purbrick, has made the wines famous and the cellars, also called Château Tahbilk, have been officially classified as buildings

of historical interest. They date back to 1860.

Seaview has always been an outstanding name and under the enterprising new proprietors will undoubtedly expand further. Seaview Cabernet Shiraz 1967 was a splendid red that went admirably with roast saddle of Australian lamb, I remember. The vineyards date from 1850 when they were founded by an Englishman, George Manning.

I have invariably found Penfold's Dalwood Hermitage very close to the Hermitage of the Rhône Valley, with the body and fullness one would expect of this notable red wine. They also make an interesting Private Bin Riesling, sherry-type wines, and dessert wines of quality. The founder was Dr Christopher Penfold of Sussex, who had been a medical practitioner at Brighton and was an advocate of the medicinal value of wine like many later doctors. He practised near Adelaide but eventually gave this up to devote himself to wine-growing and died in 1870 when his widow, like the famous *veuves* of Champagne, carried on his work.

Another outstanding name in Australian wine is that of Seppelt which has long been represented in Britain. The first time I tasted their fine Great Western Imperial Reserve, a truly great sparkling wine, was in the London cellars. Another fine wine is Seppelt's Arawatta hock, a very dry white. The company owes its name to Joseph Seppelt, born in Silesia in 1813, who became head of a family business making liqueurs and, of all things, snuff! The political troubles of 1848 sent him abroad, like Agoston Haraszthy, who went to California. Seppelt, however, sailed for Adelaide and took a considerable number of his employees with him. They settled on land they called Seppeltsfield near Tanunda and, although he first planted tobacco and then gave it up for corn, he also planted a vineyard. Some of his employees left him to join the gold rush to Bendigo, but the wine prospered and when he died in 1868 he was succeeded by his son Benno.

By the mid-nineteenth century the authorities in England were encouraging emigration to Australia and among those sailing in 1850 was Thomas Hardy of Honiton in Devon. He was 20 years old and took a job on a cattle station. He subsequently did well enough to purchase land near Adelaide and plant Grenache and Syrah grapes. By 1859 he was shipping some of the wine to London. In due course he bought other properties and when he died in 1912, outliving two of the three sons who had helped to run the firm, the business was one of the biggest in South Australia. There are estates in both the Barossa Valley and the Murray Valley. The wines include Cabinet Claret, St Thomas Burgundy and Old Castle Riesling. They also make Hardy's Fine Old Tawny, a port type of high standard.

Many firms make brandy and Angove's St Agnes' Very Old is an excellent example. Yet another doctor was the founder, Dr W. T. Angove, and this Cornishman settled near Adelaide and planted a vineyard to make red wine. It is said that his brandy, perhaps the most famous of the many wines and spirits Angove produce, was named St Agnes after the village where his family had lived in Cornwall. His eldest son was Tom Angove, who set up on the Murray River in 1910 and was one of the most successful growers there. Other Angove wines include Brightlands Burgundy, Tregrehan Claret and Bookmark Riesling.

A third doctor to found a great company was Henry John Lindeman, who left the Royal Navy to settle with his wife in Australia in 1840. He started on a tributary of the Hunter River and planted a vineyard he called Cawarra where he made dry white table wines, but he later bought other vineyards to extend his range, among them Porphyry, and Lindeman's Porphyry is a notable Sauternes type today, though the original vineyard is not now used. The Lindeman firm also makes Porphyry Pearl, a sparkling wine. Their Sunshine vineyard on the Hunter River is well known for its dry white wines, among them Sunshine Riesling. Yet another wine is Lindeman's Coolalta White Burgundy. The firm was recently bought by the Philip Morris tobacco combine.

The Australian wine story is as romantic as any other in the trade, and if the Australians themselves had been less down-to-earth people they would have made the native product far more famous than it is. But time is on Australia's side and now that international finance has brought its millions to the takeover scene the growers should not lack the funds to exploit their wines by better marketing and promotion.

South Africa

The cellars of the Cape can boast buildings as splendid as any in the world for wine-making, and in some ways their story has a good deal in common with that of California and Australia. The original Dutch settlers planted vineyards at the Cape from their first arrival, and in the middle of the seventeenth century, a hundred years before Australia was discovered, South African vineyards were flourishing. What the wine was like nobody can now know and allowance must be made for the settlers' pride in their industry. But once again, as in the story of other lands, it was a notable man who gave the lead to his companions.

Jan van Riebeeck has earned fame as the colony's founder and after he landed in 1652 with his little company he planted vines three years later. In his diary for 2 February 1659, he duly recorded, 'Today, God be praised, wine pressed for the first time from Cape grapes, and from the virgin must, fresh from the coop, a sample taken.' It was from the Cape that Captain Arthur Phillip was to take his vines to Australia a century later. During the period in between, religious persecutions in France caused the Huguenots to emigrate. By a happy chance for the young wine-growing industry 200 came to settle in the Cape and brought with them a considerable knowledge of viticulture, so the South African wines of today have inherited much of the French experience.

Following van Riebeeck's prayer of thanksgiving an equally admirable, but more lovable, character came to power in the Cape. This was Simon van der Stel who had the energy and ability of van Riebeeck but accompanied these qualities with a love of good living and ceremony. As Governor in 1690, he set his fellow citizens a splendid example in the beautifully designed buildings at Groot Constantia where he made one of the great wines of history on this estate. The wine

South Africa

☐ Principal wine-growing areas

0   50   100   150 Km.
0   50   Mi.

A view of vineyards beneath the mountains in Western Province, South Africa.

was called Constantia after his wife and it was exported across the world to England, Holland and France. The Huguenots worked enthusiastically in the vineyards, encouraged perhaps by the thought that they were sending a fine wine back to the land they had left behind. The grape is thought to have been the white grape called Muscadelle, used in blends round Bordeaux where it gives a suggestion of Muscat odour to the wine, a relation carried across the country to Alsace where it appears again in the Muscat d'Alsace.

Tragically enough, over two hundred years, the wine lost its appeal. Perhaps other wines became better made or some of the magic went from the workers as the original Huguenots and their skills died out. Groot Constantia is now State-owned and the wine is still made, but it is a medium wine and not a great one.

The power in South Africa is the Co-operative Wine Growers Association, known by its initials as KWV. It was founded in 1918 and benefited from the reintroduction of Imperial Preference in 1925, for Britain has long been an importer of South African wines. Only the bedevilment of race politics has affected interest in the wines in recent times. Now that Britain has entered the EEC there are further complications, all unfortunate, for South Africa, like Australia, has much to offer winewise.

South African sherries have won deserved renown and it is often difficult to tell them from the lesser sherries of Spain, a considerable compliment to the abilities of the makers.

The excellent medium dry Onzerust and the richer Golden Acre are good examples. Mymering is a pale extra dry and there is also the Paarlsack trio of extra dry, medium dry and cream. Before the present excellence was reached it was necessary to discover that flor, the yeast that is the basis of sherry, was present in South Africa. This was as recent as 1933 when research work at the University of Stellenbosch showed how sherry could be made. The *solera* system of Spain was also adopted and the way opened for a great addition to world wines. Normally one would talk of a sherry-type, but South African sherry is so close to the Spanish original, and the methods are so similar, that only a trade expert can tell the best apart. Other sherry ranges are Ravendrost, Cape House, Marievale and R.S.L. The more delicate sherries come from Stellenbosch, Paarl and Tulbagh while the heavier ones are made in the Worcester, Robertson and Montagu districts. The South African port-type wines are not so close to the originals as are the sherries and the flavour is somewhat different, but there are good South African brandies and the mandarin-flavoured base makes Van der Hum a liqueur to stand with any other.

At work in a vineyard near Paarl, Western Province.

The warm climate of South Africa sets problems in table wine-making, especially with the white, but hock types have been commercially successful. Steen is a good example of white wine, dry and estate bottled from the KWV. KWV also has Steen Late Vintage, a medium dry wine. Among reds, Roodeberg is a robust, full-bodied wine. Steen, incidentally, is the name of a grape variety for white wines and is only found in South Africa. For red wine, Cabernet and Syrah grapes are used, and there are many wines with their own names though the KWV wines are recognised as leaders.

Agricultural-area vineyard workers in southern Chile.

South America

Chile has long, perhaps too long, been hailed as the wine supplier of the future. Most importing countries are glad to buy Chilean wine because the standard is very acceptable and the price reasonable, although one would not call the wines great. About a hundred years ago French experts were used to help replant the best local vineyards with Cabernet grapes for red wine and Sauvignon for white. The man responsible was Silvestre Ochagavia and his action earned him another of those titles that posterity rather than contemporaries bestow, Father of Chilean Viticulture.

His example of importing *vignerons* and cuttings led the Chilean Government to support the industry with further supplies and, in due course, to finance co-operative cellars. There are now strict laws concerning wine so that production by growers is limited and this has led to their readiness to export surplus wine. But even here there are further regulations which forbid the export of poor wine. All this, of course, is good for foreign consumers!

So one can always buy a Chilean wine with a certain amount of confidence. It is much more consistent than South American politics. The winemaking methods, like the best grapes, are French from Bordeaux and though the soil in the best central region of the country has quite a lot of limestone the red Cabernet grapes do very well there.

In fact it is mostly under such a title as 'Chilean Cabernet' that you will meet them in this country, among the stockists being Harveys of Bristol. They are smooth, with a good nose, deep claret colour, satisfactory texture and a lingering aftertaste. Many are as good as the lesser Bordeaux wines from which they spring and they compete effectively with them in price.

Riesling and a local grape called Pais, a descendant of Spanish grapes brought in before the replantings, make somewhat lesser wines further south.

It is rather interesting that, as in California, wine-growing started with missionaries who wanted the wine for altar purposes. In the north wine is made from the muscat grape and there are fortified wines like port and sherry. Apart from the grapes mentioned there are also examples of Pinot Noir, Pinot Blanc, Folle Blanche and Merlot. Sparkling wines are made but Cabernet remains the best export.

Recently Seagrams of USA have arranged to act as United States and Canadian distributors for seventeen Chilean wine producers, each producer's wine being marketed under his own trademark. This farsighted agreement will help to meet the increasing demand in these two countries, and some of the Chilean firms are large ones. Since it has been suggested that the increasing rate of USA consumption alone could rise in another ten or fifteen years to a level that would equal world production, Chilean wines may yet come truly into their own.

Argentina, running parallel with Chile down South America, has an even larger wine production and ranks in the first six of the world, but the quality is not of the same standard and it is not among the important exporters. The department of Mendoza on the Chilean border provides the major proportion. However, while Chilean wine has been made under French influence, Argentinian is made on Italian lines, which in the past have been less exact. Recent strict laws, however, have tightened up procedures and Argentina seems a country of great possibilities in future.

The red wine is made from the Malbec grape and the white from a variety called Criollas, brought to the country by the Jesuits. Argentina, unlike Chile, has suffered from *phylloxera*, which has hampered improvement.

Vines near Ténès in Algeria.

North Africa

Both Algeria and Morocco produce good wines in large quantities, but it has been the custom in the past rather to look down on them, an attitude perhaps inspired by French determination to praise their home-grown product.

Like Argentina, the wine output of Algeria is in the front ranks of world production, and French control made great use of these wines for blending. With Algerian independence in 1962 many of the French growers left for their own country and it is these growers who, settled in Roussillon and Languedoc, are there raising the standards of V.D.Q.S. wines. The grapes used in Algeria, in fact, include the Carignan and Cinsault of the Midi for reds, and Ugni Blanc for whites.

Most Algerian wines, then, are good *vin ordinaire*, though there are better examples of at least V.D.Q.S. standards, but production is on very commercial, well-regulated lines that aim at quantity rather than any very high quality. They are coarse and dark by French wine standards but usually of good alcoholic content where the reds are concerned, all these factors being due to the hot sun. Recently official efforts have aimed at improvement.

Morocco is another country that owes its improved production to French settlers and the Government has taken considerable interest in the vineyards, with controls on quality and export. These wines, and those of Tunisia, have similarities to Algerian and use similar grapes but there are not quite as good prospects for future development as in that country. Tunisia has passed wine laws and has an *Appellation Contrôlée* system, which should regulate products—and ensure quality, but in most cases it is necessary to drink the wines when they are young as the climate causes early maturity.

All these countries, however, could be future providers if world demand had to turn from the traditional producers of good wine because of the high prices reached. There will always be wine for a thirsty world and it should grow better as standards are raised!

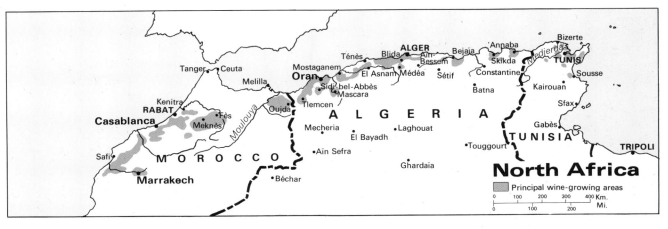

North Africa

Principal wine-growing areas

Some Memorable Menus

The wine trade at home and abroad is generous in hospitality to its friends. Outstanding meals that admirably matched wine and food are among my happiest memories. Some of them are listed here, both as a personal recollection of things past and as examples of superb choices.

The Vintage Dinner
Held at Fishmongers' Hall, City of London
October 29, 1973

Consommé à la Royale	*El Corregidor Oloroso Secco (Sandeman)*
Homard à la Newburg	*Bâtard-Montrachet, 1966 (Gagnard-Delagrange)*
Bouchée de Ris de Veau	*Château Haut Brion, Graves, 1964*
Filet de Boeuf au Primeurs	*Château Mouton-Rothschild, Pauillac, 1962*
Timbale Elysée	*Graacher Himmelreich Auslese Eiswein 1971 (Freiherr von Schorlemer)*
Les Noix	*Sandeman 1945 (Bottled in Oporto)*
Café	*Rémy Martin Grande Réserve*

Luncheon, Hedges & Butler, London
February 27, 1973

Aperitif	*Krug, Brut Reserve*
Soufflé d'Eglefin	*Bâtard Montrachet 1969 (Gagnard-Delagrange)*
Tournedos de Boeuf	*Château Mouton Baron Philippe, 1961*
Légumes Varies	*Château Montrose, 1919*
Fromages Varies	*Offley Boa Vista Port, 1954*
Café	*Rémy Martin, Grande Réserve*

Festival Gastronomique Provencal
Luncheon, Inn on the Park, London
January 27, 1972

Caille Lucullus en Gelée	*Clos Mireille, Blanc de Blanc de Provence 1970 (Domaine Ott)*
Loup de Nice en Croute Brillat-Savarin	
Carré d'Agneau aux Herbes de Provence	
Artichaut Barigoule	*Château Minuty Rosé*
Gratin Dauphinois	
Fromages de France	
Soufflé Glacé aux Framboises	*Domaine du Val d'Arenc 1968,*
Mignardises	*Cuvée de la Gravière Rouge*

Dinner following a tasting of Burgundies
Grants of St. James's, Carlton Tower Hotel, London
April 15, 1969

Aperitif   *Pommery et Greno, 1962*

Bisquit de Turbot Mère Jeanne

Ris de Veau Maréchale   *Chevalier Montrachet "Les Demoiselles" 1962*
                                                        (Louis Jadot)

Sorbet au Citron

Coeur de Filet Financière
Haricots Verts au Beurre
Pomme Berny   *Corton Pougets 1959 (Louis Jadot)*

Plateau de Fromages   *Romanée St Vivant 1952 (Louis Jadot)*

Poire de Chamoine
Café

Fêtes du Vin de Bordeaux
Dinner at Les Horizons restaurant, Bordeaux
June 25, 1971

Consommé Madrilène
Bar Braisé au Sauternes   *Château Olivier, Graves*

Côte de Boeuf rôtie Forestière   *Château Beau-Site 1967, Médoc*

Plateau de Fromages   *Château Gouprie 1967*

Omelette Norvégienne   *Château Rieussec 1967, Sauternes*

Café   *Château Filhot 1967, Sauternes*

Confrerie des Compagnons Haut-Normands du
Gouste-Vin Dinner at the Royal Garden Hotel, London
June 17, 1972

Aperitif	*Visan, 1970, Côtes-du-Rhône Villages*
La Mousse d'Asperge Crinoline	*Bourgogne Aligoté 1970 (Bouchard Père et Fils)*
Le Suprême de Sole Anastasia	*Pouilly-Fuissé, Domaine de la Chapelle 1970*
Le Contrefilet de Boeuf en Bouquetière	*Beaune Les Marconnets 1966*
Le Trou Normand	
Le Brie sur Paille	*Givry 1970*
Les Fraises de Bois Jeannette	*Corton Charlemagne 1966*
Le Café	*Cognac*
	Champagne Heidsieck Dry Monopole

Luncheon given by Peter Reynier Esq., J. B. Reynier Ltd.
in his private dining room
January 5, 1972

Aperitif	*Champagne Perrier-Jouët 1964*
Coquilles St. Jacques	*Le Montrachet 1968 (Baron Thenard)*
Faisan à la Mirabeau	*Beaujolais Nouveau 1970*
Pommes Rissolées	
Haricots verts	*Savigny-les-Beaune Dominodes 1969*
Fromages Assortis	*Gevrey-Chambertin les Combottes 1964*
Poires Waleska	*Clos de St Catherine 1964 (Jean Baumard)*
Café	*Coteaux du Layon*

Luncheon given by Stanley Williams Esq.,
Hedges & Butler Ltd. in his private dining room
June 30, 1972

Aperitif   *Champagne Krug*

Mousse de Saumon   *Chablis, Premier Crû, Montmain, 1970 (Laroche)*

Boeuf en Croûte   *Domaine du Chateau de Vosne Romanée, 1962*
Les Legumes Variés

Les Fromages

Les Pêches   *Château Coutet, 1966*

Le Café   *Graham's Port, 1935*
                                            Rémy Martin Cognac V.S.O.P.

Dinner for the European Wine Tasting Championship
given by Grants of St. James's, London
November 8, 1973

Mousse de truite garnie au saumon fumé   *Champagne Laurent Perrier Extra Dry*

Quiches-Lorraine, aux épinards, aux   *Meursault 1970, Louis Jadot*
asperges et aux champignons

Faisan aux châtaignes   *Château La Lagune 1964*
Jardinière de Légumes   *Troisième Cru Ludon*

Plateau de fromages   *Bonnes Mares 1967, Louis Jadot*

Choix de sorbets: au Cognac Courvoisier   *Champagne Laurent Perrier demi-sec*
V.S.O.P. aux coings et au cassis
Café   *Cointreau, Chartreuse, Cognac, Courvoisier*

Luncheon given by Messrs. Hugel of Alsace
Claridge's Hotel, London
April 28, 1972

Les Filets de Sole Bonne Femme	*Pinot Hugel, 1970*
La Selle d'Agneau Rôtie à la Broche	*Riesling Hugel*
Les Haricots Verts Fines Fleurs	*Reserve Exceptionnelle 1970*
Les Pommes Nouvelles Persillées	
	Tokay Hugel
	Reserve Exceptionnelle 1959 (Selection J. Hugel)
Les Fraises Rafraîchies	*Gewürztraminer Hugel*
La Crème Double	*Reserve Exceptionnelle 1969 (Selection J. Hugel)*
Le Café	*Eau de Vie Framboise Hugel*

Luncheon given by David Rutherford Esq., of
Rutherford Osborne & Perkin Ltd.
Martini Tower, London
March 4, 1974

Aperitif	*Lacrima d'Arno (Melini)*
Smoked salmon pinwheels	*Chianti Classico Fattoria Granaio 1969 D.O.C.*
	(Melini)
Cold Ham	
	Chianti Classico Fattoria La Selvanella 1969 D.O.C
Salad	*(Melini)*
Vanilla Ice Cream	*Fraise des Bois liqueur (Dolfi of Strasbourg)*

How many to the bottle?

Wineograph Vintage Chart

Opinions on the value of vintage charts vary, for even in bad years good wines are made somewhere or other. The Wineograph chart from the House of Hallgarten has the advantage of giving a range for each year so that this aspect of the vintage is covered.

WHITE WINES								RED WINES				
Year	Bordeaux	Burgundy	Rhine	Moselle	Alsace	Loire	Champagne	Year	Claret	Burgundy	Rhone	Port
1945	7–10	6–10	7–10	6–10	8–10	8–10	V	1945	7–10	8–10	8–10	V
1946	4–6	5–8	5–7	3–5	4–6	6–9	—	1946	4–7	4–6	6–8	—
1947	8–10	8–10	7–10	7–10	8–10	8–10	V	1947	8–10	8–10	9–10	V
1948	5–8	6–8	6–8	5–8	5–7	4–0	—	1948	6–9	6–8	6–8	V
1949	7–9	8–10	7–10	6–10	9–10	4–10	V	1949	8–10	9–10	8–10	—
1950	5–8	5–8	3–6	3–6	6–8	5–8	—	1950	5–8	4–7	7–9	V
1951	3–6	3–5	2–5	2–5	2–4	2–5	—	1951	3–6	3–6	5–7	—
1952	7–9	7–9	6–8	5–8	6–8	6–9	V	1952	8–10	8–10	9–10	—
1953	8–10	8–10	8–10	7–10	8–10	7–9	V	1953	7–10	9–10	9–10	—
1954	5–7	4–6	0–3	0–4	5–8	5–8	—	1954	4–7	4–6	5–8	V
1955	8–10	8–10	6–8	4–8	7–9	8–10	V	1955	6–10	7–10	8–10	V
1956	4–7	4–7	2–5	1–4	5–8	5–8	—	1956	4–7	3–6	7–9	—
1957	6–8	6–9	4–8	6–8	6–9	6–9	V	1957	6–8	6–8	8–10	—
1958	4–7	5–8	5–8	6–8	5–8	5–8	—	1958	5–7	2–6	7–9	V
1959	6–9	8–10	8–10	8–10	8–10	9–10	V	1959	6–10	6–10	7–10	—
1960	5–7	3–6	4–7	4–7	6–8	4–8	—	1960	4–7	2–6	7–9	V
1961	7–9	8–10	4–8	4–9	6–9	9–10	V	1961	9–10	8–10	9–10	—
1962	6–8	7–9	5–6(9*)	5–6(9*)	7–9	7–9	V	1962	6–9	7–9	7–9	—
1963	4–6	5–7	3–6	3–6	4–6	4–6	—	1963	3–5	3–6	2–4	V
1964	6–8	7–9	7–10	9–10	8–10	6–9	V	1964	5–9	6–9	6–9	—
1965	4–7	5–7	4–7	3–6	4–6	5–7	—	1965	3–6	3–5	6–8	—
1966	6–9	7–9	7–9	8–10	7–9	7–9	V	1966	6–9	7–9	7–9	V
1967	6–9	6–9	7–9	6–9	7–9	6–9		1967	5–9	5–8	7–9	V
1968	3–5	3–6	4–7	4–7	4–6	4–6		1968	3–5	3–6	5–8	
1969	5–8	6–8	6–9	7–10	6–9	7–9		1969	5–8	5–8	4–7	
1970	5–8	6–9	5–8	5–8	6–9	6–8		1970	6–8	5–8	5–8	V
1971	8–10	8–10	8–10	9–10	8–10	8–10		1971	7–9	8–10	8–10	
1972	6–8	6–9	6–7	6–7	6–7	6–8		1972	5–7	7–9	7–9	

(*ice wines). The numbers indicate the range of quality from 0 = BAD to 10 = FINEST.
The symbol V shows that a vintage has been shipped.

Wineograph reproduced by permission of Dr. Peter Hallgarten   E & OE

Acknowledgements

In Vino Veritas

No-one can write a wine book, however modest, without much outside assistance. To the Gentlemen of the London Wine Trade I now express my appreciation of their knowledge, charm, tolerance, good humour and generous hospitality shown on numerous occasions in the highest traditions of their splendid calling.

To Raymond Cullas, Director of Wines at Macon, France, and to Siegfried Körner of the Kaiserstuhl Kellerei, Eichstetten, Germany, I gratefully acknowledge days beside the Rhone and Rhine when they opened many bottles to expound on the wines of their respective countries.

And last, but not least, to my wife, Iris Olsen, for a tolerance beyond the call of matrimony and much advice and patient assistance in preparing these pages.

The publishers would like to express their appreciation for the help and advice provided by many individuals and companies during the preparation of this book including: Mr E. A. Tasker, Mr William A. Warre, Mr Hugh Mackay, Counsel Ltd, Food From France, Wine Development Board, and the Wine Institute, California.

Photographs and Illustrators:

(left to right, top to bottom from A)

2/3	British Library (Royal ms 2B vii f 79 v)
6	British Library (Add. ms 19720 f 80)
9	*A* British Library (Kings ms 24 f 26 v) *B* Trustees of the British Museum
10	*A,B* Landesmuseum, Trier, W. Germany
11	J. Morrell
12	*A,B,C,D* J. R. Phillips & Co.
13	*A* Bénédictine *B,C* Louis-Noël Latour, Beaune
14/15	*A* Gebr, Metz, Tübingen *B* German Embassy *C* Jim Robins
17	*A,B,C,D,E,F* Food From France
18	*A,B,C* Food From France
19	*A,B,C* Food From France
20	Jim Robins
22	Jim Robins
23	Grants of St. James's
27	*A* Food From France *B* Harveys of Bristol *C,D* P. Hallgarten
28	Puytorac Fres.
29	*A* Wines from Germany Information Service *B* Christie's Wine Department
30	*A,B* Farrow & Jackson
31	Michael Busselle
32	Michael Busselle
46	C.I.V.C. Epernay
47	Champagne Mercier
48	*A,B,C,D* Moët & Chandon
49	J. R. Phillips & Co.
50	*A,B* Food From France
51	French Tourist Office
52	*A,B* Food From France
55	Barnabys Picture Library
56/57	*A* Barnabys Picture Library *B* Food From France
58	Barnabys Picture Library
59	Barnabys Picture Library
60	Louis-Noël Latour, Beaune
61	*A* Food From France *B* Barnabys Picture Library
62	Barnabys Picture Library
63	Food From France
64	Guy et Aillet, Mâcon
65	Guy et Aillet, Mâcon
66	Food From France
67	*A* French Tourist Office *B* Food From France
68	*A* Peter Hallgarten *B,C* Food From France
69	*A* Food From France *B* Colour Library International
70	French Tourist Office
72/73	*A,C* Hedges & Butler *B* Barnabys Picture Library *D* French Tourist Office
74	*A,B* Harveys of Bristol
75	Food From France
76	Food From France
77	Food From France
78	French Tourist Office
79	*A,B* Barnabys Picture Library
80	Barnabys Picture Library
81	*A* French Tourist Office *B* Barnabys Picture Library *C* Food From France
82	Barnabys Picture Library
83	*A* Picturepoint *B* Grants of St. James's *C* Food From France
85	*A,B* French Tourist Office
86/87	*A* Colour Library International *B* Food From France
88	Colour Library International
89	Wines from Germany Information Service
90	Wines from Germany Information Service
93	Wines from Germany Information Service
94	Peter Hallgarten
95	Wines from Germany Information Service
96	Wines from Germany Information Service
97	Wines from Germany Information Service
98	*A* Peter Hallgarten *B* Wines from Germany Information Service
99	Peter Hallgarten
100	Peter Hallgarten
101	Wines from Germany Information Service
102	Peter Hallgarten
103	*A* Peter Hallgarten *B* John Morrell
104/105	*A,B* Wines from Germany Information Service
106	*A* Wines from Germany Information Service *B* German Embassy
108	*A* Hedges & Butler *B* Grants of St. James's
109	Barnabys Picture Library
110/111	*A,C* Italian Institute for Foreign Trade *B* Hedges & Butler
112	*A,B* Italian State Tourist Office
113	*A* Grants of St. James's *B,C* Hedges & Butler
114	Italian State Tourist Office
116	Picturepoint
117	Italian State Tourist Office
119	*A,B* Harveys of Bristol
120	*A,B* Grants of St. James's
122	Maderia Wine Association
123	Colin Gordon
124	*A* Barnabys Picture Library *B* Colin Gordon
125	Barnabys Picture Library
126	Barnabys Picture Library
128/129	*A,B* Wine Institute
130	Wine Institute
131	Wine Institute
132	Wine Institute
133	Wine Institute
135	*A,B* Philip H. Harding
136	Monimpex
137	Monimpex
138	Picturepoint
139	Yugoslav National Tourist Office
140/141	*A* Barnabys Picture Library
142	*A* Picturepoint *B* Carmel Wine Company
143	Colour Library International
144/145	*A,B* Australian Wine Board
147	Satour
148	*A* Satour *B* Picturepoint
149	Picturepoint
150/155	Jim Robins

Index